■ Evaluating Civic Yo

Evaluating Civic Youth Work

Illustrative Evaluation Designs and Methodologies for Complex Youth Program Evaluations

EDITED BY

Ross VeLure Roholt
Michael Baizerman

OXFORD
UNIVERSITY PRESS

OXFORD

UNIVERSITY PRESS

Oxford University Press is a department of the University of Oxford. It furthers the University's objective of excellence in research, scholarship, and education by publishing worldwide. Oxford is a registered trade mark of Oxford University Press in the UK and certain other countries.

Published in the United States of America by Oxford University Press
198 Madison Avenue, New York, NY 10016, United States of America.

Library of Congress Cataloging-in-Publication Data
Names: VeLure Roholt, Ross, 1970– editor. | Baizerman, Michael.
Title: Evaluating civic youth work : illustrative evaluation designs and methodologies for complex youth program evaluations / Ross VeLure Roholt, ed., Michael Baizerman, ed.
Description: New York, NY : Oxford University Press, [2018] |
Includes bibliographical references and index.
Identifiers: LCCN 2017057402 (print) | LCCN 2017059398 (ebook) |
ISBN 9780190883843 (updf) | ISBN 9780190883850 (epub) |
ISBN 9780190883836 (pbk. : alk. paper)
Subjects: LCSH: Youth—Political activity. | Civics. | Evaluation research (Social action programs)
Classification: LCC HQ799.2.P6 (ebook) | LCC HQ799.2.P6 E93 2018 (print) |
DDC 320.40835—dc23
LC record available at https://lccn.loc.gov/2017057402

9 8 7 6 5 4 3 2 1

Printed by Webcom, Inc., Canada

To the young people whose stories of civic youth work taught us how to understand it and evaluate it from their perspective.

■ CONTENTS

SECTION 5 ■ **Justify Conclusions**

SECTION 6 ■ **Use and Share Lessons Learned**

SECTION 7 ■ **Conclusion**

■ PREFACE

Michael Baizerman and Ross VeLure Roholt

There are direct theoretical and practical connections between the ongoing and increasing concern of young people becoming increasingly radicalized and the subject of this book. The dominant preventive narrative for interrupting the recruitment of "disaffiliated" young men (and some young women) into "radical" ideologies is said to be the creation of opportunities for "marginalized" youth to participate meaningfully in society. Participation is not only a personal choice but is also related to real "opportunity structures," which invite, encourage, and support these young people in "becoming part of the society"—its workforce, its culture (meanings, symbols, and values), and its everyday ways of living life and *being citizens* of a democracy. It is the goal of citizenship (defined by us as cultural, social, economic, and political belonging, along with civic rights and obligations) to bring youth into prevailing institutional arrangements (Bellah et al., 1985). For many young people these institutions are currently the very ones that work to marginalize them, thus contributing to their "disaffection," and in turn to their relative high risk to radicalization. Civic youth work's ethos is to both respond to young people's disaffection and marginalization and to create pathways for these youth into the sociopolitical mainstream. Is this realistic? Too conservative?

A well-designed and thoughtfully implemented evaluation study provides one strategy and process to answer this first question. The dominant current youth work and human service practice philosophy (and ideology) is "empirically based practice" grounded in proven "best practices, and "promising practices" (Baizerman, VeLure Roholt, Korum, & Rana, 2013). This is increasingly also true for civic youth work, with its focus on youth civic engagement and youth citizenship. All practice innovations increasingly require proof that it will work, or at least has worked with others, elsewhere. Evaluation, as an empirical social science research strategy, contributes to figuring out what practices work, with whom, and under which conditions, and when grounded to other social sciences methods, evaluation can also contribute to answering why a project/intervention works (or does not), and even whether its goals and aims are realistic.

Over the 50 years of its development (Alkin, 2004), evaluation practice has become increasingly complex and this, it is thought, results in better quality evaluation studies and hence a better grasp of which (youth) programs work (for whom, when, where, and how and why) (Dahler-Larsen, 2012). This book brings together for the first time approaches to and examples of evaluating civic youth work practice, youth civic engagement practices, and citizen development interventions. While evaluations on this practice and these practices are not unusual, making the designs public is unique. Too often, program and practice evaluation reports are not available to those who are not program staff and other stakeholders, thus limiting their impact on broader, interested audiences.

■ THE HOLE IN THE DOUGHNUT: "GRAY LITERATURE"

Librarians and archivists refer to reprints and other informally published written material as "gray literature;" related is "fugitive material," defined as private materials that have a short useful life as printed materials (Bryan, 2014). Both terms are important here. Examples are student theses and one-time contracted evaluation studies. It is difficult to know the universe of evaluations completed on youth civic education, civic youth work, and youth civic engagement efforts, whether (called) programs, initiatives, or projects. There is not a central registry of these, nor are many of these published in accessible sources. Typically, these are studies done under contract, with the final report only given to the contractor, who may share it with staff, more rarely with certain constituencies, and far more rarely with clients/youth participants. Given this reality in our literature review, we surely missed the vast majority of evaluations, and thus likely do not have even a good sample of the total evaluation studies that have been done on civic youth work and youth civic engagement programs in the United States and internationally. Instead, we have invited and provide examples from working evaluators who have completed several evaluations on youth civic engagement programs and civic youth work practice. These are the core of the book.

■ CIVIC YOUTH WORK: ORIENTATIONS AND PRACTICES

Civic youth work is a complex youth practice that includes multiple strategies and goes by many names. After working for many years evaluating youth civic engagement initiatives both in the United States and internationally, we recognized that often what the youth program was called matter less than what adult practitioners did within the program (VeLure Roholt et al., 2009). For example, we found service-learning programs that supported a rich and everyday lived democratic experience for participating youth, as well as autocratic and adult-led service-learning where young people simply did as they were told. Tania Mitchell (2008) expands on this idea by distinguishing between traditional service-learning and critical service-learning; we would add that even within these categories there are differences and distinctions, depending on the practitioner facilitating the process. We noticed similar differences even when the initiative was called youth-led evaluation, youth participatory action research, and youth organizing. It seemed to matter less what the program was and more how the adults and young people interacted and what practices between them became normalized and expected.

We called the practices adults and young people told us were important for their own democratic development "civic youth work" (VeLure Roholt & Baizerman, 2013). These appear in multiple youth programs across the field of youth civic engagement but always includes a set of orientations and practices.

Civic youth work refers to a set of essential orientations and practices, including cocreation, contributory, interrogatory, contextual, caring for the world, processual, open, invitational, and toward more than self (VeLure Roholt et al., 2009). For those working to support democratic, civic, and citizen development among young people, these terms are quite familiar. Civic youth work has a radical frame and definition of young person. In this practice field, young people are citizens now. It challenges traditional understandings of young person and promotes a "child as citizen" worldview (Wyness, 2000). This similar philosophical anthropology scaffolds most youth-led practices, which assume young people to have competence (Wyness, 2000). Civic youth work aims to illustrate what these families of youth work practices together have in common and how these are responsive practices that work with young people to name public issues they care about, work toward developing a deep and rich understanding of these issues, considering what together can be done, acting to address the issue, and studying whether the action they took had both intended and unintended consequences. Civic youth work describes direct practice with young people that can be found in high-quality youth participatory action research (Cammarota & Fine, 2008), youth-led evaluation (Flores-Sabo, 2008), youth-led community and social development, and youth organizing (Gordon, 2010). It recognizes and embraces youth civic engagement as a multifaceted, contextual, and responsive practice. Civic youth work is a complex youth work practice.

Primarily, civic youth work is a complex practice because it emphasizes lived experience rather than a preordained curriculum. Civic youth work cannot be prescribed because we have learned that what adults do to support young people to experience voice and power often differs depending on place and young people involved (Rubin, 2008). Civic youth workers bring together a set of practices that respond to the young people collaborating with them and allow both adult and young people involved to navigate the place of the work so that participatory and democratic practice between them can emerge and eventually flourish. In our work, and as the case studies in this text describe, the practices necessary to support youth civic engagement depend on where the work is taking place and who is involved.

For youth civic engagement, practice matters and must evolve as the work proceeds. For many groups, the adult facilitator has to be more involved at the beginning. As the youth group members become familiar with democratic practice, the adult facilitator moves into a less directive role, one that is more consultative and collaborative. This apprenticeship model has been well documented as an effective way to learn about new practices (Lave & Wenger, 1991), and it takes into consideration the time and direct modeling new members often need before they become full members of a practice. We have seen may young people who at first appear to be disinterested in the process and then are highly engaged when we return several weeks later. When asked, what supported your involvement? They often say: At first we didn't believe the adult when they said we would have power; lots of adults say this to us and then step in and take over. Civic youth workers focus on what can be continually turned over to the youth group members.

Who is involved also influences what is done and how. Rubin (2008) found that different populations of young people often require dramatically different civic engagement practices for the same outcome to emerge across groups. If the aim is for young people to be and become citizens, what the adults do often has to differ depending on the youth who are in the group. The same is true for where the work takes place. Organizations and agencies can be both spaces of possibilities as well as places where ineffective practices are kept alive long beyond their expiration date (VeLure Roholt et al., 2013); so too for communities and youth services. Civic youth work recognizes the influences place has on the work and responds to place in ways that allows for (often incremental) democratic practice with young people to take hold and grow.

■ WHY THIS BOOK NOW?

The timing of this book is propitious: We have finished three texts on civic youth work (Velure Roholt & Baizerman, 2013; VeLure Roholt, Baizerman, & Hildreth, 2013; VeLure Roholt, Hildreth, & Baizerman, 2009), and there are increasingly active journal publishing on youth as citizens, youth citizen making, and on evaluating both. There is also the recent political acts of terrorism internationally, along with active coverage of these in the United States, and increasing concern about the social determinants of health and well-being for young people both in the United States and internationally. Focus is on youth as "alienated," "disaffiliated," and "disaffected," that is, youth who see themselves as denied full citizenship or have chosen not to claim this civic identity. Taken together, the time is right to assess this field of youth work and its evaluation, explicating the philosophy, ethos, knowledge, practice, and practices of both the work and the way it is assessed and evaluated. As active practitioners and authors of civic youth work and its evaluation, and as colleagues to many who also do this work, in the United States and internationally, we are well positioned to make this contribution to these expanding practices, here and internationally.

The vocation of civic youth work is citizen making by following general youth work practices, along with those specific to civic youth work. The latter are introduced and outlined in our work (VeLure Roholt, Baizerman, & Hildreth, 2014) and herein. The vocation of evaluation is to be practical (Baizerman, VeLure Roholt, & Fink, 2014), by providing empirical, usable data for use in program/project/intervention accountability, improvement, decision making, and policy and reflections, and also for programmatic and conceptual clarifications for theory development (Patton, 2010). This book is organized to invite you to understand the connections between civic youth work and evaluation, so that you can begin to design effective and meaningful evaluations of civic youth work programs.

Chapter 1 introduces a civic youth work evaluation process. We do not provide a primer on evaluation, but we do introduce evaluation as a process. The US Centers for Disease Control Framework for Evaluation (USCDC) (2012) is used to organize the chapter and illustrate the perspectives, questions, issues, and choices that emerge throughout the evaluation process when one is evaluating a civic youth work initiative. The USCDC framework for evaluation includes six "steps" that those who have done evaluations before are likely familiar with, including engage stakeholders, describe program, focus evaluation design, gather credible evidence, justify conclusions, and use and share lessons learned. In Chapters 2–8, these steps are used again to organize the case studies. An analysis of the case studies in the book is presented in Chapters 9 and 10, whereas Chapter 11 provides some advice from an expert evaluator on what he or she has learned from evaluating complex youth programs over the last several years. The aim of the book is to both describe practice principles and provide concrete, specific examples of how these principles are often put into practice. In doing so, we describe the different ways of evaluating this work and clarify both the nuances of the practice and the level of analysis that is necessary for building an understanding of civic youth work and whether its claims of youth change are supported.

◼ WHAT THE READER COULD TAKE FROM THIS BOOK

Note that we did not write "what the readers should/will learn from reading this book"; instead, we focused on what the reader could take from this book. We did this because we want to emphasize that you have to do the major lifting, the major work; it is up to you as a reader to take away lessons. This opens up several issues:

- What is a "lesson"?
- How does one read to "take away" a lesson?

Simply, a lesson ("lessons learned") is whatever you take from the text, which you can use to think and/or act in your practice whether directly with or on behalf of young people; it is yours to name. In contrast, is what we think/believe you should "get out of" reading our book.

What is civic youth work? And youth civic engagement? What is the relationship philosophically, theoretically, conceptually, politically, and in mundane everyday life and mundane youth work between and among these and citizenship, civic practice, citizen work, public work, and the being and acting (as) citizen (the sociopolitical role) (and a way of being youth)? We begin by presenting an overview of the evaluation process and the questions, issues, and choices that emerge for an evaluator while doing a civic youth work program evaluation.

■ AUTHOR BIOGRAPHIES

Michael Baizerman is Professor of Youth Studies in the School of Social Work, University of Minnesota. He is a leading scholar in the fields of youth studies and youth work. He has published over 60 articles and books and consults internationally with governments, universities, and community organizations to build effective and sustainable youth work practice and programs to support young people's involvement in political, social, democratic, and community development.

Harry C. Boyte is founder of the Center for Democracy and Citizenship at the Humphrey School of Public Affairs, merged into the Sabo Center for Democracy and Citizenship at Augsburg College, where he now serves as Senior Scholar in Public Work Philosophy. He is also a Senior Fellow at the University of Minnesota's Humphrey School of Public Affairs. Boyte is an architect of the Center's public work framework for citizenship, an action-oriented civic agency approach, theorizing the normative civic implications of communal and cooperative labor traditions from across the world, which has gained international recognition for its theoretical innovations and practical effectiveness. Boyte is also the founder of Public Achievement, an international civic education initiative for young people now in hundreds of communities in more than two dozen countries. His most recent book is the edited volume, *Democracy's Education: Public Work, Citizenship, and the Future of Colleges and Universities*, a collection of essays by leading thinkers, public intellectuals, students, and others on how educators can be agents of change not victims of change. In the 1960s and 1970, Boyte worked for the Southern Christian Leadership conference in the southern civil rights movement and was a community and union organizer.

Charmagne Campbell-Patton is the Director of Organizational Learning and Evaluation at Utilization-Focused Evaluation. In this role, Charmagne works to support organizations working for social justice by embedding evaluative thinking across programs and operations. She brings a decade of program design, implementation, and evaluation experience to this work from across a range of fields, including youth civic engagement, education, environmental justice, youth homelessness, and philanthropy. She specializes in qualitative research methods and utilization-focused developmental evaluation. She holds a BA in Political Science from Grinnell College and an MA in International Peace and Conflict Resolution from American University's School of International Service. She has authored several articles and blog posts, including "Conceptualizing and Evaluating the Complexities of Youth Civic Engagement" in the *Handbook of Research on Civic Engagement in Youth*. Charmagne has lived, worked, and travelled in North and

Central America, the Caribbean, Central and Eastern Europe, West and East Africa, and South Asia. She lives in Minneapolis, Minnesota, with her husband, daughter, and cat.

Brian Hubbard is the AmeriCorps Individual Placements Program Coordinator for the Conservation Corps Minnesota and Iowa. In the fall of 2010 he was the Parks and Trails Legacy Strategic Plan Assistant and contributed to youth outreach for the Parks and Trails Legacy Plan. In 2015 he was appointed chair to the Parks and Trails Legacy Advisory Committee. Brian previously served as an English teacher with the Peace Corps in Benin, West Africa and is certified as an Emergency Medical Technician-Basic. He has participated with the After School Matters Practitioner Fellowship and the Neighborhood Leadership Program. He holds a bachelor's degree in communications and professional writing, and a master's of Education in Youth Development and Leadership from the University of Minnesota.

Xu Huiying is the Deputy Director of China Public Service Education Research Institute of Beijing Institute of Culture Innovation and Communication, Beijing Normal University, and former associate professor of College of Philosophy and Sociology. Xu has conducted research on teaching and learning theory of political education and moral education for more than 30 years. Her works include more than 10 books and more than 30 papers about teenagers' education. She has also been involved in public service education projects on environment in cooperation with the World Wildlife Fund for nearly 15 years, and she has produced rich theory and practice on public service education for elementary and secondary schools. Xu has also written books on a variety of topics, from environmental education to public service education.

Terrance Kwame-Ross, PhD, is Associate Professor in Education, Augsburg College, Minneapolis, MN. He holds a community faculty position in the School of Social Work, Youth Development Leadership (YDL) Graduate Program. He's taught in public schools and was the co-founder and principal of New City School, a public charter school located in northeast Minneapolis, Minnesota. Terrance holds a BA in Elementary Education, MEd in Youth Development Leadership, and a PhD in Education.

Shang Lifu, Beijing Normal University, is Director of China Public Service Education Research Institute of Beijing Institute of Culture Innovation and Communication, Beijing Normal University, PhD in Management of Beijing Normal University. From 2003 to 2008, Shang conducted surveys on the elementary education of elementary and secondary schools in 22 provinces and municipalities in China successively, and published four monographs of elementary education. With educational experiments and exploration in 22 provinces and municipalities, Shang has identified many effective methods and programs involving elementary education. He has also conducted research on teenagers involved in public service education, sponsored by the US Chou Foundation. He is currently editing a volume on a *Public Service Practice Course for Elementary School*.

Paul Mattessich has served as executive director of Wilder Research since 1982, building a research team of about 80 people from multiple disciplines, who devote themselves to increasing the effectiveness of services, programs, organizations, and policies intended to improve the lives of individuals, families, and communities. Paul lectures frequently throughout the United States and the United Kingdom, especially on topics of organization and service effectiveness, collaboration/partnerships, and major social trends. He has authored or coauthored more than 300 publications. Since 2000, he has spent several weeks each year in Belfast, Northern Ireland, working with youth development and civic engagement organizations that promote democratic skills to bring communities together and to resolve conflict. He has served on a variety of government and nonprofit boards of directors and special task forces. He currently sits on the boards of the Hamm Memorial Psychiatric Clinic and of Minnesota Community Measurement. He has an appointment as Adjunct Faculty in the Department of Youth Studies, School of Social Work, at the University of Minnesota. He received his doctorate in Sociology from the University of Minnesota.

Shi Pian is Executive Dean of China Public Service Education Research Institute of Beijing Institute of Culture Innovation and Communication, Beijing Normal University. Since 2011, Shi has started with the *Research on Forming the All-Round Development of Teenagers in School, Family and Community System by Public Service Education* and has accumulated rich experience in operation and research on teenager public service education in elementary school, family, and community in China. In the *Public Service Practice Course for Elementary School*, which is about to be published by Beijing Normal University Press, she is the executive vice-editor.

Katie Richards-Schuster is an Assistant Professor and Director of the Community Action and Social Change Minor in the School of Social Work at the University of Michigan. Her focus in her teaching and work is youth engagement, youth participation, and youth civic action. Her interests are in helping young people have a voice in their schools and community issues.

Ross VeLure Roholt is Associate Professor, School of Social Work (Youth Studies), University of Minnesota, where he teaches courses on youth development, youth work, and civic youth work. He is an active community-based participatory researcher and evaluator. Most of his research and evaluation work focuses on youth work, civic youth work, and youth involvement in democratic and social development, especially with young people from historically marginalized and contested communities.

Dr. Robert Shumer has been involved in education for the past 44 years. He has taught from middle school through graduate school, and has covered topics from Reading, Language Arts, and Social Studies, to graduate courses on Service Learning, Participatory Evaluation, and Education for Work. He holds credentials in Special Education and Counseling and Guidance and has worked as a Library/Resource Center Director, a Work Experience Coordinator, and Director of a Community School where students spent 70% of their time in the community doing project-based learning in all academic subjects. His dissertation was about a high school for Health Sciences developed in the Watts community of Los Angeles, where students spent more than 1 day per week in a medical center learning about careers and college, life and community. There has been one basic theme to all of his diverse professional roles: connecting academic institutions with community for learning in all areas of the curriculum, from math and science, to English and Social Studies, to Education and Social Work, to Civic Education and Human Development. His expertise is in the experiential learning process. Dr. Shumer is also a prolific researcher and scholar. He has conducted more than 30 studies at the local, state, national, and international levels on topics related to service-learning, civic engagement, teacher education, evaluation/research, experiential learning, and community development. He has published more than 80 articles, book chapters, and even a few books on topics related to service and experiential learning, career and technical education, special education, participatory evaluation, and civic engagement. He has conducted major studies on a variety of topics, from a 5-year study of community and national service in Minnesota, to a 3-year study of character education and service- learning, to recent national studies on career and technical education in various states across the country. He also served as the primary evaluator for the National Research Center for Career and Technical Education at the University of Louisville (and several national partners from California to New York), and he is currently the chief evaluator for the State of New Jersey on their pilot teacher education program for Alternative Licensure in Career and Technical Education.

Paul Smyth was the Chief Executive of the Northern Ireland nongovernmental organization Public Achievement. His background was in the peace movement (The Peace People) in Northern Ireland from his teenage years through to setting up their youth programs. He also worked at the University of Ulster on the "Speak Your Piece" program—teaching youth workers and teachers to handle sensitive and controversial issues with young people, the Youth Council for Northern Ireland and in addition to founding Public Achievement, Northern Ireland in 1999, he became its first Director in 2003. He has an MA in Youth Studies (Brunel) and MSc in Innovation Management (Ulster), and an Advanced Diploma in Sustainable Development in the "Third Sector." His primary degree was in Fine Art. He is married to Kim with two daughters, Raffy and Evie.

Rebecca J. Timmermans is the Coordinator of the VISION Volunteer Center at Eastern Michigan University. She is a graduate of the University of Michigan's

School of Social Work, where she studied community organizing with children, youth, and families. Her work centers on issues of diversity and social justice, youth voice, youth dialogues, and community and civic engagement primarily with young adults. For the past 2 years, she worked directly with youth policy leaders on a social justice assessment project.

Tong Xing, Beijing Normal University, is Interpreter and Translator of China Light Industry International Engineering Co., Ltd. She got her MA at Inner Mongolia University, majoring in Linguistics Abroad and Linguistics Applied. She has published papers on a variety of topics related to English translations *Comparisons and Analyses of the Translations of Qiang-jin-jiu* in *Inner Mongolia University Journal*, and *On the English Translation of Cultural Relics in Inner Mongolia Museum* in *Theory and Practice in Language Studies*. She also involved in the project of *Inner Mongolia Ethnic Culture Construction Research Project— Translation of "Travel Notes in Mongolia,"* which is sponsored by Inner Mongolia Social Science Plan Fund. Since 2012, she has involved in the *Research on Forming the All-Round Development of Teenagers in School, Family and Community System by Public Service Education* as assistant and translator, and has gained rich experience in public service education for elementary school students.

■ Evaluating Civic Youth Work

1 Evaluating Civic Youth Work

Explicating Evaluation Perspectives, Questions, Issues, and Choices

■ ROSS VELURE ROHOLT AND
MICHAEL BAIZERMAN

The end of the school day is approaching and the students are watching the clock, waiting for the final bell. During the previous 90 minutes, the students participated in a focus group interview as part of an evaluation of a nationwide youth civic engagement initiative. We had just finished up talking about their experiences, and now they waited in the room with us rather than head back to class for the last minutes of the school day. One of the participants turned to us and asked: "So what happens now that you have talked to us? What do you do with the things we told you?"

We began to describe the evaluation design and how we have talked to young people participating in similar work in three other locations and that now we will bring all of what we heard together in a report to the program staff and share the impact the program had on participating young people. One of the students, who had been listening but not fully engaged in the conversation, sat up and asked: "Will you also tell them about the changes we made in our community?" This led to a more involved discussion by the group as to what "story" the evaluation should tell. All agreed that it was more important to talk about the actual changes they made in the community than what they had learned and how they had changed. The evaluation study design accepted by the funder and managing agency did not ask for community impact data.

This book emerged from this conversation and from the remaining months of working on this evaluation study. Prompted by the students to reflect on the purposes of the evaluation study and to consider what evidence others might accept as credible, we started to change not only how we were conducting the evaluation but also expand its purpose. It was here that we began to understand civic youth work as a complex youth program, as well as the challenges this posed for evaluation of these programs (Campbell-Patton & Patton, 2010).

This chapter introduces the evaluation process, along with the perspectives, questions, issues, and choices that emerge when evaluating civic youth work, a complex youth program. Mattessich (2003) describes "evaluation as an ongoing process of doing and learning" (p. 7). We couldn't agree more; evaluation is a process (Matessich, 2003; Owen & Alkin, 2006; Royse, Thyer, & Padgett, 2010). We continue to advocate for it to be understood as a rich learning process, from the beginning when imagined until its findings are used. In this chapter, we use one well-known model of evaluation as process, the US Centers for Disease Control's (USCDC) framework for evaluation, to introduce evaluation and to illustrate how complex youth program evaluations confront the evaluator with a variety of questions, issues, and choices.

We chose to use the CDC framework because it is a simple and clear model of the evaluation process we prefer, is publically available online (http://www. cdc.gov/eval/framework/), and the CDC provides additional resources online for those who want a deeper understanding. This chapter is an introduction to and an illustration of how this framework can be used, and of the perspectives, questions, issues, and choices that can emerge during an evaluation study of complex youth initiatives, such as civic youth work.

The first section of this chapter provides an introduction to evaluation in general. Next we describe the six steps in the CDC framework and provide an example of a civic youth work evaluation to illustrate how this framework organizes evaluations. Then we use this same framework to discuss and explore important perspectives, questions, issues, and choices for practical civic youth work evaluations guided by the American Evaluation Association's Program Evaluation Standards (Yarbrough et al., 2011). A good evaluator negotiates and navigates these questions, issues, and choices to create an evaluation design that works and is accepted by stakeholders and intended users for the specific complex youth program being assessed.

■ WHAT IS EVALUATION?

Evaluation is about determining if something (in this case, a particular civic youth work program) "works," that is, accomplished what it intended to, "met its goals," and was effective (Fitzpatrick et al., 2010). All evaluation studies begin with questions, such as: Did the program work? For whom? Under what conditions? Using what data? These types of questions distinguish evaluation from social science research. Evaluation doesn't typically ask how the program works or why it worked. Those questions are typically reserved for social science research.

The American Evaluation Association's Program Evaluation Standards (Yarbrough et al., 2011) recommend that all evaluation studies begin with a rich and multiperspectival understanding of the context and history of the particular program, and of the larger field within which this particular program and practice lives. For example, a school-based civic education program that encourages young people to engage issues in the school that are troublesome to them should in our view be contextualized in the larger field of in-school and community-based youth participation/involvement/engagement studies and evaluations of these locally and beyond. However, this is rarely done. More typically, the evaluator designs an evaluation of a particular program without using the larger universe of such programs in which the particular program resides as a guide for how this particular evaluation of this particular program might best be done. The evaluator thus has a limited perspective on the program at hand. When these larger ideas are incorporated into the evaluation study of a particular program, the evaluation can provide grounding for perspectives, questions, issues, and choices thought valuable by scholar, evaluators, and practitioners working in these fields.

Other factors we have found that limit this deeper understanding of the context include the selection of evaluation teams and contractual conditions. Typical evaluations are done by evaluators who may (not) meet American Evaluation Associations Standards for Evaluation, are likely hired by contract from outside the program, and typically have a tight contract and timetable to complete a specific evaluation study. These systemic pressures make it unlikely that any evaluator will do the homework we think is basic and crucial for in-depth understanding of the deep and rich history and context of this type of complex youth program. Funders and other external and internal stakeholders of the program control the shape and structure of evaluation studies, and scholarship and disciplinary understanding rarely get included to frame the evaluation or design the evaluation study.

This is one locus of issues that an evaluator is confronted with and has to engage and resolve. This shows that evaluation is not a straightforward, value-free social science but is instead value based and political. Evaluation is filled with stakeholder interests and requires attending to power dynamics and to negotiating with stakeholders who often disagree about program purpose and evaluation purpose (Weiss, 1998). Evaluation studies are always negotiations between factual data and their interpretation, because youth program outcomes are value based and often have profound consequences for funding and program survival. Indeed, youth program evaluation often begins with how the society sees itself and its people, its citizens, and hence what it wants its youth to become and how they should grow and develop into that image.

A brief example might help clarify these points. In our experience of evaluating civic youth work programs, we have often encountered competing aims for the evaluation, even when the main accepted evaluation purpose is to provide data for program accountability. Many times there is relatively little agreement among stakeholders on how to determine whether the program has been effective. The funders often want to know about program impact on participating young people: Did participants develop civic knowledge, skills, and attitudes? In contrast, the participating young people most often want an evaluation to illustrate and then share with others whether and how their involvement impacted the community. The youth present these concerns as requests: "Can you tell others that our efforts have really transformed the vacant lot next to our school?" Seen here are the differences between and among stakeholders on what the program is, who it is for, and what an evaluation should be (its purpose), for whom, and how. Evaluation is not a rarified, acontextual "scientific" enterprise. It is a grounded, in-the-world practical practice, which aims to be scientific in its approach and procedures. How an evaluation study is accomplished and used is the evaluation process.

■ EVALUATION PROCESS

High-quality evaluations follow a normative series of steps made up of activities that, when done with integrity and skill, create a high-quality final product—an evaluation that can be used for program improvement, accountability, policy development, or learning. Here is a basic shift in purpose from social science research to evaluation research. The goal is not creation of new knowledge as it is in sociobehavioral sciences. In evaluation, a final outcome is when decision makers, stakeholders, program managers, or participants themselves use what has been learned in the evaluation in practical, real, and hopefully positive and consequential ways for assessment of merit or worth, program and organizational improvement, oversight and compliance, and knowledge development (Mark et al., 2000). The evaluation process supports use as a primary outcome of every evaluation study (Compton et al., 2004). One model of the general evaluation process is the US Centers for Disease Control's framework for evaluation, summarized in Table 1.1.

Many programs seeking evaluations emphasize either their need for credible data or their lack of experience in collecting credible evidence for use in justifying conclusions. The CDC framework makes clear that gathering credible evidence and justifying conclusions are just two steps within a longer process of doing an evaluation study. The evaluation process begins with stakeholder engagement; stakeholders are individuals and groups who care about the program. An evaluation process must support their participation throughout but especially in

TABLE 1.1. *Center for Disease Control Framework for Evaluation*

Step	Title	Short Description
1	Engage Stakeholders	Involving primary users of the evaluation and others who care about the evaluation and its findings in deciding the focus, purpose, and often design of the evaluation.
2	Describe the Program	Articulating program features and purpose. Clarify both intended program design and if it differs from implemented program design.
3	Focus Evaluation Design	An iterative process to decide evaluation questions and methods that stakeholders agree upon and find useful.
4	Gather Credible Evidence	Implementing chosen method appropriately to compile information about program and respond to framing evaluation questions.
5	Justify Conclusions	Using data compiled to make claims about the program. Conclusions should be linked to evidence and agree with values of stakeholders.
6	Use and Share Lessons Learned	Evaluator shares lessons learned with stakeholders, supports the use of findings for program decision making, and ensures participants in the evaluation had a beneficial experience.

determining how the program should be described, what the evaluation should focus on, and how to gather credible, understandable, and useful evidence. They also play important roles in helping to use evidence to justify the evaluator's conclusions. When stakeholders are involved throughout the evaluation process, the final step in this model—the use of the findings—is done more effectively. Others argue (Compton et al., 2002) that after findings (and other aspects of the evaluation) are used, evaluation of that use begins. This is the broader evaluation cycle, and it is linked to a broader program development model. This is sometimes called continuous program improvement. To illustrate this process in action, we present a short example from an actual evaluation project.

■ CONFLICT EXHIBIT EVALUATION

As with many evaluation projects, this one started by responding to a request for proposal. Invited were evaluation designs of a newly opened exhibit at a country's national museum, which focused on a particularly divisive moment in the country's history.

US CDC's Step 1: Engaging Stakeholders

The evaluator applied and was interviewed for the project. The leadership team selected the proposal and the final contract required an evaluation focus on (1) the experience of visitors to the exhibition; (2) the success of an exhibit element called the Voices Project; (3) what visitors said they learned from the exhibit; and (4) visitor enjoyment and satisfaction with the exhibit.

The evaluator arranged to meet several times with the leadership team and museum staff during the evaluation study's first weeks. The evaluator discussed with the team the project and listened to their reactions, suggested revisions, and recommendations for how to design, collect data, and generally work together to complete the evaluation study. In these conversations, several spoke of their desire and willingness to advise the evaluator during the evaluation. By the end of the first month, a formal evaluation advisory group was formed (VeLure Roholt & Baizerman, 2013). This proved to be an invaluable resource for the evaluator.

US CDC's Step 2: Describing the Program

After completing the initial interviews with both (now) advisory group members and other stakeholders in the museum, the evaluator accurately, according to the advisory group members, described the exhibit that would be the focus of the evaluation study. The exhibit included historical artifacts and recorded stories from community members who lived during this troublesome period. The exhibit designers called this the Voices Project. The exhibit design also included a Reflection Area within the exhibit, where visitors were invited to reflect on what they had experienced in the exhibit and to share comments with other visitors and staff using a moderated feedback wall. Visitors themselves could not directly place comments on the wall. Instead, museum staff passively gathered (through a comment box) and posted selected visitor comments. To the evaluation advisory group, the exhibit included all three of these components.

US CDC's Step 3: Focusing Evaluation Design

With agreed-upon aims with the advisory group (VeLure Roholt & Baizerman, 2013) and a beginning understanding of the exhibit, three types of data collection were imagined and then designed and used: a survey, focus group interviews, and individual interviews. The evaluator created the survey and interview guides and then reviewed these with the evaluation advisory group. The group members individually and collectively revised each of these before giving final approval. The museum allowed surveys to be distributed both passively (left on a table at the beginning of the exhibit) and, when this did not work as intended, actively gathered by the evaluator. The evaluator would visit the exhibit on different days of the week and at multiple times during the day and directly ask visitors to fill out a survey.

US CDC's Step 4: Gather Credible Evidence

Several times over the course of 2 months, the evaluator would arrive at the museum, walk up to the exhibit space, and then hang out, inviting visitors to participate in the evaluation. This was done at two spaces in the exhibit: near the end of the exhibit and in the Reflection Space. This proved to be a highly effective method for completing surveys. The evaluation included over 200 surveys by the end of the study.

About halfway through the survey data collection, the evaluation advisory group arranged focus groups with different community groups who came to view the exhibit. Attention to diversity, in age and community membership, shaped who was invited and who participated in focus group interviews. In total, eight focus groups were completed, with visitors from a wide range of backgrounds. Further, five individual interviews were conducted with the museum staff—exhibit developers, museum history curators, and others—to learn more about their expected outcomes and the challenges they faced in imaging, designing, creating, and mounting the exhibit.

US CDC's Step 5: Justify Conclusions

The evaluator wrote an initial report of the evaluation findings and presented this to the evaluation advisory group 6 months after beginning the study. They did not receive it with enthusiasm. They wanted greater detail about visitor experience and how this varied depending on whether the visitor was from outside of or from the local community. They also wanted to know more about local community reactions. We reviewed the contract and decided that another round of data collection was warranted. This was completed over another month, a second report was drafted, and after several revisions, the Evaluation Advisory Group accepted the report as meeting the terms of the contract.

US CDC's Step 6: Use and Share Lessons Learned

The Evaluation Advisory Group invited the evaluator to present the evaluation study findings to the larger museum staff and to facilitate a conversation about the exhibit and the final report. This took place about a month after the final report was approved, and it raised further interesting questions and recommendations for future exhibits on controversial topics. One of the evaluation advisory committee members also belonged to a national museum organization and invited me to talk at the annual conference about the evaluation process, how the evaluation was done, what was learned from the evaluation, and how that might be used in future museum and exhibit design projects.

■ THE EVALUATION PROCESS IN THE CONFLICT EXHIBIT EVALUATION

This example illustrates what an evaluation process can look like when the focus is on "doing an evaluation study" using the US CDC's framework for evaluation. Typically described as a linear process, in fact, evaluation in real life is more complex, (Forss et al., 2011) with the evaluator moving between steps and at times jumping over one step to others and then moving back again to what is said to be an earlier step. For a beginning evaluator, it is recommended to follow the steps in order. As one becomes more experienced, the process also becomes more fluid. Describing the process as steps helps make sense of the evaluation process. But it is an ideal and metaphoric: In the real world the evaluator, especially an experienced practitioner, will modify this sequence and its steps to fit the particulars of each project. Evaluators and evaluation studies are practical and situation responsive.

How the steps in the CDC evaluation framework showed themselves in this example are summarized in Table 1.2, along with the questions the evaluator asked and responded to at each step in the framework.

Even this brief example of one evaluation study process highlights how each step in the USCDC evaluation process is present in a real-world evaluation study. We included in Table 1.2 the types of questions an evaluator might use to frame how he or she will engage the issues at each of these steps. It is this and similar evaluation frameworks that can be used to guide the evaluation studies of complex youth programs, such as civic youth work.

TABLE 1.2. *The Evaluation Process in the Example*

Process Step	Example	Framing Questions
Engage Stakeholders	a. Talked with program staff b. Created evaluation advisory group	1. Who cares about this program? 2. How do they want to be involved in the evaluation?
Describe the Program	a. Evaluation advisory group meetings b. Stakeholders meetings c. Further clarified in evaluation	1. What was the intended program design? 2. How did the design change during implementation? 3. What implicit elements of the design emerged in talking with stakeholders?
Focus Evaluation Design	a. Initiated in the contract b. Expanded in meetings with stakeholders.	1. What do stakeholders want to learn? 2. What is the purpose of the evaluation?
Gather Credible Evidence	a. Initial design: surveys, interviews b. Revised design: active survey collection, comments in reflection, interviews	1. What types of data is taken as credible by stakeholders? 2. Who needs to participate in data collection?
Justify Conclusions	a. Initially with collected data b. Discussion with evaluation advisory group c. Further data collection and sharing of evidence	1. Are stakeholders satisfied with information collected? 2. Do stakeholders agree with linkages between data and conclusions?
Use and Share Lessons Learned	a. Evaluation advisory group b. Initial presentation of conclusions c. Revised presentation of conclusions d. Presentation to museum staff e. Presentation at annual meeting	1. What activities supports evaluation results to be used by intended users? 2. How can lessons learned extend beyond stakeholders involved?

■ PERSPECTIVES, QUESTIONS, ISSUES, AND CHOICES IN THE EVALUATION PROCESS

Using the CDC's evaluation framework, we now describe more generally the types of different questions, issues, and choices that can emerge during the evaluation process of a specific civic youth work evaluation study. Again, we use the same US CDC framework for evaluation as an organizing guide to discuss the different questions, issues, and choices an evaluator may encounter when evaluating civic youth work programs. All evaluations require that the evaluator respond to questions and issues that emerge during the evaluation process and then make choices to create an effective, high-quality, and unique evaluation study. Through this iterative practice of responding to questions, addressing issues, and then making choices based on what has been learned, the evaluation study is crafted, implemented, completed, and used.

We talk about evaluation as a craft activity to emphasize its processual nature. For us, it does not begin with design, which accentuates the technical tasks and responsibilities within an evaluation study. This technical process is well

TABLE 1.3. *Questions, Issues, and Choices in Complex Youth Program Evaluations*

Evaluation Process	Questions	Issues	Choices
Step 1: Engage Stakeholders	Who cares about the program?	Stakeholder involvement	Youth roles in evaluation
Step 2: Describe the program	What model of civic youth work are you evaluating?	Complexity	Using theory to describe the program
Step 3: Focus Evaluation Design	What type of evaluation study is best?	Process, outcome, or other type of evaluation	What to evaluate?
Step 4: Gather Credible Evidence	Are we measuring what we value?	Level of analysis	Whose definition of credible.
Step 5: Justify Conclusions	Will this evaluation study and these data be accepted as valid and trustworthy?	Proof	What data justifies conclusions and supports use?
Step 6: Use and Share Lessons Learned	Who and what support use of findings?	Politics	Navigating the political process of evaluation

documented in evaluation textbooks (Fitzpatrick et al., 2010; Owen & Alkin, 2006). Instead, we focus on how evaluations are crafted, discussing a range of questions, issues, and choices that arise during a civic youth work evaluation study, the focus for the remainder of this chapter. These questions, issues, and choices are summarized in Table 1.3. This list is illustrative and oriented to supporting an evaluator's reflective professional practice. We have grounded these questions, issues, and choices in a discussion for an evaluator doing an evaluation of a civic youth work program, one type of complex youth program.

■ US CDC STEP 1: ENGAGING STAKEHOLDERS

Fundamental to an effective evaluation is a process that early on involves stakeholders: individuals, groups, and organizations that have an interest in the project, who care about it, and for whom the project is important. Stakeholders can include a wide variety of individuals and groups and are typically described as having one of three roles (CDC, 2011):

- Those involved in program operations
- Those served or affected by the program
- Those who are intended users of the program evaluation

Stakeholders include program funders, community leaders, and civic groups, along with the more obvious members (i.e., program staff, participants, and funders). Attention to stakeholder engagement has increased over the last few decades as research has found that their involvement increases the quality of an evaluation study and especially the use of its findings (Patton, 2008). Evaluators must first find who is a stakeholder for this specific program.

Question: Who Cares About the Program?

In a civic youth work evaluation, the question becomes: Who cares whether civic youth work (CYW) programs exist? If they do care whether these exist, do they care if it should be evaluated? The easy answer is evaluation of CYW matters to funders (Are funds being spent on effective work?), CYW program staff (Are we accomplishing what we want to?), academics (What do evaluations teach us about youth engagement practices and about youth?), and those interested and concerned about the current and future states of our democracy. As you can see, we are back again to the larger context of this type of complex youth program and the implications of these bigger issues on this specific evaluation. Beyond these obvious stakeholder individuals, groups, and organizations, who else cares?

It is easier to answer who we think should care: youth and the youth development industry that guides and tends to young people and CYW programs, and the guardians of our democratic vision and practices. Who else? This is not a frivolous question. Rather, it is asked to concentrate attention on the stakes here and the presence and absence of active constituencies in support of this/these democratic vision(s) and practices, which includes CYW. This is so only when the reader, at least for a moment, moves from considering evaluation as evaluation research and takes evaluation in as an exploration of larger questions—the interest and commitment of some to sustain these democratic visions and practices, and their search for effective ways to accomplish this on a grand scale under ever-changing sociopolitical conditions. What do we, as a society, believe to be young people's place in our society, country, and in our local to national politics? What opportunities will we provide, and to which young people, to prepare them for their ongoing civic and political participation? The evaluation of civic youth work is not simply about these civic youth work practices; much is at stake here about our society, culture, and sociopolitical values and beliefs. All of this gets at the topic of perspective on young people, on society and culture, on youth programs and services, and on evaluation as a practice.

Issue: Stakeholder Involvement

The case studies included in this volume, and in our experience in facilitating CYW evaluations in the United States and internationally, all support the idea that the evaluation of CYW programs could (and we argue should) be undertaken as a CYW program itself: This is our belief, values, and ethos. This is more than an obvious point in our philosophy of civic youth work; it is an imperative. Several of the case studies that follow (see Chapters 2, 3, and 7) describe how young people can participate as coevaluators. Youth involvement in evaluation is more than "the involvement of young people" ritualistically (see Hart's [1992] ladder of participation); it is a call to an authentic involvement of young people as citizens who are learning a stance toward and the practices of documenting and assessing their work as citizens while being and "doing" youth citizens—their public work, their citizen work, their citizenship (VeLure Roholt & Baizerman, 2013; VeLure Roholt, Baizerman, & Hildreth, 2013; VeLure Roholt, Hildreth, & Baizerman, 2009).

In this sense, the evaluation enterprise of CYW programs is a *citizen practice*, a form of citizenship, a learning of a citizen role, and the orientation, knowledge, skills, and practices of that citizen role. It is about reflection, analysis, inquiry, and knowledge creation and use for civic betterment. Evaluations of civic youth work programs are opportunities to learn how to frame, think about, design, implement, complete, and (try to) use an evaluation. It is a priori that the civic youth work evaluation is citizen learning, citizen practice, and a practice of citizenship.

Choices: Youth Roles in Evaluation

Given this position, an important choice evaluators have to make when undertaking a CYW program evaluation is the role(s) young people will have in the evaluation study. It is preferable to work out with young people their roles in the evaluation study. Remember that the young people who are the (or a) focus of these types of programs are its participants (or, in human service terms, are its "clients"). Checkoway and Richards-Schuster (2003) provide a range of roles that young people often have in the evaluation process, including subject, consultant, partner, and director. Their work illustrates the range of roles young people could take on in an evaluation and, therefore, the possible choices for an evaluator.

Increasingly, these roles require young people to have greater responsibility and decision-making authority for the overall evaluation enterprise and for steps within the study. Their framework is part of a larger political process that has been building over decades that is often described as "norm entrepreneurship" (Rosen, 2007). Norm entrepreneurship is a political campaign to change cultural norms related to age, in this case changing the ways we read age and opportunities we assign to people of certain ages. What we have learned through this process is that young people can design and complete rigorous evaluations with support of adult coaches, youth workers, and evaluators (Checkoway & Richards-Schuster, 2003; Sabo-Flores, 2008). They can also be invaluable to the evaluation enterprise as key informants, critical friends, and advisory group members if they are not directly involved in designing and completing the evaluation. Although a great deal of attention has focused on changing the role for young people in the evaluation process, less attention has focused on how this impacts the evaluator.

Given larger social, cultural, and political norms and practices, adults and youth in our society tend to live and work in age-segregated worlds and to have few public spaces where they work together, and fewer still where they work as equals. This next point bumps up against this normative age-based understanding of adults and young people. When deciding on what role young people have (beyond participants or client) in an evaluation process, the adult evaluator is also deciding what role he or she and other adult staff will take on both in general and specifically in relation to those young people who are helping to do the study. Youth involvement succeeds when young people are invited to take on new roles, when there is a supportive structure for this, and when adults choose to take on nontraditional adult roles with them (Shier, 2001). Successful youth involvement in evaluation, as in civic youth work in general, requires adults to change how they are present to and work with young people. In many ways, adults have to *move out of the way* for young people to truly have opportunity to take on new roles. Hart (1992) and Sheir (2001) both introduce this idea in different ways, mainly through a focus on youth roles and opportunities. Roger Hart's ladder of participation describes both participatory practices and nonparticipatory practices (tokenism, decoration, manipulation), while Sheir (2001) describes how youth participation is related to "openings, opportunities, and obligations" of adult staff. We extend these ideas to suggest that there are five different roles adult evaluators can take on when evaluating civic youth work, including expert, supervisor, consultant, coach, and cocreator.

In most evaluations, the adult evaluator is seen and treated as an expert or the only expert about how to do evaluation—the six steps, at least. The evaluator is hired to design, conduct, and report on an evaluation, following normative evaluation processes, such as the USCDC Evaluation for Evaluation (2012). In some evaluation designs the evaluator may play the role of supervisor, hiring young people to assist with specific tasks, including evaluation design, recruitment, data collection, or some data analysis, but the final decisions about the final product and what it contains, how it is organized and written, remains the adult evaluator's contracted responsibility. As a supervisor, the evaluator can choose many different ways of supervising, but he or she is responsible for the final decisions.

To move toward a more collaborative working relationship with young people changes all this. The adult evaluator can work as a consultant to the project, with young people responsible for the overall evaluation study process, leaving the adult responsible for ensuring evaluation rigor. In this role, the young people have greater opportunity to design the evaluation, collect data, and share lessons from the study in ways that may not be typical for youth or for adult evaluators, while simultaneously ensuring commitment to scientific and practical rigor and accuracy.

The role of the evaluator shifts as the individual moves from consultant, the one who holds expertise knowledge but shares it openly with young people, to coach, where the evaluator is working directly with young people who are members of a larger team that the evaluator facilitates. Much like a sports team coach, the coach knows the overall process and works to build the skill and competency of the team (young people) to complete the evaluation process. The evaluator as coach also works to recognize the unique skills young people bring to the evaluation enterprise that they as adult evaluation experts may not have. Although they know about the game, they also recognize that young people may be the most skillful players of the game (evaluation study), or at least some aspects of the game.

In the final role, cocreator, the entire evaluation study process is open to negotiation and young people not only learn the technical skills of doing an evaluation study; they also work as evaluators. They discuss evaluation philosophy and methods and enter into long-standing debates about validity, reliability, trustworthiness, and accuracy. At this stage, the adult role is negotiated directly with young people, depending on what expertise emerges among group members; philosophically this negotiation process begins with recognizing that young people have expertise and it is the evaluator's job to recognize, name, assess, and enhance and broaden their expertise. In a civic youth work evaluation, the evaluator has to decide who will be consulted, how, how often, and where. All of this fits our ethos of seeing and using evaluation as a citizen development process, a democratic practice.

In this section we have named and briefly discussed several perspectives that typically emerge when evaluating civic youth work, as well as select issues and choices an evaluator can be confronted by while doing a civic youth work evaluation. We now turn to the second set of activities in the evaluation process: describing the program.

■ US CDC STEP 2: DESCRIBING THE PROGRAM

Typically, a beginning set of activities in any evaluation study is to describe the program to be evaluated. This is done through and while engaging with stakeholders; they discuss and come to agree (ideally) on the program purpose most important and necessary to evaluate, and they describe the program as they understand and have experienced it. As with all complex youth programs, involving stakeholders in describing the youth program is basic because "youth civic engagement programs can take a number of different forms and there is not agreement about a single model that will always and everywhere achieve the best results" (Campbell-Patton & Patton, 2010, p. 601). This characteristic of typical civic youth work programs works to raise questions, issues, and choices for the evaluator of every evaluation study.

Question: What Model of Civic Youth Work Are You Evaluating?

Most (semi) professionals have explicit structures to guide normative practice in their field (Sercombe, 2010), a common one being a code of ethics, promulgated by its professional group or its field. Civic youth work, like many practices within the family of youth work (Baizerman & VeLure Roholt, 2016), does not have these. As a newly named practice, it may be this very newness that explains why there is none, but the answer is likely located elsewhere, in how "youth work" is understood, trained for, managed, and legitimized in the United States. There are real and deep differences in these across countries, for example: Australia (Bessant et al., 1998); Canada (Gharabaghi et al., 2014); Germany (Sandermann & Neumann, 2014); and the United Kingdom (Jeffs & Smith, 2005).

Another issue arises when the focus is youth participation, which is basic to civic youth work. Often the participatory process required for one population of young people to enhance their civic and political participation can be less effective for another population. Rubin (2007) found that traditional civic programs had a positive engagement impact for middle-class White students, whereas these programs had less impact for students from other racial and ethnic backgrounds. Normative civic engagement programming is less effective for young people who experience prejudice and discrimination on a daily basis (Rubin, 2007). Curriculum and programs that included ethnic studies content and invited students to use their own everyday lived experiences to critique the common and idealistic stories about democracy were found to be effective and have greater positive impacts for these students. This teaches that to support youth civic engagement depends on how the program responds to the everyday lived experiences of young people in society. Hence the question: What and which CYW is being evaluated?

This is our practical concern and focus: the programmatic forms of youth civic engagement and how to find, perceive, conceptualize, and evaluate these in the mundane, everyday practice of evaluating this type of complex youth program. We begin with big, abstract issues for context and then move toward the concrete and practical.

Issue: Complexity

If there is little to no agreement on what youth civic engagement is and what civic youth workers do, and how they do their work, it is difficult to evaluate civic youth work practice as if it were a coherent, universal way of understanding young people and working with them. There will be some to great variation in "who does what to whom, when, where, how, and why" within agencies and, more certain, between and among youth-serving organizations of all types, including juvenile justice, medical and health, recreation and sports, counseling, and teaching. This is an issue that shows itself when generalizing findings within one and across several agencies, programs, and spheres of practice. This makes it far more difficult to compare and contrast programs, agencies, and workers—a basic but far more complex evaluation strategy. For example, youth-serving organizations are likely to have different answers to the following questions:

- What do you call "working with youth" in your program?
- What are its core values, ethics, knowledge, and skills? (ethos?)
- What are its core practices?
- What training do those who do "youth work" have?
- What does "youth work" look like in your program?

We argue that civic youth work is a youth work practice that works with young people to create critical democratic spaces (VeLure Roholt & Baizerman, 2013). It is seen when young people engage in community, political, and social action. Civic youth work is about young people planning and taking direct action on public issues of personal concern; it is about "doing citizen." As pedagogy, it is cocreative, contributory, interrogatory, contextual, caring, processual, open, invitational, and public (VeLure Roholt et al., 2009). This work has been around for a long time, can be found in many different places, and often goes by several names (VeLure Roholt & Baizerman, 2013), such as informal education, civics, experiential education, action learning, youth participatory action research, youth organizing, and political/civic activism, and it is related to youth civic engagement.

Youth civic engagement refers to a scholarly field, a family of practices, and programs with common desired outcomes, and to an ideology/philosophy of rights, citizenship, and democracy (Sherrod et al., 2010). The field emerged in the 1990s in response to a concern over (perceived) low levels of youth political and civic engagement/participation, especially a decline in young people's voting (Bennett, 1997; Delli Carpini, 2000). Recent scholarship has been seen as a response to Putnam's (1995) study showing an apparent high degree of "apathy" among young people and a downward trend in traditional civic and political participation among young people in the United States. Presidential candidate Bernie Sanders (2015–2016) challenged the belief in the nonparticipation of youth, at least during his US presidential campaign.

One response to this concern focused on figuring out how citizen participation when one was older (voting, political campaigning) could be anticipated by, predicted by, connected to, and supported by youth's earlier civic and political activities and educational opportunities. Scholars worked at creating social scientific indicators for youth civic participation (Keeter et al., 2003). As scholarship continued, definitions of citizen and citizenship became more diverse and complex, raising a basic question: What indicator(s) for what type of citizen? The answer has a direct impact on evaluating youth civic engagement and civic youth work. Why? Because civic youth work is about citizen making. It is a practice about enhancing opportunity for young people to participate in civic and political activities in their youth worlds and in the broader social and civic worlds of adults, both while they are youth and over their lives. How can youth civic engagement theory ground and/or guide an evaluation study?

Choice: Using Theory to Describe the Program

As a practice to invite, support, and animate youth participation, civic youth work is not new, emerging, or recently arrived. It has a long history within youth work, both in the United States and internationally, as well as within the general, often voluntary family of practice around working with young people in places of worship, communities, schools, and youth organizations. For example, in the United Kingdom it is found as informal education (Jeffs & Smith, 1999). It was named by us to illuminate what we saw as present and important, but it was missed by others because no one had the language or frame to look for it and at it, so it often went unseen and hence unnamed (VeLure Roholt & Baizerman, 2013). Although much had been written about youth civic engagement programs, little if anything focused on the practitioner within these programs who cocreated with youth participants' democratic space. Through defining a form of practice rather than a program model, we and others have now noticed this practice in many different types of programs and settings. Several of these are summarized in Table 1.4.

Civic youth work does not describe a particular funded program or project; rather, it names and describes a family (families) of ways of working with young people to support their direct involvement in democratic practice and in being and doing (active and participatory) citizen. This support can come from a variety of perspectives and in a variety of ways. It is done by several types of professionals and in a variety of youth-serving settings, often by a community or by student volunteers.

As seen in Table 1.4, civic youth work emphasizes direct work with young people more than work for, on, or on behalf of young people. It is grounded in participatory philosophies (Chawla, 2002; Driscoll, 2002; Reason, 1994), situated and experiential learning pedagogies (Lave & Wenger, 1991; Rogoff, 1990), and alternative paradigms for understanding young people, including "evolving capacity" (Landsdown, 2005), "youth citizenship" (Checkoway et al., 2003), and capability frameworks (Ballet et al., 2011); it is more constructionist (James, 2011; Morss, 1990) than developmental (Lerner, 2004), in our conception.

TABLE 1.4. *Exemplars of the Civic Youth Work Family of Practices*

Program	Peace Education	Youth Philanthropy	Youth Participatory Action Research	Youth Participatory Evaluation
Description	Respond to problems of conflict and violence nationally and internationally, as well as within personal relationships	"Programs and initiatives in which youth develop knowledge of and participate in the formal practice of philanthropy, specifically grantmaking"(Garza & Stevens, 2002).	Collective investigation of a problem that relies on indigenous knowledge and results in individual or collective action to address the problem (Morrell, 2008)	Process where young people are involved at all levels of the evaluation effort (Sabo-Flores, 2008)
Role of Young People	Agents of Change	Grant Maker	Researcher	Evaluator
Desired outcomes	"...transforming society by recognizing the link between structural violence and direct violence and working to create a means of educating for a peaceful future."	"...making philanthropic values, principles and traditions come alive for youth and communities"	"...to contest and transform systems and institutions to produce greater justice..." (Morrell, 2004, pg. 3)	Supporting environments that in turn support ongoing growth and change.

All four exemplars in Table 1.4 emphasize and value the act of participation and participatory philosophies. Civic youth work creates new opportunities for young people to participate in the world in new, although normative, ways. Young people are researchers, evaluators, community organizers, "change agents," and grant makers. Critically, they are not assigned these roles, but rather learn to do and take on these roles, thereby becoming, "being," this role. Civic youth work is not built on Romanticism; the goal is not tokenistic or decorative (Hart, 1992). Civic youth work invites, welcomes, and supports young people *to be* and *to do* these citizen roles. Although this takes additional time, often spanning months and years, the process is a substance of civic youth work, since the main purpose is for young people to have the opportunity to participate fully as actors of these types of practices, not simply to be or to be involved as "youth" members. This is citizen-making work: learning the thinking, acting, and feeling basic to the socio-political role "citizen."

All the exemplars in Table 1.4 illustrate how youth civic engagement contests deficit ways of defining and understanding young people (VeLure Roholt & Baizerman, 2013). Of course, young people have much to learn, and in our experience, they have much to contribute. Civic youth work invites, names, and promotes the contributions young people make as and during their youth and holds that by participating in cocreating creative and critical learning spaces in the present, they increase what they can and will contribute in the future. Young people rarely participate in civic activities that are for them and for adults. This is unusual, not because young people can't do these, but because they have never been given or taken the opportunity and given support to try to do this work (Yates & Youniss, 1999). Civic youth work challenges notions of "developmentally appropriate practice," arguing for a conception of youth capacity appropriate to available and newly cocreated opportunities (VeLure Roholt et al., 2009). Convincing others that young people can do this work, even after they have demonstrated their ability to do so, remains one of the biggest challenges for civic youth workers. Although everyone may not agree with how civic youth workers understand and work with young people, there remains high interest in this practice, its need, and its results. Here is where evaluation fits.

As these brief examples illustrate, youth civic engagement is a diverse and increasingly complex field (Campbell-Patton & Patton, 2010). It is also expanding, and this expansion has brought attention to program outcomes and indicators for evaluating civic youth work. In addition to a diversity of programmatic frameworks, civic youth work can also receive support from a variety of theoretical frameworks.

Typically in scholarship on evaluation and curriculum design, youth civic engagement commonly refers to an organized, intentional effort to support young people learning democratic civic and political knowledge, skills, and "attitudes/dispositions." Even with this guiding definition, the plurality of civic youth work remains. Gibson (2001) provides one mapping of youth civic engagement programs describing four theoretical frameworks: civics, service learning, social action, and youth development. Each of these theoretical frameworks suggests different practices and supports different outcomes. To complete an evaluation, the evaluator has to decide what theoretical framework to use to describe and analyze the program under investigation. The theory one chooses will shape what the evaluator will look for and therefore what the evaluator will see (and not see or attend to).

"Civic education" has enjoyed long public support as an appropriate approach to teaching citizenship. When discussion and dialogue are used to deliver civic content, these have been found effective for building civic capacity among young people (Niemi & Junn, 2005). Another approach (model) is "service learning." It originated in the United States and joins volunteering in a community (one's own or another) with school-based academic coursework. Ideally, the service site becomes another "text" in teaching citizenship, social responsibility, and civic and political agency. Scholarship on service learning continues to show that it too supports civic learning and education (Youniss & Yates, 1997). "Social action" by groups of young people is a familiar approach, which until recently received less attention as a high-quality civic education approach. Work by Cammarota and Fine (2008) and others (e.g., Checkoway & Richards-Schuster, 2003; McIntyre, 2000; Sabo-Flores, 2008; VeLure Roholt et al., 2009) illustrates how direct involvement in social action, often through youth participatory action-research (Cammarota & Fine, 2008) or youth-led evaluation (Sabo-Flores, 2010), provides substantive civic and political learning. Finally, youth development practitioners and scholars also argue that good, evidence-based youth development programs support and promote the citizenship of young people during their youth and especially so as they get older. This too has some scholarly support (Lerner, 2004).

Often, if not typically, evaluators may know only a little or nothing about the class of projects/programs they will study and about the specific project to be evaluated. Of course, this is more true of evaluators outside compared to those who work in the agency (in-house). This is a fraught situation. Without the knowledge of the world one is evaluating one is more likely to not know what "stuff" is, what is important, and what it means in that world to stakeholders and to that world, and thus that world's understanding of its own work, its own practices, its efforts, successes, failures, and the like. So what?

The "so what?" here is crucial for valid, truthful, useful evaluation of a project because it is this particular project one wants to evaluate—that is, to understand and assess in its particularities, in its concreteness and specificities—and to work so that it improves. This is an issue with a long biography, especially in the early days of professional evaluation when there were few trained evaluators and those who were received their training in the traditional social and behavioral sciences and not in professional evaluation practice. They brought their discipline and methods to the study and to the specific project, raising the possibility, if not the likelihood, that the specific, concrete, particular would not be seen or studied on its own terms. Although this situation has improved with the establishment of graduate programs preparing professional evaluators, these folks will know almost nothing about our civic youth work world in general or about a specific program. Increasingly, graduates of evaluation studies programs are technically astute in the methods of evaluation practice, but neither experienced in real-world practice in human services agencies nor theoretically oriented in the sociobehavioral sciences—especially youth programs and most especially civic youth work. Both of these facts can lead to different and problematic outcomes. This gets complicated in another way.

Not to know a world is not to have a vocabulary of that world and thus not to be able to see and to name what is in that world and how it works. That is, CYW is what it is only to those who know what it is and thus can see it for what it is (and is not). Otherwise, it is just an adult with a group of young people or a "youth worker with their kids." CYW lies both in its intention and in its practice, neither of which is self-evident: You have to know what you are looking at and looking for to find it, see it, and learn how it works.

An atheoretical evaluator who knows only or mostly evaluation theory and technical practice will likely not know—at least at first—how to grasp, understand, and make sense theoretically of civic youth work projects and practice(s). Nor will the evaluator know where and how to look for evidence of effects, and how to involve young people in collecting and analyzing data; in writing a report of findings, conclusions, and recommendations; and in facilitating the use of the evaluation findings. Now, all of this is not unusual, and an interested and competent evaluator can learn all of this with sufficient time and good teachers. But the simple lesson holds: Don't hire an evaluator assuming that he or she "gets it"; that is, that the evaluator knows what you are about and what you are made of. Prior to starting an evaluation of civic youth work, clarify ethos, purpose, and frames for understanding the practice, the role of youth participants, and intended outcomes, so staff and other stakeholders can teach the evaluator what he or she needs to pay attention to and why. An example of questions that can guide such a reflection include the following:

- Is your program based in "youth engagement?" In your program what does this mean? To you and to specific others (stakeholders)?
- Is your program "youth civic engagement?" What does this mean in your program? To you and to specific others (stakeholders)?
- Are your youth staff "civic youth workers" to themselves and to the program? What does this mean to them, to the program, and to the young people who participate?
- Do you know any evaluators who grasp and understand deeply what you are about (i.e., what you are trying to do and how)?
- Would your program hire an evaluator who does not know this? Why (not)? What must an evaluator know about your (type of) program at minimum for you to hire him or her?

- What discipline or profession prepares evaluators who best understand your type of program?
- What questions about your type of program would you ask an evaluator before signing a contract with him or her?

Once the program has been described in general, in particular, and in its specifics, the evaluator can now construct an evaluation design. Here too questions, issues, and choices arise. The practical evaluator, one who knows all of the theoretical issues discussed or does not know any of these, has to figure out, somehow, how to describe what is thought and said to be "the program"—the nitty-gritty of the day-to-day ordinary and mundane work that is the program and is also civic youth work. This is the practical bottom line—whether the evaluator is theoretically and programmatically knowledgeable or not.

■ US CDC STEP 3: FOCUSING THE EVALUATION DESIGN

Once a description of the civic youth work program has been developed, revised, and accepted by primary stakeholders and advisors, the next step in evaluating civic youth work is to decide the primary evaluation questions or evaluation study focus (CDC, 2011). The design begins with a response to the question: What will be the focus of the evaluation?

We recommend that evaluators ask not one but a series of questions to develop the evaluation focus: what is the civic youth work program, practice, or initiative that I decide will be evaluated? What is the official description of this effort and how does that compare to the lived experience of participants? What impact does this work have on participants, staff, community members, neighborhood issues, or municipal policy? What impacts were anticipated and which ones were unanticipated? These questions disclose a primary issue for evaluating civic youth work: it is not a simple program model (Campbell-Patton & Patton, 2010). To evaluate civic youth work, clarifying the design is critical and fraught with complications, because as discussed above, there is no standard model that "takes into account the specific needs, goals, and desires of the youth as well as the community" (Campbell-Patton & Patton, 2010, p. 602). The evaluator can focus (in part or entirely) on the civic youth work ethos.

The ethos of civic youth work is learning, and its purpose is to create spaces of opportunity (Moss & Petrie, 2002) wherein participants can act and be guided in reflection on their own lived-experiences of participating, draw out commonalities and connections between their lived experience and contemporary public issues and policies, and explore active ways to respond collectively and individually. Civic youth work is an experiential and situated learning process in which young people learn by doing the work and having a safe and critical space to reflect on it and to make sense out of what they have done and what they can do next. The evaluator can (also) focus (in part or entirely) on youth learning and consequently changes in their actions and behaviors.

The goal here is their learning of the citizen role—youth civic development—and the social change they want to create, typically on a small scale (work in Northern Ireland, Chapter 5, shows larger scale actions and scope). Here is the phenomenology of lived-citizen joined to the Existentialism of responsibility, freedom and choice, and the sociology of individual and collective act and action in socially, politically, and culturally normative ways (VeLure Roholt et al., 2009). The evaluator can focus on changes in participatory youths' political beliefs, on their sophisticated (in adult terms) understanding of civic life, political life, and self as citizen, for example. These and other choices are made practical in the evaluation question.

Question: What Type of Evaluation Study Is Best?

Practical program evaluation begins with evaluation questions. This is detailed in the voluminous literature on doing evaluation, i.e. evaluation practice. Our own work on evaluation capacity building (Baizerman, 1975; Compton et al., 2004; Compton & Baizerman, 2007), managing evaluation (Compton & Baizerman, 2009), and on evaluation advisory groups (VeLure Roholt & Baizerman, 2012) complement these method texts. Here are examples of evaluation questions drawn from theory, actual evaluations, and case examples in this text:

- What did youth participants actually do?
- How did the program support young people to develop or live out their civic agency?
- What impact did participating in a service project have on the young person?
- What are student experiences of the civic engagement program?
- What did students learn by participating?
- What skills did young people master?
- Based on the feedback from participants and others, how can the YCE/CYW become more effective?

A civic youth work program/project can be evaluated by looking at changes in participants (and others). It can (also) focus on the practice; what the civic youth worker did (why and how). And it can be evaluated as a program-as-such, such as a structure, which "housed" worker, participants, and practice, or as an organization as such. Evaluation question can focus on many things, for example the five levels just discussed (organization, civic youth work practice, participants, group, community) or on inputs (strategies, resources) activities, outputs, and outcomes, as in an evaluation logic model (Knowlton & Phillips, 2013). What questions an evaluator will focus on is partly their choice, and often negotiated with stakeholders and advisors. Different stakeholders may think and argue that some questions are better and more valid than others. The evaluator can act as mediator at this point and look for ways to bridge different stakeholders. If the evaluator fails, the final study will have less use to stakeholders. Of course, many times an evaluator is told what questions should be asked. These vary by focus. For example, evaluation questions based on a program logic model look like this:

- What is the program overall trying to accomplish?
- What are the program's goals, short to medium to long term?
- What outcomes do the program want to bring about?
- What is the program trying to get done?
- What are the programs inputs?
- What are the programs activities?

Typically an evaluation is done to learn if the program's goals or outcomes were met, that is "got done", for whom, using what evidence? The basic outcome evaluation question are "did [what they do] work?"; and "did they accomplish what they wanted to? These are on the *program level*. Other questions could be asked on the other four levels: organization, practices, participants, group, and community. Some of these however are less evaluation questions than social science questions:

Organizational Level

- Was any contribution to the outcome made by the way the organization was structured?
- What organization policies contributed or not (and how) to the program outcomes?
- What organization practices contributed or not (and how) to the program outcomes?
- Did the ways the organization was managed contribute to program outcomes?
- Are there elements of organizational culture that enhanced, minimized, deflected or otherwise effect program outcomes? (on the level of young people? parents? program reputation? etc.)

Practices

- How was civic youth work practiced with these young people?
- What were effective practices with these youth?
- How were effective practices done by civic youth worker?
- What does the civic youth worker think was their own effective practice?
- Why do they think this worked as it did?

Participants

- What changes in their mastery of the citizen role were found?
- How do they young people account for these?

- How do they experience and name these?
- Do others they know see these same changes?

Group

- Did the group become a true democratic social group?
- What do group members attribute changes in the group to?
- How did the group become a democratic group?
- How do group members assess civic youth worker and their practice?

Community

- Did the group project change anything in their target community?
- Are community members aware of changes in their community, and if so, to what do they attribute these?
- How does this larger community assess the youth in the group, the group, and the group's work?

These are merely suggestive questions, showing some levels and domains constituting "program" and some simple, direct questions plausible at each level to focus outcome evaluations. For other types of evaluations (process, formative) there are other typical questions. The practical work of evaluation is to get one focus or several foci—before beginning an evaluation study or, in contrast to the US CDC model, during the evaluation process if (as) new understanding of the program emerges over the evaluation study period.

Issue: Process, Outcome, or Other Type of Evaluation

The wise evaluator will use the program description (US CDC Step 2) to learn if the "program on paper" and the program described by stakeholders and others is the actual program (structures, practices, sets of activities) they are going to evaluate. To be sure, and if time, funds, and contract permits, the evaluator may want to do a process evaluation.

An important distinction in evaluation is between process evaluation and an outcome evaluation. The latter gets at final results, while the former is an early study of whether the program idea was implemented as conceived, and if so with what modifications, i.e. the "fidelity" of putting the conception into practice. Process evaluation precedes outcome evaluation logically and practically. The evaluator must know what work is actually being done, how it is named, and understood, and by whom, using what vocabulary. These must be known simply because this is the reality of what is to be evaluated! In effect, a process evaluation studies whether there is space between idea and programmatic reality, while outcome evaluation examines whether the program worked (for whom, etc.). (For a practical workbook, see Introduction to process evaluation in tobacco use prevention and control, 2008).

Outcome Evaluation

A common approach to evaluating civic youth work is to focus on outcomes (Chapter 7 provides a good example of this type of evaluation). Issues arise with this approach because often outcomes are unclear, contradictory, even unstated. In these cases what is an evaluator to do? They can work with the program to clarify these and then construct them as measureable. That is, the evaluator typically stays inside the study and the program to find outcomes. A researcher who is not a professional evaluator may look outside the program to find factors/variables to measure. Program staff often know what their program-specific outcomes are but they may not know why these were chosen and/or that others could have been chosen as primary or as complementary and/or supplementary outcomes. All of this is actually practical, concrete, and necessary stuff for the evaluator to understand and work through with the stakeholders and other advisors.

This lack of understanding can create other issues. In the case of civic youth work, efforts to design the evaluation becomes more complex, often more fraught with tension because the activity can often bring to the surface a confluence of deep social conceptions, values and power around children/families, politics/government/governance, intentional social change/social reform/social justice (typically), and (civic) education/training/preparation/indoctrination. Basically and most simply, this complex reticula of the social, political, and moral centers on children and youth being invited to learn democratic practice to be (come) and stay life-long active citizens, working individually and collectively to "make their voice be known, heard, and acted upon." This formulation works to make explicit the tensions between different, even antithetical, conceptions of child/youth—as capable and efficacious in contrast to not ready, minimally able, and "to be seen and not heard;" and conceptions about government, politics, civic life, and all the rest. Conceptually, a simple way to get at all of this is to piggy-back insights from literature onto the back of program outcomes defined by/with program staff and youth "clients" and advisors. An example is:

- What are our program goals?
- What are our goals for young people?
- Do we have a process goal for our youth work?
- How do our program goals and program outcomes compare?
- Who participated in deciding and writing our program goals/outcomes?
- What are our different levels of goals/outcomes for the program as such, young people, staff, parents, community, others?
- What does civic youth work look like in its specifics and particularities?

What we remind you is that there are categories of subjects the evaluator might focus on: program, youth, workers, funders, and community. What then should (must, could) the evaluator evaluate?

Choices: What to Evaluate?

To us, the answer to this question is political in a broad sense: it depends on the evaluator's contract and their judgment as to what "makes sense," is doable and is acceptable to stakeholders and other advisors, and to the terms of the contract (time, cost, access to data).

In civic youth work evaluations, we argue (insist!) that at least one evaluation focus be on young people in the project. Beyond that another focus should be on the civic youth work process, and another on the host organization (agency, group) as context for the work. Ideally, and at minimum, these three foci are treated interdependently—each alone and in combination—touching the others. Why? Because in the real work of civic youth work, these are intertwined, and when possible, we argue, should be understood and treated as such. All of these evaluator judgments have some degree of professional expertise involved, but the final practical decision and choices are political—it is about interests, practicalities, and ongoing negotiations by the evaluator and stakeholders and other advisors. The broad and specific evaluation questions drive what becomes for the evaluation its data (evidence).

■ US CDC STEP 4: GATHERING CREDIBLE EVIDENCE

While the design begins with some agreement on one or more focal questions and a discussion of possible methods of data collection, the next activities in an evaluation directs our attention to how evaluations can ensure that credible evidence is gathered and analyzed. In gathering credible evidence, the evaluator must consider sources of evidence, quality, quantity, and logistics. The CDC also recommends thinking about indicators for the evaluation at this step to help define exactly the focus of the evaluation. When codeveloped with program staff, youth participants, and other stakeholders, creating indicators can be a wise way to proceed. We recommend caution around the development of indicators because doing so will shape both what you are looking for and also how you look, and therefore, you may miss significant information (evidence/data) about the civic youth work program and its impacts. Instead we propose thinking about program goals: what do program staff and stakeholders want to accomplish? Starting with goals allows for a conversation about how these goals show themselves in the program, and in this way support the evaluator's gathering credible evidence, as agreed by key stakeholders. Creating goals statements does raise a question with gathering credible evidence: what is the dependent variable, the desired outcome(s)?

Question: Are We Measuring What We Value?

A basic question in evaluation, perhaps the basic question, is what outcomes are to be evaluated. A second, related question is who decides what this/these should be.

In the abstract this seems simple, even obvious, and may be. But in the concrete, it is a more complex issue. The complexity comes from several sources—project funder, evaluation contractor, theory, and earlier research, and the evaluator's priorities, beliefs, and experiencing, and the like. Here we can dispatch the second question for the moment and focus on the first.

The basic question here is: What is/are the goal(s) of a youth civic engagement initiative? And of civic youth work? Table 1.5 illustrates some common goals depending the level of analysis.

First, let us agree that any one initiative may have more than one goal and more than one objective. All of these are typically determined in collaboration with intended users.

Obviously at first review, some of these goals are about youth learning about and learning how to do activities, and also the social role of citizen; some are about changes in how a young person experiences and names themselves, while others are about a change in how others perceive the participating youth, and another is about how the program/project as an organization works to bring about all of these changes. This very simple set of program goals is obviously a set of multiple, complex outcomes. An evaluation study of these would have multiple dependent variables, multiple outcomes.

Consider that this table was completed after meeting with youth, agency staff and management, funders, parents, and community groups. This would be a reasonable process since civic youth work is a program that fosters youth participation, so the evaluator too might want to work in this way. Typically, there are multiple, competing outcomes that result from a participatory process making the evaluation even more complex.

TABLE 1.5. *Youth Civic Engagement Goals by Level of Analysis*

Level	Goals
Citizen role	- Knows how to act as a citizen - Knows how to talk about citizen - Knows how to be a group member
Individual young person	- Experiences self as citizen
Small group	- Knows variety of small group roles
Organization	- Effectively invites and supports youth's experience and mastery
Community	- Sees youth as capable of citizen work
Other	- Parents see their child as capable

Issue: Level of Analysis

As you probably know there are families of evaluation methodologies with multiple methods, tools, and all the rest; and now a huge literature, for beginner to expert. At their core, every evaluator regardless of approach and method is after the same gold ring: Trying to get at whether the program did as it hoped to and to what extent. For example, let's use an outcome on the level of participants and focus on youth. Outcome: "Youth will (be able to) display enhanced mastery (or a beginning level mastery) of citizen roles." The evaluator would have to learn first how this outcome is defined, and by whom and whether it is used, by whom, when, for what purpose? There may be a written definition which is available or could be constructed and/ or individuals to ask, including, by the evaluator's choice, the funder, project manager and staff, participating youth, or the scholarly literature. While outputs may be somewhat to fully self-evident (e.g. number of meetings), outcomes may not be; the same outcomes may be variously defined by those involved and others.

How do (funder, program director, agency director, civic youth worker, youth, youths' friends, youths' families, larger community, other stakeholders) define and understand this, to what extent do they agree with this, to what extent do they hold the program accountable to this, and do they want this to be a program outcome?

Other examples of outcomes for participants:

- Enhanced civic literacy
- Experience self as citizen
- Actively, regularly engages in citizen work
- Talks about lifelong involvement in public work

Moving from individual *level* to group *level* outcomes, some examples are:

- Members see selves as a group of citizens
- Group works democratically
- Group allocates citizen roles democratically

The evaluator clarifies this for every outcome to be studied. Whose inputs counts most? Whose is most credible?

Choices: Whose Definition of Credible?

Designing a credible study is different from developing a rigorous scientific study, and we have found for most civic youth work programs, a credible study is more than sufficient to satisfy funders and other stakeholders. Said another way, in evaluation there is evaluation and "evaluation." We are not arguing against quality data collection, but raising concerns over the over-emphasis on rigorous (often randomized blind and control group trials) evaluation designs. These may not be needed and indeed may cause harm (Campbell-Patton & Patton, 2010). And be too costly to implement. For example, why spend $20,000 to evaluate at $2,000 program if the program is not unique, not edge work, not politically important?

An evaluation study must meet certain criteria (Yarbrough et al., 2011) to be accepted first as "evaluation" and then as "program evaluation", so too must a research or an evaluation study meet explicit criteria to be accepted as "scientific." This is where the issue becomes more complicated: there is more than one type of science, as you know (and now remember). More important for us here is our assertion that a good and effective program evaluation need *not* be "scientific," in a (neo) Positivistic sense.

What we mean by this is that an effective evaluation study "in the real world" is practical research that meets the needs and wants of the person/group/organization that paid for the study. This can be true whether or not the study is scientific or, for that matter, done well (according to criteria about what a "good study" looks like). In the "real world" outside of academia, the quality, worth, utility, and usefulness of an evaluation are assessed using real-world criteria, which may or not include criteria used in academic scholarship. (For a different view, see Tavernise (2015)).

This is a crucial point, one which can't be overemphasized: evaluation studies have to meet the wants and needs of intended users and they have to be "good enough," not "text book perfect." This means in part that evaluation studies, while these may not meet academic standards, must meet a pragmatic test. It is not a question of whether a study is "scholarly" but instead is a question of whether or not it did the job asked of it "well enough" for its sponsors and other intended users, whether it is "credible" and can be used to show and argue with others.

This does not mean that sponsors do no use their own criteria of what is a good and useful study. Rather, it means that these criteria vary by funders and other users and that many of these criteria are unknown, just as *many if not most program evaluations of everyday projects/programs/interventions are unknown*: these never make it into the public realm through dissemination, by publication, lectures, or the like. This has a crucial consequence for evaluating civic youth work because it limits the universe of studies available to report on and analyze, leading to distortions in what can be said about the evaluation field of practice in civic youth work.

While common perception is that credible studies take only one or a limited number of forms, this is simply not true. Credible evaluations are those that both adhere to standards of evaluation design and collect evidence that stakeholders and funders care about and want to use. In designing and conducting civic youth work evaluations, the evaluator often has more options than initially anticipated when they begin talking with stakeholders about what kind of data they would like and what purposes they will use it for. Certainly, when evaluating a new drug to see if it has the intended outcome with patients and with limited side-effects, a randomized control study is often required. When evaluating a civic youth work program, credible evidence can be gathered using a wide variety of methods, tools, and strategies, and include interviews, observations, surveys, among many other things. What makes the evidence credible is the adherence to evaluation standards and alignment with the evaluation questions agreed upon and the intended users of the final report. And for us, because most civic youth work program emphasize youth participation, the evaluation should also include the authentic involvement of young people.

A study has to be "credible" to others, and the data must also be credible. In one sense this means understandable and defenseable to others (stakeholders). While in another sense it means that it meets some external, textbook-like, standard. It also means that it gets close to what stakeholders agree is real, accurate, complete, and can be used to answer the evaluation questions. One interrogation asked of evidence in an evaluation study is: does the evidence hold up to scrutiny? A youth worker question is: does the evidence make sense to young people? To young people a question could be: Did they get it right—as we experienced it?

■ US CDC STEP 5: JUSTIFYING CONCLUSIONS

Once the data have been collected, these have to be analyzed. Deciding how to analyze and how to present findings and conclusions of an evaluation influences whether or not it is accepted by stakeholders of the program (Baizerman et al., 2014). In our own work, we lean towards working with young people or with advisory groups (with young people) (VeLure Roholt & Baizerman, 2013) to support both the development of an evaluation and its implementation, data analysis, and on to the completion of the final evaluation reports and its use. It is important to balance the need to "speak truth to power" using evaluation with creating a willingness to use the findings (what was learned) and conclusions: Don't take for granted that because you have proof others will believe what you found and agree with what sense you make of the findings. How data are presented matters, and this too is not simple task.

Questions: Will This Evaluator and These Data Be Accepted as Valid?

Civic youth work is a form of youth work (United States) and informal education (United Kingdom and elsewhere) and as such is in a broader family of practices—each with a family resemblance to the others (Baizerman & VeLure Roholt, 2016). Civic youth work is a practice, a value, and also a way to go about working with youth, and is a term covering the acts and actions of young people who are doing public/civic/citizen work. Interestingly, even in projects explicitly on youth public engagement, it may be rare to hear the work described as civic education or civic preparation or civic youth work, and rarer still to hear young people calling themselves and their friends, classmates, or group members citizens. Youth typically say that they are working on issues which matter to them because they want "to make a difference." Youth workers typically do not use the language of civic/public/citizen work. Rather they say, they are simply "working with young people" or "doing a youth group," or "helping youth work on something in their world they want to change": Ordinary stuff using normative youth work and educational terms basic to formal and informal learning. Only in explicitly political and social action groups do the youth and adult languages become explicitly political, although often they too don't talk in a civic, citizen, or social action language.

Here we have a Wittgensteinian "language game" (Manser, 1967), and by moving from the language-world of youth practice using soft, fuzzy, metaphoric terms it becomes difficult for those in the language-world of measurement and science to grasp what is going on in the practice world and to what effect. Too often youth workers seem to be implying that what they do is ineffable (Coussee, 2009), inexplicable and surely un-measurable. To the measurers, this is nonsense—all can be measured, somehow, and somewhat. All of this is tied into larger ideologies of data-based, empirical and evidence-based practice.

Here is found a tension between expertise cultures of practice, styles, epistemologies (way of demonstrating truths), and even ontologies (philosophies of existence, as in what really is (civic) youth work and what is the image of Human Being that is basic to a particular image of youth), and also with methods claiming sociopolitical and socioeconomic legitimacy to assess this expertise. This is another space where adult, professional, and scholarly expertise can be in conflict with the expertise of key participants, such as, young people and other stakeholders. Credible evidence can be used to prove or demonstrate, sometimes to explain and, our preference, to understand.

Issue: Proof

With the goal of supporting use, an evaluator has to consider how much they will need to rely on proving conclusions in a scientific sense and how much they might have to, or best be able to, demonstrate what has been learned in the study. Even in medicine, doctors tell stories to show their practice (Hunter, 1991); this is narrative knowing and telling (Polkinghorne, 1988), how doctors think, what they do and why (Groopman & Prichard, 2007). Positivist scholars want to specify, measure, and work-out empirically exactly how the civic youth worker (and others in the human services) does (in) effective work with clients and patients. More effective (and humane) care are worthy goals, and epistemologically, philosophically, all human practices of the human service type could be so charted, analyzed, translated into and transformed into scientifically proven principles of practice, with civic youth work among these.

A competing aesthetic and epistemological orientation is towards demonstrating and understanding, not explaining, what a civic youth worker is (the role), what they do, how they do it, and whether or not this works (for whom, under what conditions). One can answer the question: Does it work? qualitatively, narratively—with stories. It is both Romantic and political in wanting civic youth work to be understood as "a way" (Mayeroff, 1971), not as technique or technology, or even applied science (for an accessible opposite view, see Groopman and Prichard (2007), or as a "practical science" (Strasser, 1985).

All of this means that we can tell you which civic youth work craft narratives appeal to us and why, and our sense of which are more or less accurate, complete, authentic, and truthful. This is more than an invitation on our part, just as it is for the civic youth worker. But it is based in part on the intuitive, ours and their trained and experienced intuition (and tacit knowledge), a powerful turn in work with young people, however, suspiciously it is treated nowadays because it is not easy to get at what it is, and how it can be "measured." So too youth work practice as "folk knowledge," as "practice wisdom," and as "common sense."

Much of this comes down to what is acceptable as credible (to whom, under what conditions) and can be justified as such in the concrete, specific, particular: this evaluation of this program to these stakeholders, now. Remember that evaluation is a practical enterprise carried out by practical individuals called evaluators. Each (more or less) tries their best to do the best, most appropriate study in the real world, here and now: that is what has to be defended. The evaluator must know the conventions of "good data," and of justifying conclusions—of good evaluation practice. This matters because whether the study will be used is based on how others assess all of this (including the evaluator's integrity). All of this goes to "credibility" of an evaluation.

Choice: What Data Justify Conclusions and Support Use?

The CDC framework for evaluation separates artificially but reasonably the processes of linking credible evidence to justify study conclusions, and the efforts to enhance the use of the study findings (and other learning from the evaluation study) (Baizerman et al., 2014). In practice there are synaptic and potentiating relations among these, in this (and in other) sequence(s): these are connected (synaptic) and build and enhance (potentiate) the others.

Use of findings (and other learning) is a philosophical and ideological issue. It is a perspective; it is a technique. In the everyday, real world of programs and evaluation it is a practice. It is the locus of whether or not to use an evaluation study for one or more purposes. The technical question is how can/will/should the evaluator and stakeholders do this; the practical question is around how to enhance appropriate use, by whom, and how to evaluate whether the use-process was effective? Then if used, did things change (and for the better) in the program? Where these changes evaluated?

To a scientist, one uses data that meets certain standards and tests for what is right, correct, and good. To lay person (non scientist) one uses whatever is at-hand to make things work better, or for another purpose such as accountability. It seems self-evident that one would not use "poor" data to suggest program changes. But this may not be so: It depends! Sometimes, poor, non-credible data by one criterion may be fine by another criterion—scientist versus teen participant. The data that make sense to the scientist may not make sense to community stakeholders or may need to be presented in a different way to make sense and be used by stakeholders. The evaluator's responsibility is to enhance stakeholder understanding so they can make informed decisions about how to use the data gathered and presented. The evaluator must decide how to present data in ways that stakeholders understand that the data justify conclusions. In contrast are those who rely solely on scientific convention or technique. The data presentation has to be responsive to the stakeholders of the program if it will be seen as credible and if it is to be used by them after the evaluation is completed. Even poor data in this situation may be useful.

Sometimes poor data are better than no data: It is a start! For us, evaluation studies have another overarching goal: to get stakeholders to reflect on the program and begin to discuss what is going on, how they make sense of it, and what are the consequences (both good and bad) of the program. This conversation is critical, and even bad data can support discussion, reflection, and action when presented in ways that invite stakeholder participation. Even with bad data, the evaluator decides how it can be used and when it might provide some justification for study findings. Whether or not evaluation study findings get used is related in part to whether or not the evaluator choose the right way and the best method to present findings and justify conclusions for this specific group of stakeholders, given what is there in the study to work with.

■ US CDC STEP 6: ENHANCING USE AND SHARING LESSONS

In our view, evaluation is not complete until the findings and conclusions are shared and put to use by "intended users" (Patton, 2008). Too often in the real world, this stage of an evaluation process receives little or no attention. In scholarship and theory it remains seen as central to the evaluation enterprise (Patton, 2008) and a standard for good evaluation (Yarborough et al., 2011) Unfortunately, in practice, many times the evaluation ends when the final report is written and handed to the funder and/or to the program staff. For us, this is not a complete evaluation. An evaluation is only an evaluation when what is learned is being used (and that use is evaluated often by another evaluator).

There is an reticula of other issues here. Is it the job of the evaluator to facilitate this use process? It not them, whom? What are the roles of those participating in the use process? Better, could/should there be multiple use processes for different purposes and with different participants (at different times, with different outcomes). Could/should different use epistemologies and practices be used, with different notions of accuracy, validity, integrity, even "usefulness?" Why involve an evaluator in these processes if that individual does not know much about this type of complex youth program, while knowing some to a lot about this particular program? The simple metaphoric image of use easily breaks down when this subject is looked at closely, interrogated, and analyzed. Clearly, use is a complicated sociopolitical, cognitive, and technical process.

Question: Who and What Supports Use of Findings?

Evaluation enterprises are also a politics of who is in and excluded, who has what interests in a study, who is invited to negotiate over content, research methods and process, and the like. None of this necessarily violates the integrity and "rigor" of an evaluation of an actual program in the real world; it simply is a fact of life in the *socio-political process* of evaluation. It is how this life is done. And herein lies one difference with social science research, if not in practice, then in its ideal-type (Gerth & Mills, 1958) form.

Evaluation practice as politics also means, in the case of youth civic engagement and civic youth work, that these are not politically or socially neutral topics. Instead these are often (highly) contested spaces because the involvement of young people in public issues preparing them for active citizen roles, their "creating mischief" and raising social tensions by their collective acts and actions, and their acting against established practices—all of these can be read as positive (e.g. developing citizens, promoting healthy development) or negative (e.g. creating "radicals", teaching disrespect for the country) depending in part on one's socio-political views and also one's take on youth and young people. Just as teens/youth/young people are not neutral ages or persons in US (and other) societies, preparing them to be active citizens is not socio-politically neutral work in the eyes of many individuals and groups in the US and elsewhere. This is the second sense in which evaluation of civic youth engagement/civic youth work is political.

What is learned (findings) from an evaluation is essentially political in its use, if not in their intent. These "findings", "conclusions", and "recommendations" are political because they (can) challenge interests of individuals and groups and because they can be used for funding decisions about a project. Both funding and defunding are never simply fact-driven only; much else typically goes into such decisions. Where this "much else is" found is where politics is also found.

Evaluation as politics and as political also leads back to intended users of an evaluation, from a felt need/want for it, for it to be done as a funding or legal requirement, all the way through to what is in the final report, written by whom, how, presented to whom, how, and distributed to whom, how (and not to whom else?). All of this is negotiable, and in that sense political, touching interest, power, funds, reputations, beliefs, and the like.

One typical user of a study is the project or agency being evaluated. This makes sense, however, often this is *not* the case! Who in that agency or project is the intended user? Only or including the leader?; the managers?; the workers?; clients?; interested others? How will the report be used, by whom, inside and outside the program? Who likely will benefit and lose form the evaluation report, depending on what is learned? These and similar every day, practical, questions point to evaluation as such and to the important notion of "intended user" as both political and as loci of politics, as Patton (2008) and many others show. There is nothing inherently wrong with this. Indeed, the more evaluation is real in its touching of project reality, the more it will be "contaminated" by "politics." This is simply the nature of evaluation, an everyday practical practice.

Issue: Politics

This using of evaluation learning is basic to whether an evaluation is undertaken and for whom (at minimum) the evaluation is done. The intended user is the customer. More often there is more than one intended user; for example, funder and program staff both may want to know whether a program is effective. Surely, so too do its clients or customers—those given service(s)—however rarely this latter group gets to see an evaluation report, especially if they are young people. Regularly, other governance structures, and "watchdog groups" also have interest in evaluation reports and so too might advocacy and policy groups for and/or against a particular type of service or youth population, such as pregnant teens and young mothers, teen addicts, teen gangs, and the like.

Intended users typically participate in negotiations about the evaluation problem, approach, methods, data interpretation, and report writing, and hold primary responsibility for using the evaluation study for program improvement and the like. Whether and to what degree they are involved in these processes depends on who is hired to do the study, the contract agreed to, and a variety of other factors, including evaluation philosophy and typical evaluation practices. (See VeLure Roholt and Baizerman [2013] for models employing very active user involvement). This discussion shows that evaluation is more than simply an objective scientific process.

Choice: Navigating the Political Process of Evaluation

In our experience, evaluations do not become political; they are political. Therefore it is important to plan and design an evaluation with this insight in mind. There are several strategies that one can use. We have made repeated arguments that evaluating complex youth programs can and should be done with young people. Doing so also addresses the political nature of evaluation within youth and youth-serving organizations. While not guaranteed, involving young people in the evaluation process allows them to argue for the merits of the program and for how the program makes a difference (or not) and where it needs to be improved, and ideas about this. Beyond young people (or in addition to) we have also seen the value of having an evaluation advisory group (VeLure Roholt & Baizerman, 2012).

An evaluation advisory group, "is a group that is based on expertise and advises an evaluator on how to best conduct evaluation and use findings. It has no governing authority, nor can it impose its advise on the evaluator who manages it" (Baizerman, Fink, & VeLure Roholt, 2012, p. 12). An evaluator can consider a wide-range of expertise to include on the evaluation advisory group, including: technical (methodological), process, and political. Forming an evaluation advisory group early on in the process can provide dividends at the end when it comes to justifying conclusions and sharing findings. Group members can recommend what to say, how, and to whom.

Is this the end? No! Evaluation begins but never ends (at least in that conception called continuous program improvement. You will never be evaluated once and for all.

■ CONCLUSION

This chapter used the US CDC's evaluation framework as a structure for understanding the process of an evaluation study. This framework provided a place to link discussion about evaluation of civic youth work programs and how this structure, and these practices can be joined in an everyday, practical evaluation study of complex youth programs, such as civic youth work. Along the way, we introduced the six steps of the evaluation framework and stopped at each step to explore in more depth issues that can arise at that step and against which the evaluator may have to decide and act; and in doing so shape their evaluation study as designed, implemented, and completed. This was our way to sensitize readers to the complexity of evaluating complex youth programs, to provide background for the case studies in the next chapters, and to invite more experienced professional evaluation practitioners to muse on these in the hope that they will contribute to the literature on evaluating civic youth work programs, projects, and initiatives.

In most ways, evaluating these types of programs is like evaluating other youth programs. In significant ways it also differs because of the politicomoral issues involved. These issues we touched on, however lightly. In most ways, youth programs of one type embody similar issues as other types of youth programs, except when they don't: It is hard to keep aware that not all youth programs are in the human services, so it is too easy to read civic youth work efforts as "services" rather than as efforts at citizen making, as civic society development, as "youth development" in the sociopolitical, moral, and personal spheres.

Small wonder that (too) many of the evaluation studies of this type of youth project are carried out by evaluators who at best have only limited knowledge of the deep and profound issues embedded into, or which serve as bedrock, to these (more or less) explicit efforts to remake and sustain both richer and more valid conceptions of young people and a vibrant, inclusive, socially just democracy. This remaking emphasizes young people as citizens in its public, civic spheres. Evaluation can be part of this moral, political, and developmental movement. How this is so and some insights and guidance on how to do this are found in the following case studies of evaluation of civic youth work.

SECTION 1
Engage Stakeholders

In this chapter, the authors describe a youth participatory evaluation case study. As an approach, youth participatory evaluation works to directly involve young people, a major stakeholder in the entire evaluation process. This case illustrates how one youth participatory evaluation took shape and how the adults worked with young people to invite their participation and to support their ongoing involvement in creating and completing an evaluation study of a youth program. The case shows clearly how young people can be involved in evaluation and how this can be a civic youth work process and practice. It tells how adults invite, welcome, and nurture youth involvement in evaluation studies. It shows that the involvement of young people in an evaluation study neither diminishes nor lessens the quality or rigor of the evaluation, and how a final report can add insight and understanding that might otherwise go unnoticed by adults, experts, and outside evaluations.

The following questions are offered to guide your reading of this case:

1. What rationale do the authors provide for choosing to use a youth participatory evaluation design? Do you agree with their choice? On what grounds? If not, on what grounds?
2. What adult practices support youth stakeholder involvement? What did the adults do to invite, support, nurture, and sustain youth stakeholder involvement? Does this teach us anything about how to involve stakeholders from other populations?
3. How long did the adults know the youth participants before starting the evaluation study? Does this matter? Why?
4. What did young people contribute to the evaluation study design?
5. What benefits did the evaluation study gain from the young people's involvement? What value was added by the youth?
6. Erase the youth from this report. Does it change the substance of the evaluation design, implementation, and conclusions?
7. Is the involvement of young people in this case simply ideological or philosophical? Does it imply romanticism by the youth worker evaluator?

2 Evaluating Youth Civic Engagement

Ask the Youth!

■ KATIE RICHARDS-SCHUSTER AND
REBECCA J. TIMMERMANS

Youth participatory evaluation is the process of engaging young people in formulating their own evaluation process and developing their own questions about their programs, processes, and communities (Checkoway & Richards-Schuster, 2003; Delgado, 2006; Sabo, 2008). As an approach to evaluation, youth participatory evaluation enables the participants to understand their learning, and it engages the youth in developing tools that reflect their own voice, situation, and experience. This approach is built on the foundation that young people are experts on their own lives and that their ideas and experiences should be at the base of knowledge development about programs.

Conceptually, youth participatory evaluation draws from theories on human rights, asset-based practice, developmental psychology, educational theory, critical consciousness, feminist and postmodern perspectives, and community organizing frameworks, among others (Cammorata & Fine, 2008; Sabo, 2008). These theories argue for the right of people to ask questions and generate knowledge, the view of young people as resources and assets in their community, the acknowledgment that young people are experts and have unique and distinct voices to share, and the belief that their voices will lead to new insights and that the process of their participation can lead to power, critical consciousness, and change (James, 2003; Noguera, Ginwright, & Cammarota, 2006).

Although youth participatory practices are emerging as a field of practice, there is still limited knowledge about their potential use, especially in programs that focus on youth civic engagement. In our work, we define youth civic engagement through a lens of policy and action. We often define this as the process through which young people address issues and influence decisions on the programs, policies, and institutions that impact their lives (Checkoway & Richards-Schuster 2003; Richards-Schuster & Checkoway, 2009; Roholt, R. VeLure, Baizerman, & Hildreth, 2013). We often refer to this work as youth participation, youth participation in public policy, youth as change agents, and youth civic engagement. Despite the link conceptually between these frames and youth participatory evaluation, there are surprisingly few efforts to centralize this approach as a core pillar of practice within youth civic engagement efforts.

This chapter focuses on a current example of youth civic engagement in a major metropolitan region and focuses on the way youth participatory evaluation practices have been embraced within the program and the implications of this approach for the overall understanding about impacts. Lessons learned and recommendations for practice are also discussed.

■ CASE STUDY: YOUTH POLICY LEADERS

Over the last decade, we have worked with high school age young people in a major metropolitan region to get involved in their schools and communities, develop projects that address key issues, and provide platforms for young people to speak out on the policy issues that impact their lives.

Throughout this time, young people have made changes in school curriculum; created new programs; developed policy resolutions at the local and state levels; spoken at local, state, and national committees; and contributed their voice to research, policy briefs, and videos about key issues in the region. Their participation has not only impacted them but also impacted the adults around them and has had visible impact on policies, practices, and programs at multiple levels.

In 2013, one team of youth leaders began working on a multiyear project to document and assess social justice issues in a large metropolitan region. The project developed from the years of previous work by youth and positioned this new team of youth for creating a platform of issues for action.

The group of youth represented a diverse team with representation across various social identities and crossing the boundaries between city and suburb. Although membership changed over the time period, about 15 youth participated as active members through the project. Most group members were female. They included youth of European, African, Middle Eastern, and Latino/a descent. They were sophomores, juniors, and seniors in high school when they participated in the project. They came from neighborhoods in the city and suburbs.

Over the year, the youth leaders met to discuss issues and ultimately channeled their ideas into the development of a survey to assess the region. Throughout many meetings, the youth developed a survey, which after pilot testing, they launched throughout the seven-county region. They wanted to hear from young people throughout the region regarding what issues they saw in their communities and their ideas for solutions. Over 1,100 young people took the survey. The team then followed up with focus groups to gather more information. Some of the issues raised in the assessment included issues around the desire for youth voice, the importance of youth leadership in the region, and the need for youth action on issues around educational equity, transportation, community infrastructure, and segregation in the region.

The results of their assessment were developed into a report for the region, a video to share their findings, a policy summit to share their findings with other youth and leaders, and, in partnership with a local community foundation, a grant-making initiative to fund projects by young people in the region to develop solutions to the pressing regional problems. In 2014, the policy leaders' work resulted in grants to 18 youth-led projects addressing youth voice, youth leadership, and youth action that had been identified in the survey findings from across the region.

■ EVALUATION DESIGN

Evaluation has always been a critical component of the project. As designed, the evaluation was attempting to capture multiple levels of impact, including the process of the project, impact of the youth leaders, and impact on the broader community. Beyond this, however, critical to the evaluation was the impact of the project on the youth who were leading the initiative.

The root of the evaluation was based in a grounding that participating in youth civic engagement impacts the skills and knowledge of young people who participate. In earlier work, we explored a multilevel impact of youth participation that focused both on individual learning but also the collective impact of working in a group with others, including social networking, intergroup engagement, and group structures (Checkoway & Richards-Schuster, 2003). Therefore, we anticipated trying to explore both the individual learning of the youth leaders and the learning from the group as a whole. Some of the specific questions included: (1) What are the changes in youth skills and knowledge? (2) What are the changes in youth's collaboration and communication within the group? (3) What are the changes in the partnerships youth form with adults? (4) What are the changes in the level of confidence to impact changes in institutions that impact their lives?

Youth leadership and youth-led assessment was, obviously, at the base of the entire project. At each stage of the work, young people were making decisions about the approach, the process, and the practices. They had a great deal of ownership over their work and their activities. The adults working with the team were very open to enabling the young people to share their perspectives and to utilize their ideas to ground how to approach the project.

When considering evaluation of the project, it seemed important to include young people's perspectives and ideas in some aspect of the evaluation. Although there are often competing demands on an evaluation that have to do with accountability to funding sources and other institutional factors, it seemed critical to have the evaluation for the assessment of the project, at least in part, driven by the youth.

Generally, youth participatory evaluation involves a set of steps, including getting organized, forming a group, asking questions (what do we want to know, what questions should we ask, what are the sources of information?), gathering information (what methods and how?), making sense of the information (analyzing), sharing the information, and taking action (Checkoway & Richards-Schuster, 2004b; Delgado, 2006; Sabo, 2008). For the purposes of this group, we were interested in thinking about what they wanted to know about their own learning. What was interesting to them about their own growth? What was important to them about their own experiences? And what would they want to know from the broader community about the impact of their work? For the youth they were thinking about questions surrounding their own development and the development of the group.

The evaluation design incorporated a set of questions driven by more institutional approaches to program evaluation in addition to a set of questions and processes that were driven by the youth. The concept of a multilevel design for evaluation is one approach to address the various needs that might occur within an evaluation and yet still allows for an approach that embraces youth voice and participatory approaches. As such, the evaluation for the youth leaders included more "traditional" methods of youth civic engagement evaluation along with youth-generated ideas.

Although the "traditional" methods focused on questions about individual knowledge, skill, and experience as well as group process, the "traditional" approach still embraced different methods, including the use of drawing, checklists, debriefings, and writing reflections as a way to build evaluation into the existing fabric of the group's approach.

However, the youth also contributed to the development of a set of questions and design for a participatory evaluation. Through a facilitated discussion of evaluation, the team discussed what they wanted to know, what questions they might ask, and what approach they would take to generate the information. This led to differing ideas, one of which I detail for the remainder of this case study.

Example: Youth-Driven Focus Groups

One example of the participatory approach developed by the youth team was youth-driven focus groups. As a method, the use of focus groups is often a traditional component of evaluation. They involve a set of themes or questions developed to further understand a process or program. The themes or questions are usually designed by an external evaluator and draw from program objectives, documents, or logic models. The process of focus groups brings together a group and involves documenting the group discussion around the questions or themes. Focus groups can be an excellent way to develop a more nuanced understanding of a topic or set of program outcomes.

Although we had been attentive to engaging youth participatory evaluation, up until that point, we had not considered the idea of a youth-driven focus group process. Because the youth leaders had conducted their own focus groups as part of the assessment process, the idea for focus group was both familiar and interesting. We had also worked to build capacity for the youth to conduct focus groups, thus giving them the skills and confidence needed for translation into their own evaluation process.

In preparing the young people to conduct focus groups as a part of their project, we brought in an external trainer who trained them on leading focus groups. During this time they also had an opportunity to role play with one another. From there they were instrumental in not only creating the questions for the focus group but also in brainstorming with whom the focus groups should be done. We believe that this deep investment in the focus group process for the project gave them not only skills but a deep understanding of the process in a way that made it feel natural for them to evaluate their own learning.

As such, we embraced the idea and worked to develop a plan to incorporate a youth-driven focus group approach as a part of ongoing project assessments and within already scheduled programming time. Although not uniquely different in their style, the youth-driven approach was a process of the youth developing their own questions for the focus group, based on the information they were interested in knowing.

Process

Once the decision was made to conduct a focus group that embraced combined youth-driven and "adult-driven" components, we worked though a process to generate the questions. These were generated by the youth during one of their meetings. After thinking about the value of a focus group, the youth broke into small teams to generate ideas about what they wanted to know. They spent time thinking about what questions they had of one another and what questions they had for themselves.

Figures 2.1 and 2.2 showcase samples from the small group as they generated questions. Although some of the questions are ones that might be expected, for example:

- How have you changed since being part of this group?
- How has this group impacted you?
- What motivates you to be part of this group?
- What opportunities have you gained from being part of this group?

Other questions were less expected, for example:

- How has this group impacted your group of friends?
- How would you describe this group to a friend? To an adult?
- Have any of these experiences impacted you in the "real world"? And what were those experiences?
- How has the diversity of the group impacted how you interact with people different from you?

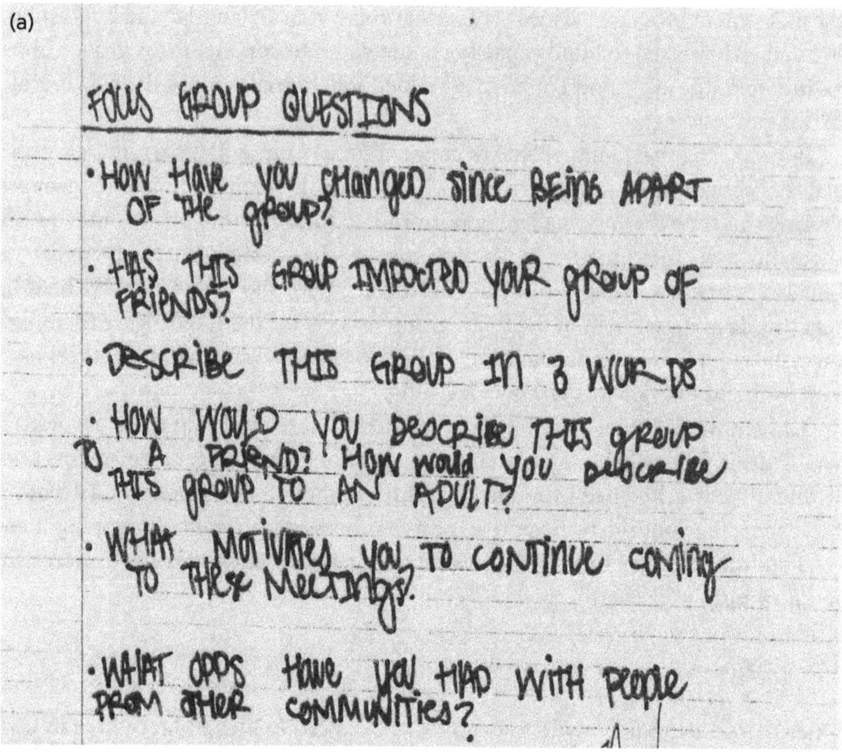

(a)

FOCUS GROUP QUESTIONS

- HOW HAVE YOU CHANGED SINCE BEING APART OF THE GROUP?

- HAS THIS GROUP IMPACTED YOUR GROUP OF FRIENDS?

- DESCRIBE THIS GROUP IN 3 WORDS

- HOW WOULD YOU DESCRIBE THIS GROUP TO A FRIEND? HOW WOULD YOU DESCRIBE THIS GROUP TO AN ADULT?

- WHAT MOTIVATES YOU TO CONTINUE COMING TO THESE MEETINGS?

- WHAT OPPS HAVE YOU HAD WITH PEOPLE FROM OTHER COMMUNITIES?

Figure 2.1 Youth Group Questions 1.

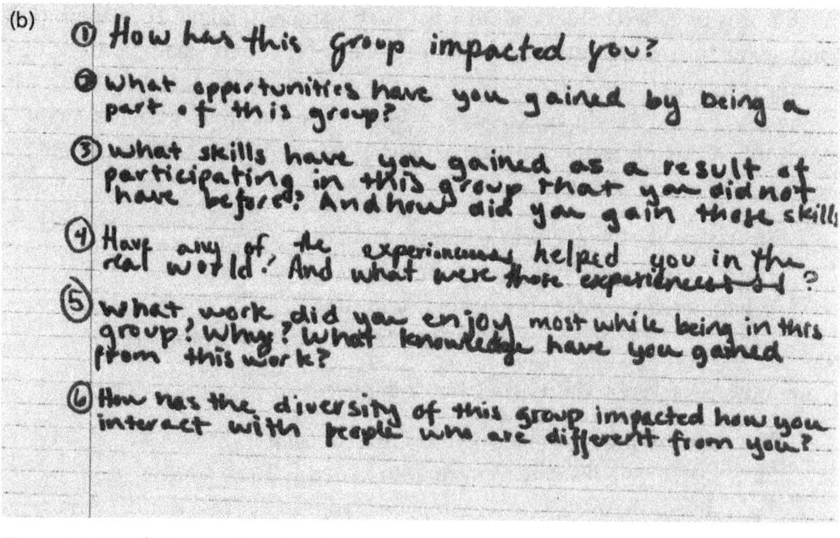

(b)

① How has this group impacted you?

② What opportunities have you gained by being a part of this group?

③ What skills have you gained as a result of participating in this group that you did not have before? And how did you gain those skills?

④ Have any of the experiences helped you in the real world? And what were those experiences?

⑤ What work did you enjoy most while being in this group? Why? What knowledge have you gained from this work?

⑥ How has the diversity of this group impacted how you interact with people who are different from you?

Figure 2.2 Youth Group Question 2.

What was fascinating was to see the depth to which they were interested in understanding their engagement and the level of impact of the group on them. These ways are not always captured in the traditional measure of youth civic engagement that often only focuses on knowledge and skills.

The youth leaders were interested in capturing knowledge and skills and how their experience impacted their sense of self and the ways in which they then interacted with others. It was also interesting to think about how young people would explain their experience—to youth and to adults—and to explore the way that those might translate into different knowledge gained.

After generating the lists, the youth team shared ideas, talked across the options, prioritized ideas, and then generated a set of cross-cutting questions to add to the focus group questions. These questions were then added and included in the focus group. Overall, the focus group generated more in-depth knowledge and youth-led knowledge about their experiences in the project and the growth that happened through the process. Some of their insights included the following:

> "Now I think young people can make an impact and before I didn't think so—I'm going to live this way and all the kids after me will live this way—but now I think I can change."
>
> "This group taught me that our voices matter."
>
> "Now, when I see something that is not right in our school, I go up and I speak about the issue, so I feel my voice is heard and I can make a difference."
>
> "If we didn't have youth from all over, we would just be guessing what do they need, just like adults guess what do youth need, so we would just be doing the same thing."

Using the Information

The information generated from this focus group combined with the other approaches to evaluation provided an understanding of both the impact as well as the process. Although this was only one piece of the evaluation, it enabled the overall project to develop learning as well as to generate consciousness in the collective and to enable them to process their own learning through their own questions. This approach also became part of the civic engagement process.

■ LESSONS LEARNED AND BEST PRACTICES

One of the main lessons learned from our approach is that a "best practice" for youth civic engagement evaluations should include participatory approaches. Youth participatory approaches enable evaluations, especially those that focus on youth civic engagement to fuse together the process of documenting impact with the development of the civic engagement. Furthermore, as an approach, youth participatory evaluation reflects and honors the role of youth as experts with the capacity to engage youth in the process. In this way, the evaluation itself is youth civic engagement.

When young people are asked to participate in the evaluation process, they come to the table with a different lens and perspective than traditional, or rather adult, evaluators would have on their own. In the case of the youth leaders and the focus group, their lens on their own individual and group process was different from what we had ourselves conceptualized. Although we would have likely only asked questions about their individual and group skill development, they were interested in a set of questions about the impact of their experience on their own peer groups and how this experience shaped interactions with their friends. In asking these questions, we were able to draw out examples of the impact of participation on a broader audience than the group itself. We did not think that there would be impact beyond the group members themselves, whereas they clearly saw impact of their participation going beyond themselves as individuals or a group.

Some evaluators and youth civic engagement organizations might, however, question the reality of youth participatory evaluation process for their work. For evaluators, youth participatory processes are either unfamiliar or contrary to the idea of "professional" evaluation efforts (Ansley & Gaventa, 1997). Or when evaluators may be conceptually onboard with the idea of youth participation, they lack the capacity to facilitate a participatory process. Similarly, whereas a lack of capacity may be the case with youth civic engagement organizations, more likely the demands of funders and other accountability structures require a "professional" evaluation process. With that in mind, it is useful to consider an approach such as the one used in the youth leaders example. Instead of conceptualizing the evaluation as an either-or (youth-led/youth-driven evaluation versus "traditional/ adult-led or adult-driven" evaluation), one could conceive of the evaluation as a "both-and." In doing so, one could consider the lesson of the youth leaders as an example of combining a youth participatory approach parallel to a traditional evaluation process. Or as the focus group example showcased, in some cases it could include combining youth-led and adult-driven perspectives in connected rather than parallel tracks.

Moving toward a youth participatory evaluation approach either as a solo approach to youth civic engagement evaluation or as a both-and approach combined with other evaluation processes requires capacity building. Capacity building, both knowledge and skills, is essential for both youth and adults. For youth, capacity building means training around evaluation—what it is and how to do it, support for evaluation ideas and the implementation of a project, and buy-in by the organization and program that evaluation efforts are used. For example, the early work that had been done to build the capacity of the youth leaders in conducting focus groups as part of their project made the process of creating youth-driven evaluation focus groups much easier. For many youth even the idea of evaluation needs to be demystified. In workshops that we have done with other groups, youth evaluation is initially viewed as "boring," "hard, " "like school." But when young people can think of evaluation as a tool for engagement, power, and change—especially youth civic engagement efforts—evaluation transforms as a part of the process and as an essential component of the work.

For adults, capacity building not only means training around evaluation skills and steps, but it also means opening spaces for youth voices to be listened to and heard. Youth participatory evaluation can be a risk, in that young people are asking their own questions about the program and the work, and those questions and their answers might not be what adults involved in the program want to hear—even for organizations that promote youth civic engagement and youth civic work.

One best practice resource for exploring youth participatory evaluation is the Wingspread Declaration on Youth Participation in Community Research and Evaluation. This declaration, which grew from a national meeting around the topic, and initially drafted by Hanh Cao Yu with a team of others, lays out a set of fundamental principles and approaches for the field (more information about the Wingspread meeting and the Declaration can be found in Checkoway, Dobbie, & Richards-Schuster, 2003). The Declaration states the following:

- Youth participation in community research and evaluation transforms its participants. It transforms our ways of knowing, the strategies we devise, the methods we employ, and our program of work.
- Youth participation promotes youth empowerment. It recognizes the experience and expertise of all young people, and respects their leadership capacities and potential contributions.
- Youth participation builds mutually liberatory partnerships. It values the assets of all ages, and fosters supportive and respectful youth/youth and youth/adult working relationships.
- Youth participation equalizes power relationships between youth and adults. It establishes a level playing field, clarifying for participants the purpose of the process and the power imbalances between groups. It structures environments that respect the involvement of young people, and train adults in supporting genuine youth decision-making and leadership development.
- Youth participation is an inclusive process that recognizes all forms of democratic leadership, young and old. It involves diverse populations and perspectives, especially those who are traditionally underserved and underrepresented.
- Youth participation involves young people in meaningful ways. Young people participate in all stages of the process, from defining the problem, to gathering and analyzing the information, to making decisions and taking action.
- Youth participation is an ongoing process, not a one-time event. Participants continuously clarify and reflect upon its purpose and content. Research and evaluation are viewed as an integral part of knowledge development, program planning, and community improvement. (Checkoway Dobbie & Richards-Schuster, 2003, p. 11)

These principles, which in many cases mirror many of the best practices of civic youth work, are crucial for consideration when embracing a youth participatory evaluation approach. In addition, the process of evaluation itself can be a tool for skill building, leadership development, and raising critical awareness.

■ RECOMMENDATIONS AND CONCLUSION

In closing, some of the recommendation we would offer based on our experience are the following:

Ask the Youth!

Evaluation of youth civic engagement should include the voices of the young people in some aspect of the evaluation process. Although each program and situation will be unique, we would encourage any program involved in youth civic engagement work to incorporate some lens of participatory evaluation. This could include young people (a) as "consultants" to the process, by giving them opportunities to give feedback to existing evaluation tools, (b) as "partners" to the process and collaborating on the design, or (c) as "leaders" in the process, and providing young people with a space to develop their own research and evaluation plan (Checkoway & Richards-Schuster, 2003). Regardless of the process, we would encourage programs to ask youth about their ideas and incorporate their thoughts on evaluation—questions, methods, outcome—into the program itself.

Build in "Both-And" Types of Evaluation Processes

Similar to the concept mentioned earlier, we would recommend that adult program leaders consider opportunities to develop evaluations that are "both-and," meaning that they incorporate both traditional concepts and tools for measuring youth civic engagement along with youth-developed ideas and tools. Although this may take some additional resources, it enables programs to move forward with evaluations that incorporate an approach that is often reflective of the traditional funding requirements, and at the same time builds in the participatory lens that often adds depth and nuance to the evaluation through the voices of youth. Eventually programs and funders may come to see the value and necessity of participatory approaches; until that time comes this "both-and" approach allows programs a way to visualize the incorporation of a youth participatory evaluation process.

Be Open to Creative and "Out-of-the-Box" Ideas

When youth participatory approaches are incorporated, program leaders should be prepared and be open to creative and out-of-the-box-type ideas. For example, in the youth leaders component, the idea of youth-driven focus groups was an out-of-the-box idea. Being open to the youth's ideas and helping them brainstorm what a youth-driven focus group could look like was an instrumental component to the process. Additionally, other creative and out-of-the-box evaluation ideas that have been used in the policy leaders' teams over the years include drawings of programs, pre- and postcartoons based on youth experiences, one-word statements, collective drawings/murals, and photography/photo-voice approaches.

Link Evaluation Processes to the Civic Engagement Process Itself

When possible, consider evaluation as an extension of the civic engagement process. If civic engagement is seen as the capacity for young people to influence and impact the institutions that impact their lives, then program evaluation becomes one tool for enabling young people to impact their own program. In addition, evaluation becomes a skill and leadership development activity, where young people can consider what they want to know, their process for gathering information, their analysis of their learning, and their ideas for taking action.

In closing, in our experience, youth participatory evaluation has added an important dimension to the overall evaluation of this ongoing project. It has helped us to understand their ideas, their thoughts, and their experiences in ways that complement and enhanced the overall evaluation approach. As noted, for youth civic engagement programs, youth participatory evaluation is about youth civic engagement. Thus, it begs the question: why shouldn't young people be involved? And for that reason, we would suggest that evaluation of youth civic engagement should always include some aspect of asking the youth.

SECTION 2
Describe the Program

The next two chapters illustrate two ways of describing programs. In the first chapter, the description emerges from practice experience and then is joined with some theoretical ideas to frame the program and to support the overall work. The second case study begins with political theory, and this is then extended and used to advocate for different ways of describing civic youth work; for asking focal questions; and conceiving, proposing, and implementing evaluation studies of civic youth work. Both chapters provide rich examples of the many ways civic youth work can be described and evaluated.

Brian Hubbard writes the first case study. In this chapter he documents his long history of working with young people directly and from this experience the wisdom he developed that supports his practice of working with and alongside young people. This case encourages organizations and practitioners to adopt participatory practices when working with young people and describes how he uses these to transform the Conservation Corps. He concludes by describing how this work is both evaluative and supportive of positive youth development.

Harry Boyte writes the second case study. Dr. Boyte is an internationally recognized scholar of democratic political theory and has developed numerous projects in communities across the globe that bring to life the principles of democratic theory and philosophy. In this case study, he describes two democratic ideas in theory: civic agency and public work. Drawing on these two ideas, he describes how they have informed the description of civic youth work programs and shaped evaluation studies of these.

The following questions are offered to guide your reading of the following two chapters:

1. How do the two approaches to describing civic youth work programs compare? Where do they differ? Which works best for you? Why?
2. What does each case study focus on in its program descriptions? How might (should) these ideas, philosophies, and concepts be used to shape an evaluation study of civic youth work programs?
3. What value can theory and scholarship provide to a practical evaluation study design? To the focal questions of a particular civic youth work evaluation study?
4. Should an evaluator use scholarship about civic youth work when designing an evaluation study of civic youth work? Whose or which scholarship?

What elements, theories, concepts, and ideas from that scholarship may (not) be used? How might these be used in drawing up (designing) an evaluation?

5. Is an evaluation study a comfortable home for abstract philosophies and theories? If so, about what? How is it used in a particular evaluation?

3 Using Action-Based Research With Civic Youth Work to Enhance Program Quality

■ BRIAN HUBBARD

Youth are often portrayed as apathetic, uninvolved, and reluctant to participate in their communities (VeLure Roholt, Baizerman, & Hildreth, 2019). Yet communities offer few opportunities for youth to participate in groups and organizations to address issues that are compelling to them and that invite and support their commitment and action (Bradford & Cullen, 2012; Sabo, 2008). Youth are rarely invited into established structures of decision making or trained to participate in decision making (VeLure Roholt, Baizerman, & Hildreth, 2014). In response, funders and policymakers request youth organizations begin to involve young people in decision-making processes (Williams, Ferguson, & Yohalem, 2013). The belief is that a request or requirement that youth participate gives young people "voice," builds social capital, generates knowledge useful for improving services and programs, contributes to political structures, and makes communities more viable, all while encouraging youth to exercise their citizenship rights (Kirby, Lanyon, Cronin, & Sinclair, 2003; Percy-Smith, 2007).

As an educator, I have seen the benefits of working with and alongside youth. I have worked at building cultures of participation with young people and adults in a variety of settings. I have not always been successful. This has led me to look for best practices, which get at the impact of youth participation on young people. I have learned that it is critical to have policies, structures, and practices in place in local youth agencies that invite and support youth involvement in a variety of decision-making processes. Also necessary are knowledgeable and skillful adults to work as partners and/or facilitators. The absence of such structures and people and/or the inflexibility of policies, structures, and practices can deflect or in other ways turn away and turn off youth who are looking for viable and authentic participation. For example, young people are often not able to attend meetings because of when these are held, such as during the school day. Or one youth will be invited to join a community advisory board of 10 adults or a committee focused on topics of little interest to them.

To build cultures and subcultures of participation, Out of School Time (OST) providers, educators, planners, community decision makers, community advocacy groups, and youth workers should invite and partner with youth in joint participatory projects meaningful to both youth and adults, as well as to their communities (Williams, Ferguson, & Yohalem, 2013). Others argue for homogeneous youth groups organized around their issues.

This call to build cultures of participation was the impetus for my development of an action-based research with youth aged 15–22 years as a way to create the Conservation Corps Youth Council, in Saint Paul, Minnesota. In this chapter, I illustrate how to create and sustain action-based research founded on democratic principles and shared power and how this contributed to my civic youth work and to their mastery of citizen roles. My approach to this work uses a particular type of informal education, civic youth work (VeLure Roholt, Hildreth, & Baizerman, 2013). As readers of this book know, civic youth work joins civic education to general democratic social work group practice (VeLure Roholt, Baizerman, & Hildreth, 2009). The goal of action-based research is to work collaboratively by using analytical and critical thinking, along with data collection, analysis, and action (Bradford & Cullen, 2012). We joined civic youth work and action-based research in an effort to develop democratic citizen skills through this research strategy and also to collect and use data for policy, planning, and (important here) evaluation. We used this approach to build the youth council, and we used data to plan and implement this, as well as to reflect on the work, on ourselves, and also on our effectiveness (evaluation). Research/evaluation done this way is a basic citizen ethos, craft, and skill, all of which are necessary for informed civic action.

I describe two specific aspects of this approach: the participatory process and the beginning mastery of civic roles and the co-production of necessary and useful knowledge—one aspect of which was evaluative. I then describe how action-based research/evaluation based in principles of social and cultural justice through inquiry and writing created an opportunity for authentic, respectful, and understanding relationships—to be established and sustained between youth and adults, thus providing a platform for crucial discussions and joint action—one result of which was the development of the Corps' Youth Council. In addition, I will address the challenges of creating and sustaining action-based research and its evaluative uses, and I will close with recommendations to enhance this practice. Note the distinction between evaluation as a social research strategy and the evaluative uses of data from social research. There are professional and scholarly lines being crossed here.

Action-based research with an evaluation orientation and evaluation use is especially important to imagine, design, and implement with young people because it can contribute to their citizenship skills and their general social competence at school, at work, in their communities, with friends, and at home. All of this is about inquiry and knowledge development and the use of these as citizen skills.

■ THE CONSERVATION CORPS

The Conservation Corps (CC) is a US nationwide nonprofit organization that provides hands-on environmental stewardship and service learning opportunities to youth and young adults, while accomplishing energy conservation, natural resource management, and emergency response work. The organization has a strong history, beginning with the Civilian Conservation Corps in the 1930s (Sommer, 2008). CC youth participants are 15–18 years old and employed in natural resource management programs. These operate throughout Minnesota and neighboring states with resource management projects in Minnesota, Wisconsin, Michigan, and North Dakota.

■ THE CONSERVATION CORPS YOUTH COUNCIL

Using action-based research/evaluation strategy and practices and civic youth work principles with youth alumni 15–22 years old and youth workers at CC, we together designed and implemented a Youth Council. Members are alumni or current CC participants, and the youth workers are AmeriCorps members (National Service Programs, 2015) who led CC youth participants in natural resource management after the school day and during the summer. The Conservation Corps Youth Council is one of the organization's strategies to engage alumni in ongoing service-learning opportunities. This was the organization's first attempt at forming a youth council. I presented my idea because it would contribute to the agency's goal of collaborating with youth. I was asked to write a proposal that would define the Council, its goals, and how it could be supported by CC.

I used this planning time as an opportunity to invite youth and youth worker alumni to work with current CC youth participants in an action-based research effort to figure out and develop a structure and guidelines for a Council. Several meetings were held with program staff and organizational leaders in the initial stages to build support. Once organizational leaders accepted the plan, youth alumni were invited to participate. About 200 were contacted by email, phone, and social media. Twelve alumni responded and attended the first meeting. Now there are seven active volunteer members from around Minnesota. Two are deaf and three are English Language Learners (ELLs). Our meetings are conducted in person, by conference call, or online in order to involve as many as possible. Deaf youth and ELLs face issues with accessibility, respect, equality, and chances for opportunities in their everyday lives (Hehir & Wilkens, 2008). The Conservation Corps Youth Council strives to empower, educate, and inspire deaf and ELL youth to work together on projects that are important to them, the organization, and their communities.

■ THE COUNCIL AS A PARTICIPATORY PROCESS

The Conservation Corps Youth Council is based in and uses principles of practice, collaboration, and cooperation. Council members, youth workers, program staff, and I work together to create pathways for youth involvement in decision making within the organization. We engage CC alumni in the everyday work of the Council, such as writing, media, planning, problem solving, and the continuing work of environmental restoration. All this is done in processes that support the mission and values of the CC and of civic youth work (VeLure Roholt, Baizerman, & Hildreth, 2014). The Council also works on evaluating our processes and outcomes.

In designing action-based research projects with the Council, our base value is youth voice. Program staff invite youth to participate in all the stages of planning and decision making. An example was co-creating the guidelines for the Council over three meetings. The group uses these guidelines to promote democratic approaches to choosing projects, agenda making, group consensus, building and sustaining the Council, strategic planning, and communicating with the larger CC about what the group is doing.

The creation of guidelines with youth is not new to the OST field, youth work, or informal education practice (Jeffs & Smith, 2010). As a civic youth worker, my approach to co-creating guidelines works at identifying the fundamental skills, areas of knowledge, and experiences so that youth and adults working together can play meaningful and powerful roles in planning, design, and implementation (Checkoway & Richards-Schuster, 2004a). Focus is always on the participatory process and the co-production of necessary and useful knowledge, and on the use of this knowledge.

Another example is when Council members were interested in planning and implementing a service project to benefit their communities. Council members decided to plan and implement a trash cleanup to benefit the Mississippi River watershed in Saint Paul, Minnesota. Council members invited youth program alumni, friends, and family of the Corps to attend the trash cleanup on April 13, 2013. Prior to the cleanup, Council members surveyed neighborhoods to identify high-need areas near the watershed. During the project, the Council members took photographs of the areas before and after the trash cleanup event. After the event, one Council member wrote a news article about her participation, and this was featured on the Corps website.

■ CO-PRODUCTION OF KNOWLEDGE

A common practice in the OST field is for adults to have youth complete questionnaires or surveys for adult-driven program evaluation and development. Adults analyze these data and use them for identifying program outcomes, which can be evaluated, and for designing programs and writing reports. Typically, youth are not invited to contribute beyond being respondents. They are not invited to be strategic partners, nor to engage in critical analysis and evaluation of relevant issues and actions. Youth and adults do not work together meaningfully to produce knowledge, nor to identify program and evaluative outcomes, design, or evaluate programs.

For example, Council members created an interview protocol for use with CC youth program participants, youth workers, staff members, and the CC Board of Directors, focusing on their perceptions and experiences of what it was like before, during, and after a CC youth program. Council members develop and use data to better understand what groups in the organization think about specific programs and how they work to achieve their goals and objectives (Sabo, 2008). Once the interviews are completed, members analyze and prepare data for presentation to the larger community—youth workers, program staff, and the board of directors. These are also evaluation data: Did it work? For whom? With what results? For example, Council members interview youth program participants on their first day of the program, during the program, in the final week, and 1 month after their participation to evaluate their experience. These data help us answer the question "Were we successful?" That is, did participants learn and enjoy the process, and did we meet our goals? The group together identifies some goals that we hope youth will achieve. Next we match program goals and youth quotes from interviews. By doing this work with adults and youth together and by linking comments to goals, we identify best practices, issues or problems, and possible future goals. These data are used evaluatively to learn whether program and individual goals are met and whether our youth work practices were effective.

The interviews and data presentations have increased reflective conversations within the CC youth programs, and these are evaluative. For example, Council members have been invited to present their findings at CC staff meetings. Youth workers have the opportunity to hear and ask questions about these data, and members have published articles and produced videos of their findings for CC's official website.

As a result of this work and these data, Council members talk about being increasingly connected to each other and to the CC. For example, one deaf Council member produced a video summarizing the data collected, and mastery of these skills led him to higher education in digital communications. Before this video, this Council member had no video editing experience. The deaf Council member worked together with a sign language interpreter and program staff member to be trained in a video editing software. A second member entered the University of Minnesota's Youth Studies Program to prepare for a youth work career. Before her council experience, she was neither aware of the Youth Studies program nor thought of youth work as a potential career. Others on the Council talk about the value of action-based research. One member explained: "By looking at the data together we were able to see how the different groups, such as Conservation Corps youth participants, the board of directors, and youth workers responded differently to our questions. The data showed us a difference in what people think the youth participants get out of the program, which is sometimes different from their lived experience of the programs. Through our research, analyzing and presenting the data, we were able to show that further training and education was needed." The comments from these Council members shed light on the evaluative nature of this research work.

To support and produce the data and youth involvement in the CC Youth Council meetings, facilitators learned that it was necessary to train adults and Council members before, during, and after meetings in action-based research practices with an evaluation orientation. For example, before the meetings it was necessary for each group to be prompted with questions they could discuss at the meeting. During the meetings, facilitators helped the groups focus on the interview protocol and goals developed by Council members. This work was the impetus for additional meetings to support training for youth workers and the Corps organization.

■ **MODEL OF THE COUNCIL**

After reviewing data from the action-based research together with Council members, a model of best practices was developed. To build this, the Council members first examined existing program models in youth development (Jolly, Campbell, & Perlman, 2004). Next, the Council created its own program model that included words that best describe practices from their work. After discussing these words, we then built a program model that could be used to talk together about the work. From our joint work identifying and building program models, we became a link joining best management practices, approaches to supporting and using action-based research projects, and a youth council. Using action-based research, adults and youth working together joined civic youth work ethos, practice, and practices to action-research ethos, practice, and practices and created a CC Youth Council, with interest and capacity for ongoing practical, useful, and usable evaluation (Compton & Baizerman, 2009) (Figure 3.1).

■ **SUMMARY**

Civic youth work using action-based research and evaluation can be done with young people. To do so, one must understand the necessary skills to facilitate and sustain this work. Basic are skills in working with diverse communities and with young people. So, too, is training in building and sustaining cultures of participation in the organization. One must work at getting organizational commitments to this work and necessary resources, including ongoing professional development (Fusco, 2012). Facilitators must know about how to implement action-based research philosophy and practice and to use this as typically written about and as modified to be evaluative—not scientific evaluation according to the American Evaluation Association and the vast literature on this, but evaluation nonetheless. These are questions, data, analysis, and interpretation, and importantly, there is action based on these: This is evaluation used for program improvement.

The Council's work is an ongoing processes of writing, evaluating, and planning for specific projects and events. Action-based research done by a civic youth worker together with young people can be useful in providing data for program

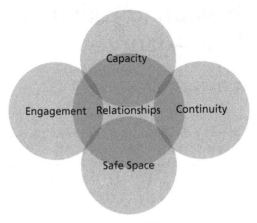

Figure 3.1 Conservation corps best Practice model.

development and evaluation, while at the same time teaching young people citizen skills—thinking, analyzing, organizing, and acting on issues and topics of importance and interest to them. This is about inquiry, knowledge building, and knowledge use. Also, this process can be used for personal and professional development by both young people and by adult program staff. By joining principles and practices of civic youth work to principles of action-based research, youth voice can be heard in evaluation and other research practices. In a deep sense, citizen work is essentially evaluative—learning, knowing, choosing, deciding, and acting on one's beliefs, purposes, and calling. Civic youth work grounds here; so, too, does evaluation-purposed action-research with young people.

4 Evaluating Young People's Civic Agency

■ HARRY C. BOYTE

> To broaden the scope of democracy to include everyone and deepen the concept to include every relationship.
>
> —SEPTIMA CLARK, *one of the first citizenship school teachers, circa 1960, on the goal of the civil rights movement*[1]

As Septima Clark's quote suggests, the civil rights movement for a time reinvigorated a broad and encompassing view of democracy, the idea of *democratic society*, not simply *democratic state* with elections at the center. This movement schooled me as a teenager and young adult in the 1960s.

My experiences in the movement shaped our approach to evaluation of young people's civic engagement and civic learning when I founded Public Achievement in 1990, as part of the early democracy work and partnerships through the Humphrey Institute. These movement traditions and experiences have continued to infuse our work ever since, including the Jane Addams School for Democracy with new immigrants, the Civic Agency Initiative with state colleges and universities, and the American Commonwealth Partnership, a coalition invited by the White House to mark the 2012 anniversary of the Morrill Act, which created land grant colleges, aimed at strengthening higher education as a public good. All have generated civic agency initiatives for young people and others, in which those involved take co-creative roles. All have been rich with lessons.

What's agency? Agency is the power to manage your life, to have real input on the decisions that affect your life, and to shape the world in which you live. It suggests an important measure of "I am the master of my fate," in the words of Nelson Mandela's favorite poem "Invictus." *Civic* agency adds a collective dimension also attentive to the well-being of the place, the civic life of a community. The Obama campaign in 2008 well conveyed such overtones with "Yes, We Can," from the Mexican American organizers' phrase, "Si, se puede." In East Africa, the term *Twaweza* ("yes, we can" in Swahili) is joined with "East African Citizen Agency Project" to describe a people's organizing and empowerment effort over three countries.

Public Achievement, launched as an international youth civic learning, empowerment, and public work initiative, later described in more detail, has embodied the goal of civic agency, collective civic empowerment, from the beginning. It has subsequently spread to hundreds of schools and communities in a number of countries. Two other civic agency initiatives whose evaluations are briefly described in this chapter, Breaking/Ground at the University of Maryland Baltimore County, and Action Research Teams in Flagstaff at Northern Arizona University, have had substantial impact on student cultures, self-conceptions, and sense of self-efficacy.

Although partners undertake evaluation of civic agency initiatives in different ways, all take the approach, which Michael Patton has called "values and vision-driven social innovation." Civic agency efforts develop pedagogies and practices that are about *empowerment of young people as an end in itself*, not simply as a means to ends like improved test scores or "overcoming the achievement gap." In fact, in education, we have found it is more useful to talk about "the empowerment gap" than "the achievement gap"—education today is something much more done *to* people (especially poor and minority people) than something people *do*.[2] At the same time, illustrating dynamics of what complexity theorists call "emergence," substantial civic agency initiatives often generate secondary outcomes such as improved confidence, increased intellectual and academic motivation, enhanced abilities to navigate settings which are open, unscripted, and filled with ambiguity, and capacities to build productive working relationships across lines of difference (Holland, 1998; Spencer, 2009).

Civic agency initiatives often also seek system changes, creating "free spaces" in which young people experience, help to build, and maintain sustainable empowering cultures (Evans & Boyte, 1992). "Complexity-based developmental evaluation shifts the locus and focus of accountability," writes Patton (2011):

> Traditionally accountability has focused on and been directed to external authorities and funders . . . charged with making sure that resources are spent on what they're supposed to be spent on. In contrast, for vision- and values-driven social innovators the highest form of accountability is internal. Are we walking the talk? Are we being true to our vision? Are we dealing with reality? Are we connecting the dots between here and now reality and our vision? And how do we know? What are we observing that's different, that's emerging? (p. 13)

The civil rights movement's democratic "freedom spirit" and its unfinished democratic work shape the main *rationale* for evaluation of civic agency—how to assess youth civic empowerment in order to deepen and enrich the experiences of empowerment. It accents *who* evaluates, in particular the central importance of collective self-evaluation. And it informs the *uses of evaluation*, to explore not only "is this working" for individual empowerment but also whether the effort is making system change.

It is helpful to highlight elements of the civil rights movement, my initial inspiration for concepts of civic agency and public work. Thus, the following recounts the roots of youth civic agency initiatives in the citizenship schools of the civil rights movement. It describes how evaluation understood as an ongoing process of social learning has further deepened and developed civic agency theory, and it gives a brief history and definition of civic agency, "the talk" we are walking, and its practice of public work. Then I describe three case studies of evaluation of youth civic agency and public work. These include a more extended look at Public Achievement, drawing on writings and analysis of Alyssa Blood, Susan O'Connor, and Donna Peterson, all associated with the special education program at Augsburg College, which has incorporated Public Achievement into its core curriculum. And, as a way to show that civic agency is not a particular program but a political approach to change, I also look at mixed-method evaluations of civic agency curricular innovations at Northern Arizona University and in the Flagstaff area; and a phenomenological evaluation of the Breaking/Ground co-curricular changes at the University of Maryland Baltimore County.

■ THE ROOTS OF CIVIC AGENCY AND PUBLIC WORK

Septima Clark, an architect and early teacher in the citizenship schools that formed the little known foundations of the civil rights movement, wrote the vision statement of the Citizenship Education Program (CEP). Whereas most public histories of the movement emphasize marches, well-known speeches, and acts of civil disobedience such as lunch-counter sit-ins—what the historian Charles Payne calls the "mobilizing" side of the movement—CEP and its the citizenship schools, begun by Esau Jenkins, supported by Highlander Folk School, and then taken up by the Southern Christian Leadership Conference, represented the "organizing" wing. Citizenship schools created everyday experiences through which people developed a sense of their power. Indeed, a close reading of Martin Luther King's speeches and writings makes clear that King shared Clark's views about democracy. In "Letter from a Birmingham Jail," King highlights the South's "real heroes," everyday citizens who were "bringing our nation back to those great wells of democracy which were dug deep by the founding fathers."[3]

From 1961 to 1968, CEP, directed by Dorothy Cotton, trained more than 8,000 people at the Dorchester Center in McIntosh, Georgia, who returned to their communities and trained tens of thousands more in community organizing and nonviolent change making. The focus was not only on skills but also on shifts in identity from victim to agent of change, as described in Cotton's (2012) book, *If Your Back's Not Bent: The Role of the Citizenship Education Program in the Civil Rights Movement*. "People who had lived for generations with a sense of impotence, with a consciousness of anger and victimization, now knew in no uncertain terms that if things were going to change, they themselves had to change them." (p. 135). Cotton (2012) calls citizenship education "people empowering" (p. 102).

Historian Charles Payne calls such citizen empowerment efforts in the movement "developmental politics." "If people like Amzie Moore and Medgar Evers and Aaron Henry tested the limits of repression, people like Septima Clark and Ella Baker and Myles Horton tested another set of limits, the limits on the ability of the oppressed to participate in the reshaping of their own lives," Payne (1965, p. 65) writes. "Above all else [leaders of citizenship education] stressed a developmental style of politics, one in which the important thing was the development of efficacy of those most affected by a problem. Whether a community achieved this or that tactical objective was likely to matter less than whether the people in it came to see themselves as having the right and the capacity to have some say-so in their own lives" (Payne, 1965, p. 68).

What is called broad-based community organizing, descending from these movement traditions (Boyte, 1999), continues developmental politics, what can also be called citizen or civic politics or "people's" politics. I began work at the Humphrey Institute in 1987, with the aim of working with partners to translate such politics into other settings, including schools, colleges, cooperative extension, government agencies, and nonprofit organizations, and also in youth work. From the start, Public Achievement aimed at developing an empowering politics for young people and also for those who worked with them, including youth workers and teachers.

Evaluating Civic Agency

> Imagine the impact on the southern freedom movement if its leaders and rank and file had to pause after each action to wait for a statistical evaluation.
> —Dudley Cocke, *founder of Roadside Theater, to a group of funders*[4]

> One popular idea when I was in school was the "continuum of service". . . that activism, service, international development, philanthropy and so on were all children of the same parent . . . . Let's spend less time congratulating each other on our impulses to do good and more time challenging each other to risk more and do better.
> —Stephen Noble Smith (2011), *"Lessons I Wish I'd Learned in College"*

We began evaluation of young people's civic agency experiences through Humphrey Institute partnerships in 1989 (though in those days we usually used the term "youth empowerment" and "citizen politics" rather than "civic agency"), shortly after the dean asked me to begin a project on democracy. From the beginning of the Humphrey work, the question of how to evaluate young people's civic agency development was a central concern, driven not mainly by the interests of funders, school officials, and other institutional leaders—though such interests should certainly not be ignored—but rather mainly by our desires to realize the democratic possibilities of Public Achievement and related civic agency efforts.

The challenge was to thread our way through the dilemmas posed by the two aforementioned quotes. We didn't want to destroy the "movement spirit," referenced by Cocke. Such spirit infused Public Achievement, and tying its outcomes too tightly to logic models and other tools of funders or other external authorities would threaten the aim of Public Achievement: for young people to develop skills, confidence, and the capacity to set their own goals, to act effectively on them in local environments, to co-create a culture of mutual accountability, and to learn that they can shape the world.

It also seemed to me, as Smith's quote about his experiences at Harvard suggests, that in youth civic engagement work good intentions and sentimentality about young people very often substitute for serious examination of how young people's civic engagement experiences can be debated and evaluated in order to deepen the work. Growth requires a tough-minded assessment of obstacles young people face, in the world and in themselves, in the way of becoming confident, bold, powerful agents of change and shapers of their environments.

As Patton observes, vision- and value-driven social innovation efforts aim "typically to bring about fundamental changes in systems, to change the world." To do this, "they have to understand how the system they want to change is operating and make changes that get beyond temporary and surface solutions." This understanding, what he calls "double-loop learning,"

> involves questioning the assumptions, policies, practices, values, and system dynamics that led to the problem in the first place, and intervening in ways that involve the modification of underlying system relationships and functioning. (Patton, 2011, p. 11)

We wanted to change the world. And we knew from the outset that Public Achievement, based on young people's civic empowerment, faced daunting obstacles in school and youth programming settings where young people are largely disempowered and given little room for self-initiating action in either individual or collective terms. Evaluating Public Achievement and other civic agency initiatives such as the Jane Addams School for Democracy and the community-wide learning coalition, Neighborhood Learning Council, on the West Side of St. Paul with this lens has provided insights not only into the constrictions of schools and youth programs but also into cultural dynamics that constrain or thwart agency in the larger society.

Middle-class young people today grow up immersed in hypercompetitive and highly structured activities that enhance certain skills and dimensions of cognitive development but that also socialize them in individualized accomplishment and dependence on authority, with few opportunities to develop capacities for self-directed initiative or collective action. Our civic agency colleague, family social scientist William Doherty, who has charted the erosion of children's unstructured play, recounts a conversation with a YMCA camp director who reported that middle-class young people have anxiety attacks during "free time" at camps, even when they are given several options.[5] In a similar vein, there is evidence that such norms themselves contribute to economic disparities, requiring poor and working-class children and young adults, from community and cultural backgrounds to make a choice between who they *are*, their cultural identities, support networks, and "interdependent values," and the demands of individual achievement and success.[6]

More generally, a positivist view of knowledge has spread through the so-cial fabric as a default, valuing credentialed subject-matter expertise but sharply devaluing common sense, local knowledge, culture traditions, spiritual knowledge, and craft and practical knowledge mediated through everyday life experiences. And we live in a highly meritocratic, individualist, meritocratic society, where "success" is an individual achievement. Nan Skelton, co-director of the Centers for Disease Control and Prevention (CDC) for a number of years and a founder of the Jane Addams School, a partnership with new immigrants, describes how much the CDC learned from immigrants about these dynamics. For instance, young, native-born American college students working with immigrants in the Jane Addams School—whose animating phrase is "everyone a learner, everyone a teacher"—were regularly questioned with amazement by elderly Hmong. Why, the older Hmong would ask, do you feel no unhap-piness about leaving your families and communities in the pursuit of career advancement?[7]

Finally, young people report that modern information technology, which generates useful tools for social networking among young people, can also substitute its own logic for theirs, divert young people from building interper-sonal relationships, and create environments of titillating but trivial pursuits (Hoffman, 2013).

Civic agency, as we have come to understand it through grounded theory building, can be described in ways that help to illuminate such obstacles. It involves people's capacities for collective action across differences to navigate and shape a world that is understood to be open, not static and fixed (Boyte, 2008). And it conceives of citizens as co-creators *of* the world, not simply deliberators *about* a world that is taken as a given, as *producers* of democracy, not as *customers or consumers* of democracy concerned only with "what can I get?" Civic agency is developed through *public work*, self-organized productive efforts by a mix of people who solve common problems and create things, material or symbolic, of lasting civic value, with reflective dimensions (Boyte, 2011). Public work also often develops a sense of ownership and connection to a place. These themes are all rele-vant factors to take in account when evaluating youth civic agency initiatives. Case studies help to illustrate.

■ PUBLIC ACHIEVEMENT IN FRIDLEY MIDDLE SCHOOL

As noted earlier, the youth civic engagement, learning, and empowerment ini-tiative called Public Achievement sought to revitalize the approach of Septima Clark and others in the civil rights movement, which I had seen firsthand in the Citizenship Education Program. In Public Achievement, teams of young people are formed, typically ranging from elementary through high school students but more recently also involving college students, to work on issues of their choice in real-world settings. They meet through the school year, coached by adults, often young adults or college students, who help them develop achievable goals, learn to navigate the local environment, and learn political skills and political concepts.

The first year of Public Achievement proved highly demobilizing for young people involved in a failed strike about a "no-hats" rule in a local area high school, and we came to understand the need for preparing young people, of any age, to understand the cultural and local dynamics of their environment if they are to become serious change agents.[8] St. Bernard's Elementary School proved the vital incubator for such learning. St. Bernard's was a low-income and working-class Catholic school in the North End area of St. Paul. Public Achievement became the centerpiece of the school's culture in the early and mid-1990s, through the leadership of then principal Dennis Donovan. Insisting that young people learn everyday political skills, and that all forms of work in the school, including teaching, have public and empowering dimensions, Donovan helped us realize the potential for "Public Achievement-style education" to grow revitalized civic sites of power. Since its founding, Public Achievement has spread to several hundred communities and schools in the United States and to Poland, Northern Ireland, Gaza and the West Bank, Israel, and elsewhere.

We moved the Center for Democracy and Citizenship to Augsburg College in 2009 partly out of the belief that departments and programs in a medium-sized liberal arts college like Augsburg, with a strong citizenship mission and the spirit of an "urban settlement," have freedom to innovate largely missing in today's research universities, with their incentive systems inextricably tied to rankings wars and with highly meritocratic and individualistic cultures. At Augsburg, special education, the PhD transcultural program in nursing, environmental studies, and other units of the college are beginning to incorporate civic agency themes into curricular and co-curricular initiatives.

From the beginning of our move, Dennis Donovan, who had become national organizer for Public Achievement, worked with the special education preservice program to experiment with Public Achievement as an answer to the critique of special education emerging from within the field. Students in special education are placed in programs, often segregated from mainstream students, because they are identified with a disability under one of 13 categories, defined by the state and deemed to interfere with educational experiences of both themselves and others. Those placed in special education often suffer lifetimes of trouble with mental illness, unemployment, and incarceration—one study suggests that as many as 70% of special education students will go to jail at some point in their lives (Reid et al., 2004).

Susan O'Connor, director of special education, wanted to try something different. "Special Education generally still uses a medical model, based on how to fix kids," she said. O'Connor observed that the literature in the field has produced an internal critique, disabilities studies, which questions such a medical approach based on positivist science. As Jan Valle and David Connor (2011) summarize the argument:

> Critical special educators . . . foreground issues such as special education's insular, re-
> ductionist approach to research; an overreliance on the remediation of deficits; sus-
> tained use of intelligence testing; commonplace segregation based on disability and/
> or race; the professionalization of school failure; and the continued medicalization of
> disabled people. (p. xii)

Donovan, O'Connor, and Donna Patterson, another faculty member, partnered with Michael Ricci and Alissa Blood, graduates of the Special Education program. Their goal was to design an alternative class in the Fridley Middle School using a Public Achievement–style approach. Over 3 years the results were often dramatic. "Problem" students, mostly low-income and minority students, who in many schools would be strictly confined to their classes, became public leaders on issues like school bullying, healthy lifestyles, campaigning against animal cruelty, and creating a support network for terminally ill children. They built relationships and received recognition in the school, and also in the larger Fridley community. Their Public Achievement work brought them into contact with school administrators, community leaders, elected officials, and at times media outlets like the local paper and Minnesota Public Radio.

For her master's thesis, Blood-Knafla (2013) used a qualitative methodology, conducting face-to-face conversations with five individual participants, making detailed observations of young people's behavior and interactions, and recording activities on videotape. She found substantial impact on student self-image, sense of empowerment, and behavior. "They believed that they were more capable then they had ever thought they were in the past," Blood-Knafla (2013) writes. "The students believed that they could be positive citizens and that the people who believed differently about them were wrong. This is a very powerful belief for any student in middle school."

Many expressed new pride and confidence. "I feel more mature and happy," said one. Another commented, "it makes me think I can do stuff that I haven't [before]." "I feel like we can change a lot of things in the world," said Katie (a pseu-donym). "The kids get to decide." Blood-Knafla (2013) observes that participants "began to express their feelings of power beyond the realm of Public Achievement." Allen (a pseudonym) commented, "If you set your mind to it, you can do it." Spud described feeling that "we can change a lot of things in the world [like] Martin Luther King did." Finally, involvement in Public Achievement had notable effects on student behavior. "It is a good way to learn to be more respectful," said one. Katie observed, "We don't normally get to work with each other. It was nice to learn you have to take in what other people want and you can't just insist on doing everything yourself. This is a group effort." Spud put it, "I didn't care about nobody but me. But now it makes me open and I care about other people. Like my friend, I make sure his little sisters get home from the park okay. The old Spud would have been like, 'whatever.' I think I have changed. It may be slow, but I am getting there" (Blood-Knafla, 2013, p. 68).

This Public Achievement approach also transformed the work of Ricci and Blood-Knafla. "My role is not to fix things for the kids but to say, 'This is your class, your mission. How are you going to do the work?' Our main task is to remind them, to guide them, not to tell them what to do," explains Ricci. The teachers became partners with their students, who choose the issues and learn how to work to address them effectively. Issues this last year included rewriting the school's bullying policy, making murals to motivate peers to get exercise, and educating the public about misconceptions regarding pit bull dogs.

Tackling such issues, students build up their citizenship identities, habits, and skills such as negotiation, compromise, initiative, planning, organizing, and public speaking. They also develop what Blood calls "a public professional persona." According to school officials and the principal, the project has also improved and deepened connections between Fridley Middle School and the Fridley community. Since this experience, the special education program at Augsburg has changed its core curriculum so that all 27 preservice students are now coaching in seven Public Achievement sites.[9]

■ CIVIC AGENCY AT NORTHERN ARIZONA

In Northern Arizona University (NAU) and Flagstaff, leading partners in the Civic Agency Initiative we launched in 2008 in association with the American Democracy Project of the American Association of State Colleges and Universities, Blase Scarnati and Michelle Miller bring faculty together in the First Year Learning Initiative. They develop faculty members' civic agency through collaborative experiences that enrich courses through active learning methods. In CRAFTS (Civic Engagement for Arizona Families, Transitions, and Communities), a second pedagogical innovation led by Scarnati and Rom Coles, nearly 1,000 freshmen in the school year 2014–2015 will undertake action research projects in conjunction with local community organizations and engage in public work on a variety of issues, from energy conservation and school reform to immigration and bullying.

Evaluations of ARTS combine standard measures, such as studies of student retention, with qualitative ones. The retention rate for minority students who successfully complete First-Year Seminars with ARGS is 16% higher than for non-ARTS minority students. For female students, the retention rate increase is 9%. Faculty report that ARTS experiences also significantly increase engagement with learning activities involving diversity, cultural influences, and multiple perspectives (Boyte & Scamati, 2014, p. 85).

The meaning of student experiences comes alive in the words of students. Rom Coles and Blase Scarnati (2014) report that "many have stated that this work has simply changed their lives." Questioned about their sense of agency, a student who had coached Public Achievement in a low-income elementary school (Public

Achievement is one option in the ARTS seminars) lifted his forearm straight up at a right angle from the table. "Before this experience, all the problems of the world just seemed like walls that were impossible to move or get around," he said. "But now, after seeing what a team of kids can do with a little coaching—they learn to work collaboratively together to identify, research, and act on an issue—everywhere I see challenges I'm starting to see pathways" (Coles & Scarnati, 2015).

The experiences in Flagstaff have also generated new concepts related to civic agency, like a "craftsperson ethos" among faculty, and the idea of "transformational ecotones," borrowing from ecological science, where overlaps among different pedagogies, practices, cultures, and issues generate new creative energy.

■ CIVIC AGENCY AT UMBC

The University of Maryland Baltimore County (UMBC), another lead partner in the Civic Agency Initiative, is a mid-sized public university with a strong history of public service and community engagement, and a national reputation for innovation in the STEM disciplines, especially for minority students, under the leadership of President Freeman A. Hbrabowski, who participated as a child in the civil rights movement in Birmingham, Alabama. Over the last 6 years, organizing by students, coached by student life professionals, has transformed student government into a center for student empowerment, while impacting student culture broadly. Deep insights have emerged in the process about the worlds in which young people grow up today.

David Hoffman, a key staff person whose position description, Assistant Director of Student Life for Civic Agency, itself conveys something of the changes, undertook an in-depth "phenomenological evaluation" of undergraduates' civic agency journeys, *Becoming Real*, as his PhD dissertation. He describes their views of "an everyday world that often seems fundamentally synthetic, structured around falsehoods, hidden agendas, or scripts" (p. 157). As Yasmin Karimian, who won the student government presidency in 2009 on a platform of civic agency, describes, "I grew up in a society that everything I did wasn't real, it was just practice for something that's real." Students also recount the new sense of authenticity, consequentiality, and democratic possibility as they learn to be effective change agents. "[We've] become alive," says Karimian, "[seeing] that you can make a difference on what reality really is . . . I wake up in the morning and think, 'I have so much to do and so many people to affect.'" (Hoffman, 2013, p. 157).

Hoffman reports that his initial round of discussions lasted 221 minutes. "In those interviews I used the words 'real' and 'really' a grand total of seven times. The students, on the other hand, used the words 'real' and 'really' 314 times . . . often in order to express the strength of a conviction or emotion." Hoffman notes that the term "real" comes from medieval Britain and France, where the word referenced the objective, concrete existence of a thing beyond people's imagination, and also the beauty and majesty of royalty. "Many of the students' invocations of the term seemed to carry resonances of both these definitions of genuineness and tangibility that was also special, rich, and noble. 'Real' people and communications were honest, open, and humane rather than phony, manipulative, and mechanical. 'Real' situations were organic and fluid rather than manufactured and predetermined" (Hoffman, 2015, p. 154).

■ CONCLUSION

Feelings of powerlessness have become more pronounced in the opening years of the 21st century. Lay citizens generally share the view of opinion elites that choosing the right leaders is the way to fix our country's problems—even if it repeatedly fails to do so.[10] The sense of powerlessness is acute in higher education, where educators also feel besieged by cost-cutting, profit-making colleges, "MOOCs" and other distance learning, and demands that higher education be narrowly geared to the needs of today's workplace.

Yet the dawning realization that leaders won't save us—that "we are the ones we've been waiting for," in the words of the old civil rights song—has also begun to generate a new movement in which citizens themselves reclaim responsibility for democracy. Signs of citizens aspiring to be the central agents of democracy are multiplying, in the United States and around the world.

Civic innovations developed over the last generation contribute practices as well as theory to civic agency. These include deliberative practices of many kinds; citizen-centered governance of common resources, which won the late Elinor Ostrom the Nobel Prize for Economics; broad-based community organizing; asset mapping of low-income communities; and an emerging effort, civic science, which aims to dismantle the "cult of the expert," reintegrating scientists into democratic society. The new volume edited by Peter Levine and Karol Soltan, *Civic Studies*, brings strands together in the field focused on agency and co-creation. Civic agency is also at the heart of traditions such as the Black Consciousness tradition in South Africa (Mangcu, 2015).

The Center for Democracy and Citizenship and our partners have integrated these themes in the framework of citizenship as public work, aimed at deepening civic agency. The public work framework reimagines settings like schools, colleges, businesses, government agencies, and others not as part of a static "system world" but rather as human inventions, communities that can be reorganized to become enabling environments for agency. We need a "long march through the institutions," to recall a phrase of transformation from the 1960s, making work more public—more collaborative, open, filled with public purpose—if we are to create sustainable foundations for the civic agency movement.

This also requires a process of social learning, which can be described as developmental evaluation, which operates in open situations of high complexity and helps us to build our collective powers to shape the future.

■ SECTION 3

Focus Evaluation Design

In the next chapter, Michael Baizerman illustrates the wide and diverse foci that an evaluation study of civic youth work could take. Dr. Baizerman has a long history of doing civic youth work program evaluation studies both in the United States and across the globe. This chapter describes the evaluation plan he developed while working with a civic youth work agency in Northern Ireland. It emerged from conversations with stakeholders about how they could evaluate both their program and then the work of the entire agency. What resulted was a "fantasy" evaluation plan describing what evaluation studies could focus on and how these could be measured. His idea was to move from a typical face-to-face encounter between a youth (youth group) and civic youth work to evaluating the possible effects of many such encounters on the level of the nation. This evaluation fantasy was intended to stimulate stakeholders' imagination of the possible (if not likely) effects of their program nationwide (and on their nation). It also sought to show how their everyday, mundane civic youth work could have profound, broad, far-reaching consequences nationwide.

The following questions are provided as a guide to reading the case study:

1. Which of the foci do you think will be accepted as legitimate by funding agencies? By young people involved? By program staff? By youth civic engagement scholars?
2. Given the evaluation studies you have read about in this book and worked on so far, which of the following questions and foci described in this case have you seen included? Which of the foci are most likely to be excluded or not recognized as possible foci? Why?
3. How does this broad and diverse plan enhance our collective understanding of evaluating the impacts of civic youth work programs?
4. Is this fantasy evaluation plan really a fantasy plan? In what ways?
5. What utility might such a schematic provide? To whom? How?

5 A Schematic Fantasy Evaluation Plan for Public Achievement in Northern Ireland

■ MICHAEL BAIZERMAN

Simply put, the basic idea of this evaluation plan and design was to think through and then try to realize a small, relatively new project with new-ish practices. This combination of civic youth work and youth civic engagement might be evaluated in multiple ways and on multiple levels to learn if it "made a difference" in a country ("nation," "province," "society"—all politically contested terms in Northern Ireland then and now). The intent was to show how a ripple effect might result from small-group work; the plan was based on the dreams and hopes of the project co-creators, staff, and participating youth and adults. Years ago, philosophers and scientists talked about how a single butterfly using its wings could have multiple, distant consequences on weather. This plan uses this as its inspiration.

For example, a Public Achievement (PA) community group of six youth and a local university student coach (or a PA staff coaching) could lead to changes in the role and acts, actions, and behaviors of young people with their friends, at home, in sports, at church, and so on, and also and likely consequently, in how schools understand and respond to their students and churches to their youth members, and further outward to how a block, a neighborhood, and a community saw young people. This would apply to the social role and in general, as well as how particular youth were seen, and on to the possible results of those on the public role of "youth" and on these particular young people, and on the public, citizen role of youth in elections, and on and on—a ball striking a ball that strikes a ball in a type of chain reaction or a type of multiple, sequential consequences.

I want to focus on several points in these paragraphs: First is the broad conception of Public Achievement as a project, one which could influence how a country/province sees young people/youth. The local can become national and could have significant effects and consequences. Thinking big in this way changes project plans and practices, hopes and dreams, and evaluation. It works to expand young people's and staff's notions of "what we are about" and of what we might accomplish, putting our small, seemingly local, even marginal or insignificant group meetings into an expansive, powerful frame of possibilities. This motivates, even if it frightens. "What we are doing here can matter, and matter 'big time.'" "We can make a real (that is, broad) difference."

Second, we focused earlier first on the social role youth/young person, and then on individual young persons/people. This fits with our conception of youth—the social role and youth—the idea as social structural and cultural notions which correlate to age and vary by sex, social class, and other local distinctions; this is the social construction perspective on age roles such as child, teenagers, youth, and young person (VeLure Roholt & Baizerman, 2013).

For example, teachers and other school staff perceive and respond to their young people as "students," expecting students to act, think, and feel in certain socially and culturally normative ways appropriate to being and performing the social role of student. Experienced teachers and staff surely individualize and can and do make distinctions between and among students, for example, who is super smart, who is best at football, who is more likely a student leader. The focus here is not on exceptions but on the social structure; this is often "the majority" or "the typical" or "average" when put in numerical terms. This means that a change in the idea "student" and in the social role "student" is a change in the expectations held by school, family, community, society, and school bureaucracies about what is and who is "student" and how "student" should be performed/done/accomplished (each of these is a different theoretical frame). When there are changes in how "student" is understood and expected to be performed, then there is a social structural change, and that is a *big deal*. An example is that students were supposed/required to sit quietly in their seats and take notes on what the teacher was saying for a later exam. Now students work in groups on the topic the teacher is lecturing on. This means also that individual young people and most/all young people will have to learn how to do/perform this new conception of "student," and this will have consequences on and for self-conceptions, behavior/acts/actions, feelings, and thoughts. All of this can be thought out and played out also at home (son/daughter, babysitter, economic earner, caretaker, protector), at church, on a playing field, and the like.

To make this a bit more complicated and to make it fit more closely into this text's subject, "citizen" too is a social structural "social station," that is, social role, and a young person can do "student" in ways which fit with, complement, or disclose (youth as) citizen. All of this lies in how the social roles of student, son, parishioner, or midfielder are performed.

Public Achievement is about citizen making, so the small youth group with the adult civic youth worker (coach) is a co-created space for co-creating the citizen role and for practicing in taking on this role with the intent of performing it in other life domains, life spaces, and life moments.

It is in these ways that the micro world of young people and youth workers can ripple across the near worlds of friends and family and beyond to church and civic society—locally to nationally.

None of this is especially new or an unusual way of thinking about civic youth work and youth civic engagement. What may be somewhat different is how these ideas were imagined and used for drawing up an evaluation plan. Joined in this plan are ideas, practices, and the realities of civic youth work—nothing more.

Yes, the evaluation plan contributed to thinking about, planning for, and working toward ways that Public Achievement could "make a (real) difference" in Northern Ireland, for Northern Ireland, and for its young people.

No, this evaluation plan in its entirety was not implemented.

At this moment (January 2018), the very contours and substance of civil society in Northern Ireland are contested, with drastic economic retrenchment in the public and economically dependent voluntary (nonprofit) sector, with dire consequences for the fully flourishing vitality of Public Achievement Northern Ireland (since unfunded and closed) and many other community-based local and province-wide youth programs, agencies, and projects.

■ INTRODUCTION

The following grand evaluation plan was written in 2000 for the purpose of imagining a nationwide evaluation of a youth program, and for using this fantasy to create local, low-cost, practical, and usable evaluations that could be brought together into a larger understanding of what was done; this process of bringing together data in this way came to be called "evaluation synthesis" (Patton, 2008).

Basic to the fantasy plan was the basic notion that evaluation is essentially comparative—actions against "outputs" and "outcomes;" youth work practices against changes in young people's knowledge, attitudes and values, and skills; a specific program against itself over multiple times periods, and very important then for an organization going nationwide, local projects compared to each other at one time and over time, among other possibilities.

Back then, and to a large extent still, our assumption was that the focal organization, Public Achievement Northern Ireland in contrast to PA in the United States but similar to Popular Achievement in Palestine, could be shown to have local, nationwide, and national-level accomplishments.

This evaluation plan remains a fantasy, but pieces of it have been used within PA as an organization and within its specific projects. What has proved enduring besides the dream of using this model is an evaluation ethos that is now in the social and managerial structures of PA, and to a large extent permeates its culture and practices, too; and beyond it to other youth projects and agencies, along with government and funders. Social norms, regulations, and practices are becoming institutionalized, that is, built into how youth services are performed and assessed.

■ CONTEXT: FALTERING LIGHT, FRACTURING TOUCHSTONE, FALLING CIVIC SOCIETY, BUT NOT AN OBITUARY

After about 16 years, Public Achievement Northern Ireland, a vibrant, innovative civic youth and youth work project and, more important, a presence, is at risk for severe diminution, even closure: It could be closed because public and philan-thropic funds are completely cut, or, if partially cut, a project or special activity could be eliminated, such as work with police on youth policing or with the fire brigade on the prevention of young people's car accidents. PA might close itself or choose to join with others in a new configuration, with the same or a new identity for itself or for the new entity.

I have been involved with PA since 1999–2000, spending weeks there most years as a consultant on youth work, youth programming, and evaluation, working always to imagine and then try to bring about ways of engaging young people in nonviolent, inclusive citizen work primarily with these Catholic and Protestant youth. I brought an evaluation gaze and a sense of how everyday, mundane youth work outside of the UK/NI youth club model could fit into reciprocities between youth development and community development; later this came to be called civic youth work there (VeLure Roholt, 2005) and more widely (VeLure Roholt & Baizerman, 2013; VeLure Roholt et al., 2013).

In Northern Ireland, with traditional UK "youth clubs" (Jeffs & Smith, 2005), Public Achievement was innovative and edgy, using, for example, European Union funds to create a 3-year, multination annual meeting on Youth Work in Contested Spaces (Magnuson & Baizerman, 2007), which focused directly and precisely on practices in societies in civil unrest, before and after conflict, in conflict-laden areas—all forms of "contested spaces." Our later coedited work on evaluation in such spaces was begun there (VeLure Roholt & Baizerman, 2012).

As you likely know, Northern Ireland has a fraught recent history of "sec-ular" tensions between Nationalists who want it to join Ireland in political union and Unionists who want it to remain within the United Kingdom ("Britain," or "England" to most in the United States). A peace accord was signed in 1998, and after civic space opened, older and new organizations developed new (non–youth club) approaches to young people, including a variety of community-based public health services, outdoor individual and group development experiences, and services for homeless youth and for LGBTIQ young people. Exchanges of young people to the United States and elsewhere expanded, and among other changes and openings, spaces became available for developing young people as citizens and, accordingly, civic youth work.

"Citizen" had a different ideational and political biography in the United Kingdom (including Northern Ireland) than it did and does in the Republic of Ireland or in the United States. It was more about voting and related formal rights and responsibilities than about—citizens joining in "voluntary association" to pe-tition government for redress, to promote their interests or to protect these, and in effect to train youth to be lifelong, active, responsive, and responsible agents for democracy, as it is imagined in the United States. With this came active, safe public work (VeLure Roholt & Baizerman, 2013), the work of (for and on behalf of) the group, neighborhood, nation, or society.

Active youth work in this civic domain is civic youth work (VeLure Roholt & Baizerman, 2013), and PA adopted and then adapted this ethos and practice to their sociocultural and political setting. Founded by Harry Boyte, Nan Skelton, Dennis Donovan, Roudy Hildreth, and associates at the H. H. H. Humphrey Institute, University of Minnesota in the early 1990s, PA was developed there, then diffused elsewhere in the United States, then to a few places internationally. PA in Norhtern Ireland made the founding idea, ethos, theory, concepts, and practices its own, crafting all of these to fit local realities, and by so doing, developing through practice an indigenous model, with far more focus and work as an organization on local youth issues than did its US founders, attending to local, and in Northern Ireland—a geographically small place compared to the United States and to most US states—the national (or in the Northern Ireland context, nationwide). The core issue there is whether Northern Ireland is a nation, a country, or only another region in the United Kingdom. In any event, the local can quickly, even easily become national and nationwide, and PA did this by making spaces throughout NI—rural and urban—for young people to be invited to and supported in being citizens. This involves doing citizen work and applying this to issues that were meaningful for them, and, to them—issues they cared about and wanted to do something about. In this work, by design and by effect, they joined the emergent movement there to enrich and make experiential the pedagogy of civic education: to learn by thinking, doing, and reflecting. This fit well with what is called "youth work" in the United States and "informal education" in the United Kingdom (Jeffs & Smith, 2005). By promoting the core grounding of citizenship as an imperative to act thoughtfully, as an ethos of public response and responsibility, as a lived practice no longer age-graded so as to exclude young people, and as a way of being-in-the-world, PA brought new and ever-evolving conceptions of citizen and of youth—as idea, practice, and promise, and of youth as citizen.

PA contributed actively and mightily to the civic dialogue in Northern Ireland (and beyond, e.g., in the larger United Kingdom) and to a larger, more vibrant, active, and civic responsibility-oriented conception of citizenship. It also contributed to youth work, and to civic youth work as a (informal education) practice that is citizen making and is about co-creating with young people spaces for responsible practice in becoming and engaging as citizens.

PA is at risk for diminution, if not closure, because of local politics and postconflict political structures. Deep and drastic cuts in public monies for civic society groups, organizations, programs, and services have resulted.

There is a shrinking of civic space, seemingly by design, in South Africa, in Uganda, and, yes, here in the United States, in Russia, and worldwide. Our recent elections (2014) will doubtless accelerate the closing of civic (oppositional) spaces, using not only "terrorism" as the rationale. The January 2015 events in Paris and later ones in Denmark and elsewhere will no doubt accelerate this process of shrinking civic space for youth (at the same time, we argue in the Preface and elsewhere that space can be preventive and ameliorative for "alienated" young people).

Look online at PA (and listen to BUSH Radio, Cape Town, South Africa, 89.5, streaming online) to get a sense of what is at risk here.

The fantasy Public Achievement evaluation plan has been contextual and introduced. It remains to be presented.

■ EVALUATION PLAN FOR NORTHERN IRELAND

[*Note*: Not all cells were filled in 2000 and are still empty (i.e., marked as "Not Done.")]

Method: PA creates small groups of young people with a trainer coach/civic youth worker, and they together democratically co-create and co-sustain regular weekly meetings during which they work to make changes to a public issue they care about. In this coach-guided process, each young person takes on several roles to carry out the group's work (project), always with guided individual reflection on self and group evaluation of its work.

I. Young People
    A. Role taking
        1. *Citizen role*: Citizen is both a sociostructural position and, in its democratic form, a way of doing public work. Young persons can take on and effectively carry out citizen roles in PA and elsewhere (by "citizen role" is meant "working on public issues/doing 'public work' "). Effective role taking (and effective carrying out) means meeting local and/or their own expectations of democratic civic work, alone and in a small to large group, by being a leader, doing group "jobs" (e.g., secretary, fundraiser, publicist, member). Citizen role is structural (i.e., group secretary), personal (e.g., when I act in that way, I do X because), and self (e.g., this is what it is like to be me when I am doing/being the group secretary).
        a. *In PA*: PA is young people working together in groups doing public, civic work on issues of their concern. Each PA group has formal roles, coach, member (leader, secretary, publicist, fundraiser, etc.).
            • Outcome: By the end of their PA involvement (e.g., 1 year), young people will have demonstrated:
                1) Knowledge of all of the group's citizen roles
                2) Understanding of the place of each role in the group's structure and work/practice
                3) Ability to do self-reflection
                4) Understanding of self-in-role
                5) Skilled evaluation of own and others' role taking (e.g., accuracy, competence, self-awareness, etc.).

b. *Elsewhere*
  - Outcome: By the end of their involvement (e.g., 1 year), young people will have, for example:.
    1) Done citizen work on a public issue outside of PA
    2) Learned about their democratic citizenship now as young people
    3) Learned about self from the experience
    4) Learned to evaluate such experiences
2. Other roles
  - *In PA*
  - *Elsewhere*

B. PA self
  1. *Citizen self/civic self:* Beginning ability and willingness to use own voice and to act democratically on public issues of concern in "contested spaces." The being and doing in democratic ways of one's authentic voice and one's authentic engagement in public issues of concern. Doing so in "contested spaces" means particular attentiveness to context (historical and present), situation, and biography of participating young people and adults.
     - Outcome: By the end of their PA involvement, young people will have, for example:
       1) Experienced democratic public work focused on issues of their own concern/interest
       2) Mastered, at an intermediate level, the ability to speak their voice
       3) Mastered, at an intermediate level, the ability to tell their citizen experience while in each role
       4) Mastered the ability to reflectively assess their citizen experience over their period of group involvement
       5) Learned to do safely group and individual work in the contested space
       6) Mastered, at a beginning level, the ability/willingness to talk about themselves as citizens (civically engaged, etc.)
       7) Mastered, at an intermediate level, the ability/willingness to talk about the contrasts between themselves as citizens and as noncitizens (trying to get at the postmodern notion that each is a "multiple self" of "multiple selves")
  2. *Reflective self:* This self can name one's lived (living) experience(ing) (van Manen, 1990) in ways phenomenological and existential, in terms descriptive, situated, and contextual, including lived self (lived time, lived space, lived body, lived relationships). All of this is focused on the meaning of the lived experience, on what it is like to be them,

there, in the moment, in a role, in a meeting of their PA group. This self could precede all of the others.

- Outcome: By the end of their PA involvement, young people will be able to, for example:
    1) Describe at a beginning level their lived experience of (a) each PA group role, (b) their citizen self, (c) other selves (see later), and (d) their lived self (body, time, space, and others)
    2) Tell "what it is like to be them" in other ways than #1
    3) Contrast their ability over the period of their PA involvement to reflect on themselves and to tell this to others
    4) Tell what PA "means to them" in their everyday lives outside of PA
    5) Talk about how they have (not) "changed" since being an active PA member
    6) Tell/write their "PA biography"
    7) Tell what it is like to experience and (try to) understand what goes on with them (and others) in "contested spaces"

3. *Vocational self*: This is the self who lives "the way of response" (Buber, 1975) to a vocational call or worldly address to civic work (public work), civic engagement, citizen(ship), and so on. For this self, PA is an opportunity to empirically test and reflect—to discern whether (and to what extent) citizen(ship)/public work is a way for the person to be responsible, authentic, and transcendent. This can be the citizen/civic self (or another self) experience and thought about in terms of vocational calling.

    1) Outcome: By the end of their PA involvement, young people will be able to, for example:
        1) Tell if and how they have been called/addressed to do citizen work
        2) Tell the living (lived) experience (reflective self) of being invited and compelled to be citizens and to do citizen/public work
        3) Tell how they went (or are going) about discerning whether this was a true call
        4) Tell in vocational terms/meaning what it is like to do/be citizen(self)
        5) Contrast what it is like to be called to citizen work, to when they had no call/address or a different one
        6) Imagine their vocation in 3, 5, and 10 years
        7) Tell how their vocational self experiences "contested space" in PA and in their everyday lives
        8) Tell in what occupational/hobby or other forms they expect to live their vocation and avocation(s)

4. *Ethicomoral self*: This self is grounded in and oriented to personal and social values and to bodying and living these in everyday life. For PA, these include democracy, nonviolence, social justice, equity, and inclusiveness. Each of these values is understood phenomenologically as a way of being-in-the-world, as well as more typically as a belief and/or idea (or thing).

- Outcome: By the end of their PA involvement, young people will be able, at an intermediate level, to:
  1) Tell their "core values"
  2) Compare their values to those of PA
  3) Tell stories about how they "live their values" in PA and elsewhere
  4) Describe the lived self of these lived values (in terms of body, time, space, and others) (e.g., nonviolence to another's body)
  5) Tell stories about those with different core values with whom one (dis)agrees
  6) Tell how living their core values works for them in PA and in their everyday lives.

5. *Caring self*: This self experiences oneself in PA primarily in terms of "caring," "helping," and "giving back"—as "service," as "charity" or philanthropy. All of these may be at theoretical odds with PA citizen/civic/public work, but it may not be at odds experientially and/or in terms of meaning. The caring self may be an alternative gaze on the vocational and the citizen self. For PA it is especially important to distinguish word choice from personal meaning and from lived experience; there may be great discrepancies among these, with young people using in an everyday sense a word which may have multiple technical, political, and rhetorical meanings and uses, for example, "helping" or "caring." This issue obviously is directly related to the policy issue and derivative practices about whether there is to be a PA language which must be used and its use assessed. All of this ties to the reflective, citizen, vocational, and other selves. In what languages is each self spoken? Outcomes here and throughout depend on resolving this and related issues.

- Outcomes: By the end of their PA involvement, young people will be able at an intermediate level to:
  1) Speak in their authentic, personal voice of caring
  2) Tell their personal meanings of caring, helping, and so on
  3) Describe their lived experience of caring, helping, and so on
  4) Tell how citizen/civic/public work can (but need not) include helping, caring, and giving back
  5) Contrast how helping, caring, and so on are understood inside and outside of PA

6. *PA self:* All of these situated selves together constitute the PA self; each works as a facet or plane of a fuller, more complex, integrated, and complete human being. Each of these five selves is also a language world and young people in PA learn to speak and name themselves in each of these (or others). The PA self as such is an outcome of the work.
   - Outcome: By the end of 1 year, young people will have at a beginning level: (a) a "PA self" composed of multiple other selves (see #1–5); (b) which can name oneself and one's PA knowledge, attitudes, and skills.

C. Learning

PA is intended to be a learning experience for young people, coaches, site coordinator, the site, and the host community, as well as for policymakers and the larger society. The first concern is with the young people: What does PA want them to learn and what of this do they learn, to what extent; and what else do they learn and to what extent? Some of the desired learning was taken up in the selves, as discussed earlier. Here, focus is on concepts (language, other knowledge, attitudes, and skills). All of this could be organized in several ways, for example, as knowledge about versus knowledge how to.

1. Knowledge
   a) Concepts: Participants are expected to learn a family of concepts basic to participatory democracy, citizenship, and nonviolence in this "divided and contested society" and in the everyday "contested spaces" in their lives.
      (1) Democracy
      (2) Citzen(ship)
      (3) Nonviolence
      (4) Power
      (5) Politics
      (6) Equality
      (7) Equity
      (8) Social justice
      (9) Justice
      (10) Public issue (vs. private issue)
      (11) Contested space
   b) Northern Ireland
      (1) As context and site of PA site work
      (2) As "divided and contested society"
      (3) As the site for a new citizenship
      (4) As site for a new democracy
      (5) As the site of multiple "contested spaces"

c) Contested spaces

d) Public issues: PA is a group process of engaging ("working on") public issues by doing "public work" (in contrast to "voluntarism" and required, juridical "community service"). Young people choose and work on a meaningful public issue and thus are expected to learn about this issue.

- Outcome: By the end of their project work, young people will be able, at an intermediate level, to:
  1) Talk in detail about the public issue
  2) Give examples of how young people and/or others are affected
  3) Show their research on the public issue
  4) Tell how the research was done
  5) Tell what changes in the public issue they are working toward

2. Attitudes/values: Participants are expected to try out, adapt, and/ or adopt at least a family of attitudes toward others, toward citizenship and democracy, toward public work, and to justice, equality, equity and nonviolence, and the like. These are values and beliefs that are foundational to an open, inclusive, democratic and learning society, as well as to PA. These "attitudes" (as with the ethicomoral and the caring selves) can be trusted as such or, as preferred, as embodied, lived realities, that is, ways of being-in-the-world in everyday life.

- Outcome: By the end of their involvement, young people will be able, at an advanced level, to:
  1) Speak in an authentic and responsible voice of the ethicomoral self
  2) Speak in an authentic and responsible voice of the caring self
  3) Use accurately and appropriately the PA family of conversation and debate about these "attitudes"
  4) Engage with others in reasonable conversation and debate about these "attitudes"
  5) Reflect on the presence of these attitudes in themselves and their lives
  6) Reflect on the place of attitudes in "contested spaces" in PA and elsewhere in their lives

3. Skills: PA creates opportunities for young people to develop a range of skills necessary and useful for democratic practice. These skills cover several life-worlds, only several of which are explicated herein. Indicators for assessing skill level have not been developed or adapted for use here.

a) Role taking

b) Reflecting

    c) Evaluating

    d) Group skills

    e) Public speaking

    f) Research on public issues

    g) Leadership of group

    h) Contract with adults in community and around group's issue

    i) Taking of minutes

- Outcome: By the end of their involvement, young people will be able, at an intermediate skill level, to perform consistently and effectively the following skills.

4. Act(ion)s

    a) In PA

    b) At home

    c) In school

    d) At site

    e) In community

II. PA Group

The group is the main context, environment, situation, and setting for individuals in PA. It is the site for being exposed to, learning, and practicing democracy. It is where and when role taking occurs and where reflective and evaluative attitudes and skills are mastered. The group's major output is its "groupness," while the major outcome of the group as such is its project.

A. As a group (Not Done)

B. The project

- Outcome: By the end of their time together, the group will have completed the following work on their project:

    1) Named an public issue

    2) Researched the public issue

    3) Begun to take action on the issue

C. Changes in public issues (Not Done)

III. Coach

The PA coach guides, consults, and offers technical assistance to the group. Coaches are trained in the PA ethos, approach, methods—civic youthwork—and embody and live these out with young people, as "models." Thus the coach must master and perform skills in working with a group, must explore her own reflective citizen and other selves and must learn concepts, other knowledge, attitudes and skills appropriate to PA. Basic are group skills.

- Outcome: By the end of training (Not Done)

    A. Roles (Not Done)

    B. Learning

       1. Knowledge
       2. Attitudes/values
       3. Skills
          1) Building a group
          2) PA group in a divided and contested society
    C. Citizen self (Not Done)

IV. Site Coordinator

The PA site coordinator is responsible for faciliting group meetings and other on-site activities. There are several required roles, along with the mastery of PA knowledge, attitudes, and skills, and always, in PA at least, a reflective self.

A. Roles (Not Done)
B. Learning
       1. Knowledge
       2. Attitudes/values
       3. Skills
C. Citizen role (Not Done)

V. The Site

The site hosts PA and as such can become part of the process, just as does the larger surrounding neighborhood and community. Often, young people choose site practices, issues, conditions, and so on for their work, thus transforming the site for context to player. Thus, there are site outcomes for it as host and others that may emerge with it as an issue.

At the end of a year as a host for PA, the site's people and the organization are expected to show some changes as a result of PA's presence. These include the following:

A. Staff
       1. Learning: The site is expected to learn about PA.
         • Outcome: By the end of one year, site staff will:
           1) Have a basic understanding of PA, its ethos, and practices
           2) Have a basic understanding of civic youth work
           3) Become involved in PA, for example, as trained coaches
           4) Understand the "contested spaces" within its organization and program
       2. Practices (Not Done)
B. Site
         • Outcome: By the end of 1 year, the site as such will show moderate progress in putting in place:
           1) Policies, activities, and practices encouraging and supporting regular and systematic youth participation in decision making (using Hart's "ladder of participation)

2) Policies, structures, and practices encouraging and supporting regular and systematic youth consultation on issues meaningful and important to their young people

3) A vocational statement about its ethos toward young people, including democratic civic youth work

4) Responses to how young people live and understand "contested spaces" within itself, its organization, policies, practices and activities.

VI. The School (Not Done)
VII. The Community

"Community" means (1) the geographical area of the site; and (2) the organized politico-religious worlds in and of that area. Because PA is site based, it is expected to have an impact on the host site and, by extension, the host community. And because young people live their everyday lives in estates, blocks, neighborhoods, or communities, they typically choose public issues to work on which show themselves in or as part of "how everyday life works for young people in this community." This involves PA as "social change": PA's model of reciprocities between and among youth development, community development, and civic development—or among citizen, civic, and community development.

Thus, there are two sets of outcomes, one for site presence and the other if community is a focus of the group's work.

A. Presence/host
- Outcome: By the end of 1 year (can add year 2, 3, 4), young people of this community and the politico-religious and organizational community will:
  1) Be aware that PA is in its community
  2) Have a (beginning) understanding of PA's ethos and practices
  3) Show (some) acceptance of these
  4) Become (somewhat) more responsive to the address/call of young people
  5) Have (or begun to put in place) infrastructure, policies, and supports for the regular, authentic, meaningful, and practical democratic civic engagement of young people
  6) Monitor and support the constructive engagement among PA, paramilitaries, and young people
  7) Be aware of the contested geographical, social, cultural, and other spaces experience by young people

VIII. Universities/Youth Work Certification

Educators in schools and (non)informal educators (youth workers) must be trained in civic youth work ethos and practices. PA is one model of civic youth work. PA's long-term success (and the success of young people's social action) will depend in part on the training and educating of workers. This is typically done by higher education and by youth service organizations. PA will try to influence their practices in part by creating its own. There are outcomes related to this.

A. Postsecondary institutions
- Outcome: By the end of _____ year, Queens University, (Belfast), School of Education and University of Ulster will have:
  1) At least an awareness of PA ethos, practices, and training
- Outcome: By the end of ___ year, they will:
  1) Have at least a moderate understanding
  2) Have a beginning acceptance of PA ethos, practices, and training
  3) Invite PA participants and staff to study
  4) Invite PA staff to teach in their courses
  5) Invite PA staff to develop course materials, modules, and so on

B. PA training/certification
- Outcome: By the end of ___year, Queens University, (Belfast), School of Education and University of Ulster, George Williams College (National YMCA College, London) will:
  1) Be aware of PA training
  2) Have PA-trained civic youth workers who will move into bachelor's, master's, and other training/education courses

IX. Policy

PA is an effort to invite and train young people to take on and master democratic citizen roles and to work on public issues of their interest and concern. The long-term outcome is a viable, nonviolent, just political democracy of committed and engaged citizens of all ages and a just, equitable, fair society. All public policy could be assessed against these outcomes. All proposed policies should. All youth policies must. Hence, there are possible PA outcomes related to each of these policy domains:

A. Youth policy
- Outcome: By the end of ___years, public policy will:
  1) Perceive, categorize, and respond to young people as citizens
  2) Promote and fund based on applicants proposals for inviting, encouraging, and supporting regular, authentic, and meaningful efforts to enhance young people as citizens

B. Youth service(s) policy
- Outcome: By the end of ___years, public youth service policy will:
  1) Promote and fund youth services which inviting, encouraging, and supporting regular, authentic, and meaningful civic engagement and citizen development

    C. Youth work policy

- Outcome: By the end of ___years, public youth work policy will:
  1) Promote and fund democratic civic youth work practice as a practice of choice

X. **Northern Ireland**

XI. **Project-Specific Outcomes**

XII. **Conceptions of Youth**

"Youth" is an age-graded social category that changes across historical time, geography, social class, and the rest. "Adolescence" is the scientific understanding of the youth, the adolescent. "Adolescent" is also the young person of scientific development theory.

PA is an effort to change the very substance of the idea of "youth" by including within it the notion that young people are citizens and that the society needs their substantive participation for its own development. Young people doing and being democratic citizens is a goal of PA, and thus an outcome for PA is whether and to what extent the social and cultural youth role is changed to include the conception of young person-citizen.

    A. Young people's citizen role

- Outcome: By the end of each year, there is detectable (and "measurable"):
  1) Change in the age-graded social role "citizen"
  2) Change in youth involvement rates on public issues
  3) Changes in gendered youth involvement rates
  4) More inclusive youth citizen engagement

    B. Changes in the youth role

    C. Youth as such

- Outcome: By the end of PA, there is detectable (and "measurable"):
  1) Change in what "youth"/"young people" means
  2) Change in "what and how 'young person' is produced and carried out"

XIII. **PA Staff**

■ DISCUSSION

This schematic fantasy evaluation plan has many spaces empty, but it may not be a (full) fantasy. It is easy to imagine that the plan could be implemented, with data collected and used for the program, for funding, and for broader political purposes. Indeed, some of the sections have been used to evaluate this civic youth work program.

It is presented to raise questions about how an evaluation of your project can be envisioned, designed, and implemented, so as to expand your conception of your work and its impacts.

S E C T I O N   4

Gather Credible Evidence

The following chapter is written by a group of scholars from both the United States and China. This case study describes an evaluation study of a civic education program in China that included a substantial service-learning activity. It describes how the study was designed to gather credible evidence on both the program participants and then also on the curriculum itself.

We left the text as it was written, allowing the authors to present their piece as they wrote it.

We offer the following questions to guide reading of this case study:

1. Is the program adequately described? If so, what did the authors provide that you can use to understand the program? If not, what more do they need to provide to make the program clear to you?
2. What evidence did they gather? Would you consider these data credible, given the evaluation study described?
3. What other evidence might you want to have gathered to increase the evaluation study's credibility? Why would you take these new data as credible?

6 Engaging the Whole Community to Assess Civic Engagement of Youth

■ ROBERT SHUMER, SHANG LIFU,
XU HUIYING, TONG XING, AND SHI PIAN

Many programs have been instituted around the world to produce successful adults. They often include elements of intellectual and personal growth, focusing on establishing goals and desires to become productive individuals who function in the social and economic portions of society. Foundational to the development of these programs is the necessary element of assessing and measuring the success of each component; of ensuring that the original goals of the effort are being achieved and attained.

A key component of this assessment of goals and outcomes is an evaluation design that provides the kind of information and knowledge that helps both the participants and program implementers understand the success of the effort. In some cases the assessment includes the actual participants (youth participatory evaluation) in the design and evaluation activities. In others, the program people responsible for the effort help to create the evaluation to ensure that policymakers and government officials are assured that the project is meeting its stated goals and outcomes.

■ EVALUATION FOCUS

The focus of this chapter is to examine a program that is designed to help young people set goals for themselves and to create opportunities to develop the character and values necessary to be responsible, caring adults in their communities and country. One such effort, Civic Service Education, is designed to engage youth in service-learning projects to help them develop caring, responsible behaviors, and to understand how to assess personal learning and community impact. Included in that design is full inclusion of the youth in participating in the complete evaluation of their learning and the program outcomes. As a full mixed-method design, the evaluation also includes additional input in the evaluation from university faculty who provide a second dimension and perspective on the youth-driven data.

■ THE GOAL OF CIVIC EDUCATION

The program and initiative mentioned earlier were instituted to engage young people in civic actions to develop their civic knowledge and skills, as well as to involve them in the understanding of the civic responsibility of citizens in a society. Although both have clear goals and program elements, whether these efforts actually result in civic outcomes of knowledge, skills, and dispositions is another story. Enter the world of research and evaluation. Without data and information that demonstrate these lofty goals and expected outcomes are achieved, the civic models presented are nothing more than well-intentioned efforts to create knowledgeable citizens.

■ CHINA PROJECT

Civic education for youth has seen a dramatic increase in the last several years. Whereas early programs, especially after the Revolution in 1949, focused on development of the China Youth League, more current efforts have been driven to include civic activity, especially service-learning efforts, in schools and community programs. Perhaps one of the best efforts currently being undertaken is the Civic Service Education program promoted through the Beijing Institute of Culture Innovation and Communication and the School of Social Development & Public Policy at Beijing Normal University. The project is funded and sponsored by the Ping & Amy Chao Family Foundation. The goals of the "School, Family, Community Intercoupling Service Learning" model are as follows:

> to develop students' civic service awareness; to improve students' responsibilities in serving family, school and community through after-school civic service practicing activities; to encourage students to make further progress on civic service by combining student self-evaluation with the judgments from partners, teachers, parents, as well as community workers. (Huiying, 2012, p. 2)

Activities of the program are focused on involving elementary-age youth in service learning in their schools and communities. The program developers have prepared various curriculum materials (*Morality and Life Form Standards*) that include PowerPoint presentations and lesson plans that teachers use to develop interest and knowledge about various topics covered. For example, in the fourth grade, students explore "feeling the difficulties of those in need, and giving them a hand." Students receive instruction in the classroom about what it means to have various kinds of needs, such as the need for food or friendship, and then devise personal plans to address some of those needs in the community. Students can choose to work in their homes, as well as work with others in their community.

The Civic Service Education initiative is designed to get students involved in various activities that raise their understanding of being a citizen in a community.

They go from focusing on being a member of a family in first grade, to studying specific civic needs in sixth grade.

The purpose of the evaluation design is to engage students and community members in the study of the impact of service activities on the lives and attitudes of all involved. As stated in the opening description, the evaluation focus is on student self-evaluation, coupled with evaluation activities that involve collecting information/data from those impacted and involved in the service.

▪ EVALUATION DESIGN

The evaluation system utilized in the Civic Service Education program is based on models of youth-led/youth participatory evaluation (Sabo Flores, 2008; Shumer, 2007). In such designs young people are responsible for developing the evaluation system, and they participate in both the design of the program and the collection and analysis of the data. In this example we will see how the youth use reflective journaling, interviews, survey development, and other evaluation methods to collect data about both how to initiate the questions and topics studied, as well as to actually process the information.

An additional component was included, external research conducted by college faculty, because the funder requested that there be other kinds of evidence produced that demonstrated more general program effects. Faculty from Beijing Normal University, the program initiators, also had individuals who were expert in evaluation systems and agreed to follow the program to examine elements of interest to the funder and the university, as well as unique contributions of the youth involved.

As part of the evaluation process, for example, students conducted a study of problems of the blind and use of guide dogs in their community, focusing on how to educate the blind and the public to support each other in helping blind individuals negotiate buses and public transportation. They are then able to interview blind individuals to see whether the program has helped them to have better public access.

As an example of the program development/assessment process, children interviewed a blind person who had a guide dog in order to become aware of the difficulties she encountered at public places. Through the interview the students learned that the existence of dogs in local areas is still quite unfamiliar to the public. In some places, such as supermarkets, buses, and even subways, guide dogs are forbidden from entering. Most people know little about the guide dogs and often mistake them for ordinary pets.

After the interviews, students designed a questionnaire (see Appendix) and conducted research among teachers and students in school. People's concerns about the blind and their guide dogs were the focus of the surveys. Bus drivers were also interviewed to understand why guide dogs are not allowed to take buses.

The students analyzed the results of the questionnaires and interviews, and came up with the following conclusions: Lives for the blind are quite inconvenient, yet guide dogs could help them in many aspects of life. However, due to the lack of awareness of the public about guide dogs, and some concern that guide dogs might actually hurt people, most public policies don't allow such animals to accompany their owners in many public places.

To address these problems, students searched the Internet for ways to help the blind. For example, to improve the blind people's access to sidewalks, several actions were taken: increasing Braille materials in public, providing paid taxi service in public places, publicizing awareness of guide dogs among the public, increasing knowledge about the differences between guide dogs and ordinary pets, and enhancing the training of the guide dogs to avoid public contact.

The students collected many stories about guide dogs, made a brochure, and sent information to other students and teachers. In addition, they also broadcast information about guide dogs to everyone during class or noon breaks.

Some of the information shared, as mentioned earlier, was based on surveys of students, parents, and community members. They determined what the general public knew about the blind and their guide dogs.

■ UNDERLYING THEORY

The underlying philosophy for this civic service education program comes from Chinese educator Tao Xingzhi. He studied with John Dewey in the United States at Columbia University and returned to China to develop many important educational reform programs, notably teacher education efforts in rural China. He believed that "teaching without practicing cannot be called teaching; learning without practicing cannot be called learning." Thus, all activities in the program required students to both learn in the classroom and practice in real-world settings.

In the Civic Service Education program, students study the principles behind the service and then are required to develop a service project with members of the community. They might teach their parents or siblings, or they might work with different groups of people in the community. In each case, they monitor the activities through evaluation to determine what happens as a result of their service work.

Evaluation of the service activities is an essential component of the program. Students are expected to do self-evaluation by entering information in a "Feeling Book" to record their personal changes as they perform their service. Such assessment helps them to understand the impact of the service on both the service recipients/community and on themselves. Because the goal of the program was to engage students as active, concerned citizens, such reflections helped them to understand how they were developing in those areas of skills, feelings, and dispositions. During the evaluation, youth describe the activity process and share their findings, in addition to changes in their affect and attitudes.

In a more specific example, sixth-grade students at Beijing Leifeng Primary School took on the activity of "Care for the Blind and Concern About Guide Dogs." A typical journal entry from a student reflection describes what students did and learned:

> During the winter holiday, some classmates in our class went to visit Chen Yan, a blind tuner, and brought New Year's greetings. Through our communication with Chen Yan and interaction with her guide dog "Jenny," we were surprised to find Chen Yan's unyielding spirit on one hand, and how their confidence was strengthened because of this public service activity.

Another student discussed her feelings and said:

> It is too inconvenient for the blind to go out. Even if Auntie Chen Yan has got "Jenny," which is like a pair of bright eyes for her, they would still suffer from a lot of exclusions from society. They can only take the "illegal taxi" of their neighbor, and they can only go to the one "CSF Market," which can accept "Jenny" to go shopping. We have to call on more people to care about the blind through our activity, and help them to get around with our practical actions.

Several other students reflected on what they did and what changes occurred as a result of their service experiences.

> At the very beginning of this semester, we contacted the "Capital Lei Feng Taxis" and told them that we hope the uncles and aunts in the team can take guide dogs. Wang Fengjin, the leader of the "Capital Lei Feng Taxis," was very happy after hearing our suggestion (on how to make accommodations) and promised to do so immediately, and also get in contact with Chen Yan. Now, Mrs. Wang has already carried Chen Yan and her guide dog "Jenny." After that, Mrs. Wang said to us, "The dog is a Labrador. Chen Yan has prepared a seat cushion for the dog, and it is very well behaved along the way!" Moreover, the "Capital Lei Feng Taxis" have promised that if Chen Yan makes an appointment, none of the 70 drivers in our team will refuse to carry "Jenny." Apart from Chen Yan, this service will also extend to other blind people with guide dogs.
>
> Through this series of public service activities, we have learnt to care for others, and we will try our best to help those people around us. Though we could not help every blind person to have a guide dog, or always get taxi service by our activity, we can let them know that they are not forgotten. Even if the world is dark, a light-filled heart can drive darkness away! We also believe that, with the care and help from more people, every blind friend can step out of their homes, infuse themselves into the society, and get the feeling that the world is full of brightness and warmth.
>
> Through study and practice, we got to know something about the public service class, and we are now much more interested. We also hope to take the public service classes like this in the future.

In addition to these great examples from student reflections, the program also encourages students to gather feedback from others, such as parents, teachers, and community members. Such information helps them to get a better understanding of the impact and quality of their efforts. Other participants, such as teachers, also provided feedback in the evaluation process. They often discussed the impact of the program on their students, as well as the community and the instructional program.

In the following example, from the "Care for the Blind" project, a teacher describes the impact of the project on students and community. He explained:

> For the entire activity, all the students have been involved. Through the process of making an on-campus public service activity plan—conducting questionnaire and interview research, concluding research and study results, making publicity materials and presentations—the activity was implemented step by step. The children did all these by themselves, and their initiatives were fully displayed.
>
> Through these activities the children have learnt to care for others and helped the people around by everything within their power. Though students' activity cannot help every blind person to get a guide dog or have access to specific taxi service, their actions can involve more people in the care for the blind. They publicized this activity to all the teachers and students in the school, as well as parents and neighbors, and created a strong collective effort to address the issues. This fully showed that they could not only dedicate themselves in the activity but also call on the social responsibilities of more people. For example, the children also noted: "We are in sixth grade now, and we will graduate soon. We hope students in lower grades can continue with our activity and go on with the project and carry on building the specific taxi service for the blind uncles and aunts and creating convenient conditions for the blind to go out. They can continue with building the taxi service between the blind and the Leifeng taxis. After they enter the junior high school, they will publicize our guide dog activity with the teachers and students, and make even more people know about guide dogs and care about the blind, and try their best to assist those who need help. We also call on residents in the community, as well as friends around us to reunderstand guide dogs and join us, and make our own contributions to the blind and guide dogs together!"

He also comments on parent feedback on the project.

> Parents found their children have changed to some degree after taking part in all kinds of public service activities. The children were fond of helping others before, but now they like to help others even more. During holidays, they would go to the communities on their own initiatives to get involved in public service activities, cleaning the poster board and helping older people in the gerocomium.

Several specific teachers made comments about changes in student behavior. They verified that involvement in service-learning efforts actually led to real change. Zhao Yingying, a third-grade teacher at BeijingYanshan Qianjin Second Primary School, said:

> Pan was a child who did not like speaking or expressing himself. After involvement in the public service course of Caring for Others, he expressed himself bravely in the

activity at the gerocomium, and danced the Gangnam style to bring joy to the old. Zhu was an irritable girl. After involvement in the public service course of Care for Others, in the activity at the gerocomium, she prepared not only musical instrument performance but also a handmade object: a small house, which is very exquisite in making. This has cultivated her taste.

Gao Xin, a fourth-grade teacher at Yong Tai Primary School in Haidian District, Beijing, said:

> After getting involved in the public service education courses for primary students, children's public service awareness has been increased, and they started to care about doing public service activities in society. For example, in the low-carbon environmental protection activity, students collected the old batteries of their families on their own initiative and put them in the recycling box at school. Students like Yiran, Yuanyuan, Yuxuan, and others and some voluntary parents also took use of the holiday time and sent advocacy materials to the community residents and publicized the harm of littering with old batteries. They then called on residents to take joint action and recycle old batteries in a correct way, which has made a big contribution to the public environment protection and was highly praised by the community residents' committee.

Yang Min, a third-grade teacher at Jiao Dao Central Primary School in Fangshan District, Beijing, also explained that:

> Students' writing skills are generally improved. Public service activities have provided writing materials for students' compositions, and students like Xinrui, Yuhao, and others are quite outstanding; some students have improved their speaking skills. Others have seen a spark in their interest in painting and have pursued a new desire to paint.

Wu Xianli, a fourth-grade teacher at Yong Tai Primary School in Haidian District, Beijing, explained that:

> After taking part in the public service activities, students have changed their roles in their families. J is a spoiled boy at home. However, after taking part in the activity, his grandmother told me that surprisingly he now helps to clean up the chopsticks and bowls after dinner and also helps her wash dishes. The child has grown up and become thoughtful!

Finally, Hou Xiaoqin, a teacher in Beijing Leifeng Primary School, related that:

> After entering into sixth grade, the students have got a new subject, which is research study. After the public service education in grade 4 and grade 5, students improved their ability for independent learning, organizing, making PowerPoint programs, and creating picture posters. Mengao, Shaohui, Jianing, and others who participated in the programs actually stood out in the new subject . . . they demonstrated improved knowledge and skill in doing assessment.

These stories about change and impact help to provide evidence that the Civic Serve Education program is making a difference. Clearly youth are developing more personal skills, more concern for public issues, and are changing their behavior to become more responsible and engaged citizens. They also reinforce the research on youth participatory research (Checkoway & Schuster-Richards, 2002) that indicates when young people become involved in evaluating their own programs, they become more proficient in related topics, such as mathematics and problem solving, and actually go on to help create new formal learning opportunities (classes) in research and evaluation methods.

In addition to these reflections on student behavior and growth, assessments from community members informed program operators of the results of student involvement in projects. Take the activity of "Advocating Civilized Dog-Keeping." Community residents have signed the "Civilized Dog-Keeping Promise" based on the advocacy and publicity of the students, and actively follow the community dog-keeping rules. Community service workers found that they can create a better community environment if the students dissuade residents from any of the uncivilized dog-keeping behaviors. Meanwhile, the children have improved their communicative and organizing abilities through their interaction with residents.

■ FORMAL EVALUATION FROM UNIVERSITY PERSONNEL

A formal evaluation was also implemented by Beijing Normal University, one of the program developers. Faculty from the university have been conducting surveys and interviews with students, teachers, and with parents/community members to better understand the impact of the curriculum on the teaching process and the impact of the effort on the development of character and attitudes of the children involved. A summary of the research/evaluation is reported next.

The overall assessment indicated that the practice of public service courses has benefitted students, teachers, and parents, as well as community service workers. First, students' initiatives were developed primarily by students. It didn't matter if it was in class or after class, the courses were dependent on students' personal efforts and activities. Students directed their programs based on their interests. Students helped develop their own learning agendas and moved from knowledge to action. Through such efforts and practices, students' intelligence, ability, and morality were enhanced. This conformed to the current educational reforms, which strongly engages the current educational practices of "setting up morality and building up people." Development of students' public service awareness and ability to serve the society was also promoted.

Secondly, teachers' creativity was highlighted. The challenges of doing community service caused teachers to modify their classes and instruction to meet the new issues raised by the community work. It helped force teachers to use alternative approaches to instruction, thus enhancing their own teaching programs. So the opportunity to do service learning actually helped teachers to be more creative in the way they did instruction in their classes.

The practice of service learning and public engagement actually led to improved knowledge and abilities of parents and community service workers. By engaging parents and other people in projects, students engaged public officials and community members in collaborating on projects and in implementing actual community improvement plans. So student growth was not only produced in the classrooms; it was also affected by family members and society. Because parents and community members were frequent partners on projects, they often helped students to learn more . . . and learned more themselves.

The Civic Service Education program prepared young people for citizenship by including school-based lessons and service activities as a regular part of the educational process (Yiyung, 2012). It intentionally focused student learning on family, on school, and on community and required students "practice" what they were learning through real-world applications. It required students to reflect on their learning, their experiences, and their service to better understand their relationship with society and with their community. Although still considered a program in its early stages, there is much that has already occurred to indicate that Beijing Normal University and their *Morality and Life Form Standards* curriculum will be spreading across China and influencing schools across the country to take a more active role in preparing young people for civic life. And reflection and self-evaluation, and other formal evaluation practices will lead the way to demonstrate that civic service education does have an impact on youth—and on the communities they serve.

We acknowledge that children and youth need to learn to become citizens. In many places that process of developing citizen knowledge and dispositions is left to chance. They engage their children and youth in learning civic action and skills through educationally based efforts. Schools and universities are involved in the work of preparing youth for citizenship.

In some cases, part of the civic process is to actually engage young people in the evaluation of their own programs. As seen in this Chinese example, such efforts help youth to reflect actively on their own experiences and those of others to better understand the goals and outcomes of the programs. And in some unique situations the evaluation actually becomes the pedagogical intervention for change and civic involvement. Youth who conduct evaluations experience the knowledge and skills to go beyond traditional understanding. They form their own groups and develop a collegial environment that empowers them to do extraordinary things. They go beyond the normal expectations and begin to become active in the implementation of their programs, helping to modify them to make them more successful.

Evaluation activities are the key to active citizenship programs. In fact, evaluation is a civic act and children and adults should be required to do it on a regular basis. It appears that the act of reflecting upon and evaluating civic actions can, itself, produce the very civic engagement intended by the original program. Let's make young people active partners in the assessment and evaluation of civic education programs. Such action appears to be promising because young people will have the knowledge and skills to participate as informed, critically thinking adults. And that should make society much better.

■ APPENDIX

Student Survey Civic Education Program

What would you do if you saw a blind person going across the street?

What would you think if you were made a blind person for one day?

What do you think are the challenges for the blind to get around?

What accommodations could be made to help them get around in public?

Do you have any good suggestions for the difficulties the blind meet when they go out?

Have you heard of guide dogs?

Do you know what guide dogs do?

What is your first response if you see a guide dog going out with a blind person?

Do you think it is possible for Chinese culture to change to help the blind and their dogs travel comfortably in public?

SECTION 5
Justify Conclusions

The case study in Chapter 7 describes an evaluation study of a civic youth work program in Belfast, Northern Ireland. From its design to the sharing of lessons learned, the case study illustrates an example of a highly skillful evaluation that utilized multiple strategies to justify conclusions. Although the US Center for Disease Control and Prevention's framework for evaluation (2012) delineates steps in the evaluation study process, with justified conclusions coming toward the end, this case study describes how the justification of conclusions is itself a process, one created throughout the entire evaluation process. From the beginning to the end of the study, evaluators are focused on what they do, how they do it, and what data they gather, and how all of this can be used to justify their conclusions.

In this evaluation study description, we see several processes the evaluators used to build justification for their conclusions, including the involving of stakeholders in the evaluation process (some stayed from beginning to end), constructing a clear design that framed the evaluation study and built agreement among stakeholders about what evidence would be accepted as credible, their triangulation of data (using multiple data sources to learn about the same foci), their presentation of data, and their clear explanation of these.

The following questions are provided to guide the reading of the case study:

1. How did the evaluation study design work to support the justification of conclusions at the study's completion?
2. What strategies did the evaluator use all through the evaluation to justify final conclusions?
3. Did the evaluator present the findings in a format that you found credible? Did this presentation support the justification of conclusions, in your judgment? How?
4. What else could the evaluator have done to further justify the study's conclusions?
5. Would you have chosen similar strategies to justify conclusions?
6. How much more and/or different work did the evaluators take on to design, implement, and complete the study as they did? Are you willing and able to do the same for your evaluation studies?

7 Evaluation of WIMPS

A Case Study of Civic Youth Work Evaluation

■ PAUL MATTESSICH AND PAUL SMYTH

This case study describes the evaluation of a civic youth work program, run by the Belfast-based nongovernmental organization Public Achievement, called WIMPS ("Where Is My Public Servant?"). The program intends to make politics more relevant and accessible to young people. As a project and a website, run for and by young people since 2004, WIMPS attempts to teach young people skills to organize, to campaign, and to bring views directly to politicians in order to influence decisions that affect their lives.

The work of WIMPS occurs in the context of a Northern Ireland that continues to live with the consequences of a long conflict, and in the context of a divided society, with new and evolving political institutions.

The chapter portrays how the evaluation of WIMPS supports program improvement, program accountability, and program sustainability. In addition, as this case study demonstrates, the process of evaluating WIMPS aims to accomplish several objectives broader than those of traditional evaluation. Public Achievement seeks to increase the capacity of the young people who participate to develop their skills to do evaluation—that is, their capacity for sound, critical observation, information collection, analysis, and systematic representation of how programs have an impact on their lives. Public Achievement also seeks to contribute to the increase of evaluation capacity broadly within the youth-serving sector. In the long term, the evaluation of WIMPS aims to evolve the practice of civic youth work to a new level in Northern Ireland and elsewhere.

■ WHAT IS WIMPS?

WIMPS states its vision as:

- To help create meaningful relationships between young people and the decision makers who influence their lives.
- To be informative, inspiring, unbiased, and accessible to everyone; creating, sustaining, and multiplying educated and empowered young people as a significant force for good in Northern Ireland and the world.

WIMPS attempts to communicate the voice of young people to public servants, both elected and appointed. It accomplishes this through political campaigns, articles (Web and print), films/videos, and other means.

Crews, normally comprised of 5–10 people aged between 13 and 18 years, exist at each of 14 community-based sites in Northern Ireland. Each crew has at least one coach (a volunteer or a WIMPS staff person). Crews meet approximately weekly, from September through May. Public Achievement also organises summer activities such as media camps for teenagers.

Crew members receive education regarding the political process, as a regular part of the program's curriculum. They also receive training and supervised experience in interviewing, the use of technology, and political campaign management. Each crew plans and develops media and political projects/campaigns. A number of successful campaigns have launched under the auspices of WIMPS, including a unique and effective campaign to end paramilitary beatings and shootings known locally as "punishment attacks" in Northern Ireland. Other campaigns include campaigning for vote rights at age 16; a campaign for first aid and suicide prevention training in schools; campaigns for better rural transport; and a host of other issues.

The WIMPS program has developed a highly interactive multimedia website (http://wimps.tv). The website contains tools such as a political search where young people can identify and send messages to their elected representatives, and a bespoke set of campaigning tools—allowing young people to set up and run their own campaigns. The site is also a repository of the work of the local crews—including interviews with politicians, films about issues that the young people are concerned about, and articles and discussions created by young people.

In the past 2 years, more than 260 young people have participated in WIMPS as crew members and coaches. Significantly more young people are engaged through the website content and events run by Public Achievement both online and (mainly) in the real world.

■ WHAT OUTCOMES DOES WIMPS HOPE TO ACHIEVE?

WIMPS builds upon a program theory that incorporates elements of youth development, youth civic engagement, and the values related to participation in democratic civil society. This theory permeates the thinking of staff and coaches, who consciously attempt to use it to shape their day-to-day interaction with the WIMPS crew members.

The WIMPS program hopes to achieve both individual and societal outcomes. For young people as individuals, WIMPS intends to produce the following:

• Increased knowledge about, and interaction with, politicians
• Increased skills for conducting political campaigns
• Increased skills with technology important for communications
• Increased social capital

TABLE 7.1. *Logic Model—WIMPS*

Inputs	Activities	Outputs	Outcomes Short Term	Outcomes Longer Term
Young people	Recruit, train, develop Crews	WIMPS infrastructure in Northern Ireland	Policy changes based on youth advocacy	Stronger sense of citizenship and commitment to shared society
Staff, volunteers	Develop web content	Crew engagement with politicians	Bridging among cross-community groups	More young people sustain political skills as adults
Equipment	Initiate campaigns	Crew meetings and activities	Strong links between young people and politicians	New models developed for youth advocacy
Web Site	Develop evaluation	Cross-community activism	Beginnings of international youth advocacy network	Greater evaluation capacity in youth advocacy community
Delivery Partners		Youth content on website		WIMPS as convener of international network
Income				

For society (in Northern Ireland, at a minimum), it hopes to:

- Influence the political decision-making process
- Improve the well-being of young people
- Create bridges among groups and communities who have been separate from, and sometimes hostile toward, one another
- Support a stronger sense of citizenship and a commitment to a shared society
- Create new models of youth advocacy, youth advocacy training, and capacity building
- Increase evaluation capacity within the youth advocacy community

A logic model, depicting the civic action theory of WIMPS, appears in Table 7.1.

■ HOW HAS EVALUATION OCCURRED?

The evaluation of the WIMPS project has the following purposes:

- To understand effectiveness: What impacts does the project have? What outcomes does it achieve (e.g., establishing itself as a youth advocacy tool, building the skills of young people to engage people in power, changing policy related to youth issues, building social capital, etc.)?
- To contribute to the development of the project: Based on feedback from participants and others, how can WIMPS improve?
- To build the capacity of young people to do evaluation: Young people participate in the design of the evaluation and the interpretation of results. This distinctive

feature of the evaluation enables young people to develop critical thinking and evidence-gathering skills, which they can apply in other situations.

- To demonstrate the potential value of WIMPS for other organizations: Results from the evaluation will be presented to and discussed with others in the field of youth work locally and internationally.

Similar to all elements of WIMPS, the design of research and evaluation of the program involved a group of young people working in partnership with WIMPS staff to identify evaluation questions and methods. A team of international evaluators has facilitated the evaluation process, which began formally in April 2011 and remains active. WIMPS formed an evaluation committee, comprised of program participants (both coaches and crew members) from several sites; several WIMPS staff; a local evaluator; and the international evaluators. Over the course of the evaluation, some turnover has occurred among the members of the committee.

Design Process

The evaluation committee made major decisions regarding the evaluation design at a series of weekend residential meetings held every 6–12 months. About 20 young people (crew members, plus a few coaches), four Public Achievement staff, and three consultants (two international; one from Northern Ireland) participated in each Friday through Sunday meeting during which the group focused intensively on evaluation. Each meeting had a similar format:

- Review of the background, aims, and activities of the WIMPS program.
- Education regarding evaluation, delivered by the international evaluators. This had two purposes: to enable the group to contribute more productively to evaluation discussions, by virtue of understanding evaluation concepts and terms; and to further the aim of building evaluation capacity among young people and youth advocates.
- Discussion and decisions regarding the design of the evaluation. Meeting participants co-created every element of the plan for collecting, analyzing, and reporting information.
- Review of findings (at the later meetings).

To fulfill the WIMPS evaluation goal, "to build the capacity of young people to do evaluation," the overall design of the evaluation process, as well as selection and design of specific data collection instruments, occurred co-creatively among WIMPS crew members and coaches, WIMPS staff, and the external evaluation team. Young people participated fully in all aspects of the design: identifying key questions that the evaluation should answer; determining data requirements for assessing the project; and specifying procedures to maintain the objectivity, relevance, and usefulness of the evaluation results.

In selecting and designing data collection instruments, young people assessed with the professional evaluators which instruments would have the greatest reliability and validity. They contributed to the generation of the initial drafts of instruments; they tested and critiqued the drafts to produce optimal final versions.

Evaluation Research Questions and Instruments

In its initial meetings, the evaluation committee identified the major research questions that the evaluation would address. First, the committee members framed questions based on the components of the logic model. Then, they formulated additional questions that would elicit data useful for program accountability, improvement, and sustainability.

Within this process, the program staff and the evaluators educated everyone regarding the background and operations of WIMPS and regarding the contents of the logic model. The committee split into small groups, each assigned to a different topic or to a different component of the logic model. In small groups, evaluation committee members drafted research questions. The small groups reported back to the full committee; after additional discussion, the full committee recommended questions for the evaluation to address.

After identifying the major research questions for the evaluation, the committee considered which instruments would best collect the desired information. The conversation about instruments led to the revision or elimination of some of the research questions. This occurred, for example, if it appeared that data collection for certain information might not be feasible, or that it might not be a worthwhile use of resources relative to its potential value.

During times between meetings of the full evaluation committee, the WIMPS staff and the evaluation consultants developed instruments to fulfill the design plan established by the committee.

A list of the evaluation questions and of the instruments intended to provide data addressing each question appears in Table 7.2.

Data Collection

Ongoing data collection has included the following:

- Registration forms completed by crew members and coaches. At the time of joining WIMPS, each crew member and coach completes a registration form, online or paper version, which gathers information on demographic characteristics (e.g., age, gender, community); extent of prior interaction with politicians; type of political participation; media production experience; and use of news sources.

TABLE 7.2. *Evaluation Questions and Methods*

Questions We Want to Answer	Method(s) for Answering Questions
CREW: How many young people are crew members? What are their social characteristics, community backgrounds?	Registration form (online or paper), indicating age, gender, postcode, Protestant/Catholic
CREW: Have crew members met politicians before?	Registration form (online or paper) Online survey (6-month intervals)
CREW: What is the technical competence level of the crew (before WIMPS, during participation)?	Registration form (online or paper) Online survey (6-month intervals)
CREW: How do crew members think WIMPS has helped them have an influence on the Northern Irish scene?	Online survey (6-month intervals) Interviews by external evaluators
CREW: How has WIMPS impacted crew members' perceptions of other communities and of politics/politicians?	Online survey (6-month intervals) Interviews by external evaluators
COACHES: What experiences have coaches had with young people and politicians (before participating, and after)? How do coaches feel about being a coach? Do coaches feel supported and valued?	Registration form for coaches Interviews of coaches by external evaluators
CREW and COACHES: Do they feel that WIMPS differs from other youth programs? If so, how?	Online survey (6-month intervals)
CREW and COACHES: How do they feel that we could improve WIMPS?	Online survey (6-month intervals) Survey of other youth organizations and schools Focus groups
CREW and COACHES: What do they feel are the strongest points to persuade people to join WIMPS? Why do the people come back? How do we create a safe space for people to speak out? What skills do you need for that?	Focus group of staff, crew, volunteers Survey of same Survey of other youth groups
CREW and COACHES: Have WIMPS participants' connections with other communities and traditions increased? If not, why? Have participants' abilities to relate to sensitive issues increased?	Online survey (6-month intervals) Focus groups
POLITICIANS: How well is the WIMPS program known by politicians?	Survey of politicians
POLITICIANS: How do politicians think that WIMPS has helped highlight youth issues in Northern Ireland? Would they have been as aware of youth issues without WIMPS?	Survey of politicians and/or staff? Interview of politicians periodically (external evaluators)
POLITICIANS: How many politicians have been contacted? How has it changed them?	Database records Survey of politicians and/or staff Document the process of doing interviews with politicians
CREW: Are people at WIMPS involved with other groups?	Online survey (6-month intervals)
CREW: What did young people learn that they hadn't known before coming to WIMPS?	Interviews with a sample of young people, by external evaluators

TABLE 7.2. *Continued*

Questions We Want to Answer	Method(s) for Answering Questions
WEBSITE: Number of comments and the quality of the conversations	Site statistics
	External evaluator analysis of conversations
	Monitor authors' engagement in conversations
WEBSITE: How useful is the site in lobbying and campaigning?	Google analytics
	Interviews of users (who did lobbying/campaigning) by external evaluators
	Possible comparative analysis of options
	Media monitoring
Has WIMPS had an impact on public policy?	Interviews of policy staff by external evaluators
	Records in political system
Has social capital formed/increased between WIMPS and political groups?	Online survey (6-month intervals)
Has social capital formed/increased among crew members?	Interviews by external evaluators

- Surveys of crew members. Crew members complete online surveys approximately every 6 months. These surveys gather information on the same topics covered in the registration form; they also gather feedback regarding the WIMPS experience. A small number of crew members are selected for in-person interviews and focus groups with the external evaluators.
- Coach interviews. Coaches participate in interviews with the external evaluators, covering topics similar to those in the registration form, plus other topics related to their experiences and to the WIMPS program overall.
- Website usage monitoring. Google Analytics provides site statistics.
- Interviews of program staff. The external evaluators conduct occasional interviews with program staff regarding the volume and types of activities; the interviews also obtain staff observations on how well the program is performing, what is going well, what is not going well, and so on
- Survey of other, youth-serving organizations. Other youth-serving organizations responded to a survey that measured their knowledge and opinions of WIMPS.

■ WHAT ARE THE INITIAL FINDINGS?

Results of the evaluation[1] so far have demonstrated that, as a result of participation in WIMPS:

- Young people's knowledge about their politicians increases, as does the amount of interaction they have with politicians—at local and national levels.

- Skills in using audio and video technology increase.
- Acquisition of information about local, national, and world politics and affairs increases.
- The social capital of participants increases.

As of now, the evaluation includes data at two time points: baseline information for program participants (that is, measurements at the time of joining WIMPS); and one wave of follow-up information, collected approximately 6 to 9 months after program entry. Selected, initial findings, comparing baseline to follow-up, appear in Table 7.3.[2]

■ **WHAT ARE THE MAJOR LESSONS?**

About the Program

This type of civic youth work program can effectively increase youth civic engagement. Demonstration of positive changes in the knowledge, skills, and behavior among the young people involved in WIMPS appears in the before–after data collected through the evaluation so far. Participants in the program increased their familiarity with politicians, their interaction with politicians, their interaction with others regarding politics, and their skills for political campaigning. In addition, they broadened their sources of information about current events.

Interpretation of these findings, for a cohort of initial participants in WIMPS, suggests that WIMPS creates a space where young people with different histories and outlooks can come together in a relatively safe environment to pursue civic projects collaboratively. WIMPS creates an alternative youth environment within the unique context of Northern Ireland.

About Evaluation of Program Impacts on Social Capital

Early results suggest that WIMPS does increase the social capital of young people. The data show that WIMPS activities offer participants the opportunity to interact with other young people of both similar and dissimilar backgrounds. Participants include females and males, young people of different ages, and members of both Protestant and Catholic communities, thus bridging social and cultural divides. WIMPS participants tend to inform other participants about the program and invite them to join.

About Involving Young People in Evaluation

Young people, such as those who participate in WIMPS, can collaborate productively in, and add value to, the design and implementation of a program evaluation. This experience has demonstrated that young people without formal evaluation training can grasp the basic principles of evaluation and use those principles to develop overall research questions and to participate in the selection and design of reliable, valid evaluation data collection instruments.

TABLE 7.3. *Changes Experienced by WIMPS Crew Members*

Characteristics of Crew Members	Status Prior to Participation in WIMPS (Baseline)	First Follow-Up (Approximately 6 to 9 months after Joining WIMPS)	Second Follow-Up (Approximately 6 to 9 months after First Follow-up)
	Interaction with politicians		
Number of local councilors crew member knows by name	None: 52% 1–3: 37% 4 or more: 11%	None: 13% 1–3: 25% 4 or more: 62%	None: 0% 1–3: 2% 4 or more: 98%
Number of local councilors crew member met	None: 56% 1–3: 38% 4 or more: 6%	None: 12% 1–3: 37% 4 or more: 51%	None: 0% 1–3: 44% 4 or more: 56%
Number of MLAs crew members met	None: 72% 1–3: 24% 4 or more: 4%	None: 24% 1–3: 52% 4 or more: 23%	None: 0% 1–3: 63% 4 or more: 37%
Frequency of talking with councilor or councilor's office staff	Never: 68% A few times: 29% Monthly: 3%	Never: 19% A few times: 52% Monthly: 29%	Never: 2% A few times: 65% Monthly: 34%
	Political participation—member of, or participated in		
Political society in school	11%	17%	20%
Political society	8%	20%	23%
Campaigning organization	13%	17%	19%
	Media production experience—experience using:		
Video camera	No experience: 28% Little experience: 29% Some experience: 27% Experienced: 11% Very experienced: 5%	No experience: 6% Little experience: 7% Some experience: 9% Experienced: 29% Very experienced: 49%	No experience: 3% Little experience: 0% Some experience: 2% Experienced: 23% Very experienced: 32%
	Media production experience—editing of:		
Audio files	29%	71%	85%
Video files	36%	76%	83%
Pictures	59%	87%	95%
	Posted comments, photos, videos, links, or status updates on:		
Facebook	93%	98%	100%
Twitter	42%	66%	72%
Another site	39%	44%	63%
	Sources of news		
Watch/listen to news programs	Never: 8% Once: 4% A few times: 34% Every month: 11% Every week or more: 43%	Never: 4% Once: 2% A few times: 16% Every month: 16% Every week or more: 64%	Never: 0% Once: 0% A few times: 3% Every month: 22% Every week or more: 76%
Websites	Never: 19% Once: 3% A few times: 32% Every month: 11% Every week or more: 35%	Never: 5% Once: 0% A few times: 19% Every month: 14% Every week or more: 63%	Never: 2% Once: 0% A few times: 11% Every month: 9% Every week or more: 79%
Read newspapers/magazines	Never: 12% Once: 7% A few times: 33% Every month: 14% Every week or more: 34%	Never: 5% Once: 4% A few times: 17% Every month: 16% Every week or more: 58%	Never: 3% Once: 5% A few times: 20% Every month: 19% Every week or more: 54%

The perspectives of the young people on the WIMPS evaluation committee injected new dimensions into the evaluation on at least two levels. On one level, those perspectives enhanced the operationalization of concepts that evaluation instruments would measure. At another level, the input from young people on the committee ensured optimal alignment with the contemporary vernacular among youth. That input also significantly shaped expectations regarding the logistics of evaluation data collection, thus improving the completeness and richness of the information collected.

Involvement of young people presents special challenges. School schedules dominate their lives and largely dictate their availability, for example. Over time, circumstances can sometimes change so as to preclude continuation with the work. Young people may progress into a new school, accept new employment, or change their residence—resulting in a change in their ability to participate in WIMPS. Nonetheless, this case study shows that an effective process that genuinely involves young people in meaningful co-creation of an evaluation can overcome those challenges. Those young people whose schedules permit remain engaged over time. Others cycle in and out of participation, but nonetheless contribute substantially.

■ WHAT RECOMMENDATIONS DOES THE EVALUATION OF WIMPS LEAD US TO MAKE FOR THE EVALUATION OF YOUTH CIVIC ENGAGEMENT AND CIVIC YOUTH WORK?

Based on the program evaluation of WIMPS, we make the following recommendations for consideration by the field of civic youth work evaluation.

Incorporate a Triangulated Approach to the Collection of Information

As noted earlier, the WIMPS evaluation made use of several data collection instruments—obtaining information from young people who participated as crew members, from coaches, from staff, and from other, youth-serving organizations. In this way, the evaluation reflected multiple perspectives.

Involve Young People in the Evaluation Design

Collaboration between WIMPS participants, staff, and the evaluators enhanced the evaluation in the framing of evaluation research questions, the operationalization of concepts to be measures, and the shaping of logistical procedures for optimizing the collection of as much reliable information as possible regarding the impacts of the program on participants.

As a community-based research strategy, this approach requires features differing from a top-down, more standard evaluation research approach. In working with young people, and community members more broadly, evaluators need to act with flexibility and openness, viewing staff and youth participants as having an equitable voice in the research design, instruments, and other elements of the research. A cookie-cutter approach to evaluation does not benefit the organization or other stakeholders.

Finally, as well as enriching the evaluation, the involvement of young people presents important development opportunities to those young people (and to evaluators).

Allow Adequate Time

Design and implementation of effective evaluation of a program similar to WIMPS cannot occur overnight. Evaluators considering such work need to allow sufficient time for (a) consultation with primary intended users of the evaluation, (b) genuine involvement of young people (program participants and potentially others) in the evaluation process, and (c) the process of collecting data using various instruments with multiple constituencies.

Social Capital Theory Can Assist in Understanding Impacts

Social capital theory presents a valuable frame for looking at the civic and social impact of programs such as WIMPS. Looking at how the networks of young people develop and the increases in several kinds of social capital provide valuable insights into the potency of informal educational and situated learning approaches. In particular, the compensating impact of positive social capital is a strong rationale for adopting the approaches outlined here.

■ CONCLUSION

The experience of evaluation of the WIMPS program in Northern Ireland demonstrates a productive joining of civic youth work, youth civic engagement, and program evaluation for program improvement (providing sound, relevant information for decision making), accountability (offering transparency to all who have a stake in funding, operating, and/or participating in the program), and sustainability (delivering to funders and prospective funders valid, empirically based evidence of effectiveness). The evaluation also demonstrates how young people can join in the co-creation of an evaluation of their own program, increasing the strength of the evaluation.

At a time when many in the world are panicked about the apparent disengagement of young people from politics, this evaluation gives a vital insight into approaches that engage and orient young people—and also public servants—to create new forms of civic discourse, centered on the interests and passions of young citizens.

SECTION 6
Use and Share Lessons Learned

In the last case study, Terrance Kwame-Ross describes how evaluation became an ongoing, everyday activity at the charter school he developed and where he was principal. Here we see how evaluation and evaluation studies can also be embedded in the ongoing activity of civic youth work organizations and programs, not only for accountability purposes but also to extend learning and to shape daily decision making. This process often works to amplify use and the sharing of lessons learned. This is an example of youth and adult participation, within and across each age group, youth and adults together.

This case study illustrates how the use of a study can be made more effective and mundane when evaluation studies are conducted with stakeholders and are embedded in the everyday activities of a civic youth work strategy. As an everyday activity, evaluation foci emerge and respond to the mundane realities of activities, programs, and practices. Evaluations studies designed together with participants can support the collection of evidence, credible at least to the "intended users" of the evaluation study. Justification of findings can also occur collaboratively, and this supports the use of the findings for a variety of purposes in the organization. Reading this case as a metaphor and analogy extends the lessons beyond a school and into other civic youth work programs, agencies, and organizations. An emphasis on how to structure programs and evaluation studies to enhance use and the sharing of lessons can be seen in the mundane and taken-for-granted, and thus almost invisible, everyday activities that support the evaluation process.

The following questions are provided to guide the reading of this case study:

1. What activities seem to have supported the ongoing evaluation described?
2. What strategies does the case study illuminate to support the use of evaluation findings and the sharing of lessons learned within the organization?
3. What role(s) did the principal play in the evaluation process? In supporting ongoing evaluation as a strategy and activity? In supporting the ongoing use of evaluation findings? In developing and sustaining continuous program improvement?

8 School Meeting Structures as Forms of Civic Engagement and School Evaluation

■ TERRANCE KWAME-ROSS

The State of Minnesota is located in the most northern region in the United States. It is known for its freezing cold and ferocious snowstorms. Each winter, the first few snowfalls bring angst to the entire state. During these times, everyone is on alert and in a preparedness mode. The state prepares roads for public safety; municipal governments and ordinary citizens plan and prepare for physical and logistical hourly shifts to remove snow from streets and sidewalks; and students at one school in the state, New City School, prepare for one of the biggest community decisions of the year: Whether or not snowball throwing would be allowed during school hours and, if so, what rules should guide this play?

At New City School, a 30-minute community meeting circle is held each year on the first Friday after a snowfall. All 140 students aged 5–14 years, teachers, staff, and community visitors sit in a circle in the school's basement, which is named the City Center. In and around the circle are chart stands and paper, colored stickers, markers, and volunteer student and adult "recorders" assisting in capturing everyone's knowledge in the forms of feelings, thoughts, and experiences with snowball throwing.

All of the school's meetings open with a community greeting, followed by something shared about a group or individual topic, and it ends with singing and/ or playing. After these community-building activities, the principal presents the agenda, which is then restated by student volunteers from each grade. Students' abilities to state and restate the issue or problem are opportunities to practice their ability to tell their understanding of the issue at hand and to hear student voices. All of this information from students and others is for use in reflecting and responding to the following questions, specific to the snowball decision:

In this school today, with the people in this circle, what are our feelings, thoughts, and prior knowledge around snowball throwing? Is this an activity that we want to continue to enjoy at this school? If so, then what will be the ground rules for keeping everyone safe, given our various ages, abilities, disabilities, and strength levels in our school? What happens when we forget rules or intentionally break the rules around snowball throwing? How should we take care of the people who break one of the rules we set?

The meeting begins and the City Center buzzes with excitement. This topic of snowball throwing elicits a school-wide collective worry and related problem-solving orientation as the community works at the issues surrounding snow and safety. This happens every year.

Students are divided into small groups of 8–10 to listen and discuss the issue with each other. The goal is to reach consensus on the first question: Will snowball throwing be allowed at New City School this year? Students and adults are note takers, time keepers, and facilitators in the groups, and this helps the process.

Students return to the large group circle and report their feelings, thoughts, and findings. Discussions begin about both individual and group "fears and excitements" of throwing and getting hit by snowballs. Students are given colored sticky dots "to spend"/use by placing them on the chart labeled "Snowball Throwing: Yes, No, and Not Sure Yet." The entire school community is given 3–5 minutes to caucus with whomever and then to vote by placing their dot under one of the three columns on one of the charts.

After the vote, volunteers count the vote and announce the results. When the tally is complete, a decision is made. The next step is to negotiate the rules for keeping all school members safe.

On charts are outlines of three parts of the body: shoulder-to-head; shoulder-to-waist; and waist-to-feet. A discussion begins about the whole community as a body and about a person's body, including visible and invisible physical and psychological characteristics, strengths, and challenges, and how to keep these in mind so as to keep everyone safe, given the student's and staff's ages, abilities, and disabilities. The school quickly comes to an agreement about placing a red X through the shoulder-to-head level. It is self-evident to them that snowball throwing at and above the shoulder-to-head level is off limits. This leads to a discussion and vote on the two other body levels. Everyone is given two colored stickers to vote for the area of the body that will be okay to target. The group takes 3–5 minutes to caucus and use their dots. The vote is tallied and results revealed. Usually, both areas of the body from shoulder-to-waist and waist-to-feet are accepted targets.

Using crumpled recycled paper, the community engages in a wild game of throwing snowballs for an intense 2–3 minutes. Afterward, four questions are asked and discussed:

1. How did we follow our agreement in keeping our snowballs in the two areas of shoulder-to-waist and waist-to-shoulder?
2. Did anyone have a difficult time following the rules?
3. How were problems resolved?
4. What should happen if we forget or intentionally break our rules for throwing snowballs?

The meeting is closed with directions for each classroom to create a data collection sheet for marking and tallying both positive and negative experiences with our rules, which will be revisited at the next meeting.

The meeting ends with the All School Recitation:

We are one school together,
We are one school apart,
We are one school together
    Heads, hands, and hearts (gesturing to each while speaking)

This anecdote is a description of one 30-minute meeting format. From an outside perspective, what took place in the meeting may seem unimportant or even "just" ordinary." However, from an insider's view, the meeting structure, agenda item, decision-making processes, and data collection plan were all interconnected and crucial because these helped to facilitate high student engagement in both social and academic affairs and to feed into the overall evaluation plans for program and school improvement of decision-making, conceptual clarification, accountability, and policy making. All these are used in order to make sense of and improve New City School.

■ NEW CITY SCHOOL: THE INTEGRATION OF SOCIAL AND ACADEMIC LEARNING FOR RESPONSIBLE CITIZENSHIP

Emergence of a New School

In 2000, I began a 3-year planning process to open: New City School, a public charter school located in northeast Minneapolis, Minnesota, now in its thirteenth year. Its vision was and continues to be "to create a supportive community which actively engages students to build knowledge, ask meaningful questions, designs solutions, open their mind, care for others and their community, and become skilled, responsible citizens of the world" (http://newcitycharterschool.org). Essentially, we wanted to create a new way to educate families and children by actively involving them in creating, monitoring, assessing, and changing how this school worked. School was a site for the practice of democratic values. One such practice is the personal development of a deep connection to and engagement in both the intellectual and social affairs of school and society. In short, New City School aligned itself with the American values of individual and group hard work and literate and active individuals. It believes this produces effective citizens and a more robust civic life.

For the founders, teachers, and parents, learning to be literate and to participate fully in society required more than arriving at "high or higher" scores on academic achievement tests. At the time New City School opened (2001), the No Child Left Behind law (NCLB) was passed. This shifted educational policy in the years 2001–2009. NCLB was intended to be an earthquake in public K–12 education.

Out of the NCLB and its focus on academic achievement, there emerged a public narrative about the failures, challenges, and models of success for public schools. Attention and public resources were allocated for academic achievement gaps and "back to basics" practices. Marginalized were attention to the civic and to the broader human development models of schooling and learning, including the role the schools in the development of the whole child. As a result of this academic achievement gap discourse, policymakers, principals, teachers, and school district personnel pushed schools to strengthen their already highly bureaucratic, authoritarian, standardized, and prescriptive curriculum and pedagogy and to marginalize or eliminate other school and learning goals and practices.

Despite the sociopolitical reality of more and tighter constraints on schools, the NCLB used a highly simplified problem-solution analysis. Much of what had to be done in education was to close the "academic achievement gap." New City School emerged at the very moment when it would be a true alternative to then ascending norms of practice and related ideology. There the child was not only a "student" (in student role) or an "academic student," but a whole person who would be treated as such and taught as such. One aspect of this wholeness was the civic self and the civic child.

In school and educational terms, New City School was a vehicle created to change and improve the ways children and adolescents engaged in learning and school. It embodied this and became an actual school, a site, and an idea for working out one of the fundamental questions and purposes of public schools: What are the skills and knowledge, in both the academic realm (math, reading, language arts, social studies, science and technology) and social realm (character, civic youth engagement, and social-emotional education), that children as citizens need in order to become full, flourishing, and productive children and, later, competent and productive adults and citizens at home, at work, and in their community?

This anecdote shows one example of the pedagogy used to invite and support youth to learn about becoming and acting as citizens and to use this in their everyday individual group and collective lives.

■ SCHOOL MEETING STRUCTURES AS FORMS OF ENGAGEMENT AND EVALUATION WORK

Meeting Structures as Forms of Engagement

On the campus of New City School was a reoccurring sight: Teachers and students huddled in circles. Community meeting in circles, such as the All School Meeting, symbolized and actualized sites for inclusion and opportunity for all school members to see, experience, and feel what it meant for everyone to be seen and heard. Circles as cultural symbols are known to signify closeness, tightness, and togetherness. To this end, circles were used as a civic engagement metaphor and a strategy for helping school members, especially students, develop comfort and confidence in their abilities and responsibilities to actively and fully participate in the everyday decision-making opportunities and processes co-created with some others and with all others as a school experience. The All School Meeting was not only a metaphor; it was a real-world structure and practice for group engagement in finding problems, discussing the issue and possible solutions, brainstorming choices, deciding on options, setting up rules, and outlining data collection for assessing the intended and unintended consequences of whatever action was taken. This is both evaluation and civic engagement together as one.

The simple but powerful notion of "circle time" at New City School provided all students and other school members a strong sense of group belonging to this school, this school community. "Circling up" at New City School was serious business. It was a time for students and adults to actively listen and interact. The circle gathering was one method for community members to receive information, ask questions, and participate in short- and long-term group discussions, decisions, planning, and evaluation. It was an opportunity to reflect on learning, demonstrate knowledge, model and practice routines and procedures, evaluate and reflect and review, and make decisions about school structures, systems, practices, and protocols.

Circles were often used to present real-world school dilemmas to students so that they could co-develop responses. There was role taking to see and reflect on multiple points of view and rehearsals of potential social and academic problems and their resolutions. In these ways children and youth practiced and experienced types of empathetic understanding basic to being a responsible community member, a citizen of the school (community). We learned from and taught each other, helped and cared for each other, and showed concern for the whole community—civic/citizen orientations and values (only if ideal) in our society and culture.

All of these structures, practices, and processes produced "data" about the school, about learning, about individuals, and about the collective and communal. Yes, this was learning "school stuff," including citizen roles. Yes, it was evaluation, although not its typical scientific clothing but evaluation nonetheless. It takes discernment to know this and to use these data; it usually takes a keen eye to see the real possibility of the real and real-time evaluation opportunities that the school world and the worlds in the school present.

Meeting Structures as Forms of Evaluation

Evaluators ultimately tell a story about a process, program, or characteristic of participants and/or all of these to make judgments and decisions about the worth of things, practices, and people: Did it work? Who says and on what grounds? What are aspects and the effects of the good? Who were involved in making this happen? These are all important everyday and long-term questions to ask in day-to-day interactions in school and more systematically through periodical student and staff self-ratings, and in more formal evaluations. Let's look more closely at how the circle meeting structure was used as a form of evaluation.

Staff highly valued and practiced child-centered pedagogy, one that promoted creating and sustaining positive human interactions in the context of all the everyday ordinary ways of learning in and outside of class. Vygotsky's (1934/1986) ideas were implemented, especially, his recognition of the importance of social interaction in helping children learn and develop cognitively. Also used was Rogoff's (1990) recognition that children are learning all the time; adult and child and everyday interactions are opportunities for guided participation and reflection.

Here is where evaluation fit into the ordinary school's structures, practices, and daily life. For example, after each lesson, the children were asked to reflect on their learning, using such questions as:

- What sorts of feelings and thoughts did this lesson or class period stir up for you? Did you learn anything new? How would you explain to someone what we did today?
- Were there any social problems that came up and we dealt with but you are not quite satisfied with the outcome?
- What were a few strengths and weakness of our time together?
- Should we think differently about any routines that hindered or helped our learning today?

In experiential learning terms, our pedagogy attended to both process and product. By using circling structures in a variety of ways, the community knew how to quickly gather as a large or small group to define a problem, get agreement, dream up solutions, and monitor and evaluate implementation. In teacher talk, school life was organized by a big lesson plan and structure: Plan, Do, and Review. This was one way to develop students who were engaged in their school and outside communities and not afraid to ask questions, live conflict, and resolve issues empathetically and fairly. How best to do this depended on using everyday teacher and school agreed-upon pedagogy to help all of the school members feel comfortable assessing our social interactions, structures, practices, pedagogy, and policies. All of this feeds the big evaluation of New City School measured by standard and typical school evaluations by outside professional evaluators, as required.

Seen here is that there is more than one way to evaluate a structure, practice, and practices. These are not "scientific" in classical Positivist frames but are practical, useful, helpful, and worthy in a human science frame. Academic arguments aside, for a practitioner—the school principal—these were especially useful because these were done in "real time." New City School was constantly evaluating its work and its impact on students and others in the school in several ways.

Evaluation Practice and Design in School

There was a big problem in realizing New City School's vision, given the enactment of NCLB. There were tighter and tighter rules imposed on schools by these funding sources and by others. This resulted in several partial formative evaluations of school success for individual students and for the whole school. High academic achievement was the gold standard outcome. As we know and has been shown, those tests are partial and shallow for getting at the dynamic, emergent, innovative learning strategies for basic academic as well as other curriculum content. With a vision and tools, viable curriculum, pedagogy, and structures, New City School needed an evaluation design that would assess the entire place, the complete experience there, and its effects on the whole child—the learner. The evaluation design we settled on attended to all of this.

There was a process evaluation to learn what of the vision was implemented and how; that is, the fidelity of the actual program in relation to its vision. There were outcome evaluation questions, answered in the short and long term, to supplement and complement required academic testing and reporting. How our evaluation differed is seen in the type of questions we wanted answered regarding process and short- and long-term effects:

Questions Regarding Process

- Characteristics of participants: What are the characteristics of students in the school? What are the characteristics of parents/families (e.g., ethnicity, family income level, language)? What are the characteristics of teachers and other school staff?
- Participation: What is the turnover? (How long do students remain in the school?)
- Instruction: What educational experience do students have? What strategies are used to foster student achievement and/or social emotional skills? Are strategies developed for diverse language and cultural groups?
- Satisfaction of stakeholders: How satisfied are school staff, parents, sponsoring organization, and others? What do they find beneficial? What do they suggest for improvement?
- Staff professional development: What type of training do teachers receive? Do teachers receive adequate training and follow-up support after their training in order to implement what was learned? How effectively are school-wide teaching practices being implemented?

Questions Regarding Short-Term Effect

- Attendance: Do students attend school regularly? What is the tardy and absenteeism rate?
- School climate: What is the climate of the school? How is the relationship between students and teachers? Do students feel that they get along with each other? Who is involved in the decision making? Are students motivated to achieve at school?
- Parent support and involvement: What types of parent involvement activities are available? What is the level of parental involvement in their children's education?

Questions Regarding Long-Term Effect

- Student achievement: Do students' performance in math and reading improve over time?

- Social skills: Do students' social skills improve over time, and do students' social skills correlate with students' academic performance?

Our evaluation was contracted to a local nonprofit firm, which used both quantitative and qualitative data collection tools and procedures, including the following:

- Longitudinal data: Measurement of student activities, behavior, and achievement over time comparing and following grade cohorts of students
- Primary data: Self-administered questionnaire and interviews of students, teachers, staff, administration, board members, and sponsoring organization
- Secondary data: Academic test scores, attendance, and discipline

These data were brought to different groups in the school community for analysis and decision making. For example, students' math scores on Minnesota's standardized comprehensive assessment showed in a 2-year period that about a third of our students continued to score comparatively lower in math than reading. The outside evaluator presented the finding to a small evaluation committee of teachers, parents, and the principal. The committee disaggregated and analyzed the math data by subcategories and found a discrepancy in math subcategory scores. The data indicated that, on average, students scored consistently lower on the math computation section. First finding: Math computation fluency skills and knowledge construct is lacking. This is one example of an evaluation finding. Briefly, here is how we took this finding and used it:

- Principal and teachers reviewed and adjusted time allocated to teaching math computational fluency skills.
- Teachers self-reflected and assessed their own knowledge and skills in teaching math computational fluency skills and developed individual, partner, and team professional development plans.
- Student and parent groups discussed the findings and brainstormed self-initiated and directed activities and lessons that were student and parent friendly.
- Staff development calendar and budget reviewed for opportunities for math support in the area of computation fluency.
- Partnership developed with local teacher college to assist with reviewing the school's math curriculum and pedagogical instructional method.

■ DISCUSSION

New City School placed high value on active and engaging learning activities, which are typically more dynamic and time consuming than traditional learning settings and methods that may not require as much student and teacher engagement and time. Our model intentionally provided many learning opportunities in school to choose how to learn, what materials to use, and how to work—along or with others. These types of learning activities that incorporate student's voice, choice, mistakes, plans, and conflicts require more time for teachers to plan and students to learn compared to more formal and traditional ways of learning such as learning math facts by rote and memory. The former type of learning is dynamic and may not show results or gains as measured by achievement test immediately or later or even by traditional school evaluations. Here is where innovation has its place.

In our context of using innovative pedagogies to teach and develop the whole person, we differed significantly from local public and private schools. And we began and continued this ethos and structure, and practice while No Child Left Behind was becoming more influential as a learning policy, along with evaluation policy, strategy, methodology, methods, and tools. With some of this we had to comply because our public and private sponsors required this. But we decided not to be bound by NCLB. Instead, we complemented and supplemented those evaluative requirements with ongoing innovative merged evaluations, which integrated learning curricular context while evaluating one's own and the school's effectiveness.

For the purpose of this book, which happily fits our ethos and practice, these evaluative practices came together in student, staff, and principal civic roles—citizen roles, roles as participants in civic evaluation, and civic leadership.

Evaluation was an opportunity for citizen-making. Because evaluation was a communal civic enterprise, it was a natural fit with our curriculum and pedagogy, building student and school social capital inside the school community for use there and outside, at home, in the neighborhood, and beyond.

This shows that evaluation can be a perspective, a structure, a process that looks like, feels like, walks like, and is simply *life*—as it is at New City School.

Evaluation was real and useful and pedagogically potent—whether or not the way we did it was scientific.

I helped create a new, innovative community-based charter school and co-created daily the school's ethos, structures, practice, and practices, with members of the school community. We wanted to know if were successful and effective. So we wanted and carried out daily reflective practices and more formal evaluations, and we used the data to make learning more effective. After 13 years, New City School remains a leader locally among charter and public schools as evaluated by standard measures of student achievement.

By our evaluations, we, like Garrison Keilor of Minnesota Public Radio fame, have a school where everyone comes to be above average.

■ SECTION 7
Conclusion

9 Designing Civic Youth Work Evaluations

■ ROSS VELURE ROHOLT AND
MICHAEL BAIZERMAN

The case studies illustrate diverse evaluation designs for civic youth work (CYW) and provide a beginning understanding of how high-quality evaluations can be designed and used for multiple purposes. In this chapter, the seven case studies were analyzed to further conceptualize and understand civic youth work evaluations in these ways: types of evaluation questions, primary evaluation focus, use orientation and practice, and roles of participants in the evaluation process.

This preliminary analysis of our small sample of CYW evaluations, our exemplars, aims to demonstrate what could be learned from a more thorough analysis of the "gray" and elusive literature, especially CYW evaluation reports. Because most of these studies are done locally and often used internally, much of what has been learned about the field remains invisible to the broader field and its stakeholders. The cases in this book and our analysis of these demonstrate another use for evaluation studies: to guide future evaluation designs (programming and programs) and to map ways similar programs and practices could be evaluated.

This analysis also highlights what may be missing from typical CYW evaluation designs. As described herein, most civic youth work evaluations remained focused on the outcomes on individual young people. Often missing is a broader understanding of the field of practice and the possible and often documented "impacts" such programs can have, not only on the participants but also for the community, for broader youth policy, and for changes to youth services. Although the case studies demonstrate expertly crafted evaluations, they also illuminate the political process for determining evaluation foci with funders and other stakeholders more concerned with individual youth outcomes. As a whole, the case studies didn't always attend to the broader range of impacts of CYW programs.

The case studies included in this analysis do not constitute a representative sample. These were invited from respected and highly productive evaluators to illustrate different evaluation designs. This purposive sampling procedure supports the development of a conceptual model to understand the possibilities of how CYW could be evaluated and to draw out lessons the case studies together provide for those who want to develop a better understanding and capacity to design and evaluate CYW. But the data and the discussion cannot be generalized across the field of complex youth programs or even across civic youth work evaluation studies. Instead, the analysis provides suggestive foci and themes. The analysis of these case studies reveals where evaluation designs converge around the types of questions used to frame an evaluation. We begin here.

■ TYPES OF EVALUATION QUESTIONS

> Always the beautiful answer who asks a more beautiful question.
>
> —E.E. Cummings

All evaluation and research begin by creating the framing questions. The questions that are chosen frame the entire study, and deciding on these is not an objective or neutral process; it is a political process of negotiating among interests and power (Velure Roholt, et al., 2009). These initial questions direct and structure the rest of the evaluation process. They both illuminate by directing the evaluators' attention toward certain programmatic aspects and obscure by ignoring others. In this section, some different question types are analyzed to deepen our understanding of what types of questions can frame civic youth work evaluations. These case studies illustrate how civic youth work evaluators can choose questions that focus on a few to many and on a narrow to broad range of subjects—from understanding the impact on young people all the way to measuring the larger impact on community, policy, and the social image of a young person—held by community, school, and adults.

Focus Is Primarily on Student or Participant Impact

All the case studies included questions that direct attention to the impact of the program on participating young people. This is not surprising because most funders and program stakeholders define success most often as "what the program does to reduce problem behavior" or increase young people's knowledge, skills, and attitudes about citizenship or some other subject. These case studies exemplify how these concerns come to be conceptualized and then put into an evaluation as guiding questions. All of the case examples included questions directed at individual participant impact. The basic question was a variation of "What (kind of) impact(s) did the program have on students?"

Most of the studies focused on documenting and describing the knowledge students "gained," the skills they "learned," and the "dispositions" (orientation) they "took on" as a result of participating in the program. These included knowledge of social issues, a broader understanding of diverse civic experiences, learning civic skills, including issue research and campaigning, and a beginning mastery of civic agency. Although all of the evaluation case studies focused on impacts of participating, many also directed attention to programmatic impact on others, whether directly involved in the program or not, such as adult facilitators in the program, the other teachers in the school, young people's groups of friends, politicians, and young people's family.

Moving Beyond Participants to Explore Impact on Others

Many of the studies recognized that these projects don't only have an impact on involved young people. Civic youth work not only supports young people in doing new and different activities; often it also requires that adults who work with young people to also change what they do and how. A focus for some of the case examples was the roles and the practice of the adult workers. Shumer et al. describe how teachers developed skills in new "active pedagogies" when they had to support student service learning; the case study by Boyte describes how teachers changed their teaching style after being involved in the project. Finally, Mattessich et al. focused on how the project had an impact on the politicians young people contacted and worked with over the course of their project. These are some of the ways evaluation studies focused on two aspects of the programs: the impact of the program on youth and on others and how these impacts were conceptualized and measured. The extent to which these same changes are found in all CYW efforts is unclear, mainly because so few evaluations focus on changes in adult youth workers. Even less clear is the impact these efforts have on communities, public policies, and the image of a young person (see Baizerman case for how this can be conceptualized).

Community Change Strategies With Limited Understanding of How Well They Work

Most of the case studies evaluated CYW programs that were similar in approach and strategy. All of the CYW programs supported young people in taking direct action on a personally meaningful public issue. Working to address a public issue, either through service, education, or social action, remains a primary activity, practice, and example of CYW practices. Surprisingly, most evaluations do not include questions about the impact of the young people's work on their community or on the focal communities and public issue they took on. Even in the case studies included here, only a few included such questions. Although many of the cases mentioned this impact, much of these data are anecdotal and studies only noted successful group actions, but not group failure. In contrast, a couple of the case studies directly focused on evaluations designed to focus on the broader community impacts of these programs, both those brought about by young people to address a particular issue and also beyond this on the secondary impact—the work, the youth, and the citizen social roles—a changed understanding of who young people are and what they can do. For example:

- The case study by Baizerman provides a rich schematic of how an evaluation can focus on questions beyond individual impact and include how the program shapes the organization, the community, and youth policy for a region, and attitudes in the larger community about who young people are and what they can do.

- The case study by Richards-Schuster and Timmermans describes how young people were also interested in learning how their work in this group impacted their friends.
- Kwame-Ross included questions about how satisfied stakeholders were of the program (school).

In general again, missing from most of the case studies was attention to how civic youth work strengthens local social capital such as youth skills, an active citizenry, adults attuned to young people as civic resources, and the like.

Increased Social Capital as an Outcome of Civic Youth Work

This focus may be a result of work on youth civic engagement and social capital that argued for clearer understandings on youth outcomes, rather than on larger social capital impacts, whether local or broader (Winter, 2003). Recently, more scholars and practitioners are advocating for a renewed attention to social capital and the impact it has on young people's well-being and development (Allan & Catts, 2012). In the group of case studies analyzed here, only a few talk about evaluating civic youth work through a social capital framework. Mattessich et al.'s case study directly attends to impacts on social capital. In this case study, a primary focus was on how the program impacted the social capital of young people. It mapped the connections young people made with others in the community and the results of those connections: This is rare. Those that do this draw attention to the value of expanded social networks for young people and how these create a more inclusive space for them and often for other young people in the community. This initial direct analysis of evaluation questions also reveals four major types of question used to focus on evaluation.

■ PRIMARY EVALUATION FOCUS

It was found in the literature and in these case studies that evaluation questions typically fall into one of four categories:

- Foreground citizen and background youth
- Foreground youth/young people and background citizen
- Treat youth and citizens as two entities; as two social roles on the same level
- Treat youth and citizens as a single entity, a single social role

Many of the evaluation case studies framed questions in ways that foreground the citizen role and background youth and young people as a role. These questions focus attention and study on youth civic engagement programs/projects as "citizen building" and treat young people and youth (both the social role and actual person) as almost incidental, giving little to no attention to the personal, social, cultural, political, and other realities of being a young person or in the age-graded social role of "youth." Evaluation questions within this frame include the following:

- Did students learn the rights and responsibilities of civic life?
- Did students learn the primary characteristics of "citizen" in our (that) society?
- Can they demonstrate citizen behavior (as typically and normatively described)?

Much of the early work on youth civic indicators used this frame. A second frame reverses the order and prioritizes youth and young person rather than citizen(ship).

Several evaluation and research projects in recent years have foregrounded youth and young people and moved citizen to the background. Here questions focus attention and study on youth civic engagement programs/projects as "youth development" in the civic domain, as "youth citizenship," and treat citizenship, the social role, as a space within which a young person can develop in several dimensions and within which a young person can show/disclose youth as such, and what it is to be a particular young person. These evaluation questions read in these ways:

- Do students act more like citizens now than before they participated in the program?
- Have individual young people changed in their thinking about civil society as a result of participating in the project?
- By participating in this project, did young people develop greater self-confidence?

Here the focus shifts from learning whether the youth have learned direct and specific citizen knowledge, skills, and attitudes toward understanding youth development impacts of civic youth work. A third frame treats citizen and youth as two entities and focuses on both simultaneously.

In treating youth and citizen as two social roles, questions focus attention and study on youth civic engagement programs/projects as an available social role (youth) and an achieved social role (citizen) resulting from mastery of how to do "citizen" in age-appropriate ways. For example:

- What have participating young people learned about being citizens from being in this project?
- What can participating young people demonstrate about how to act as citizens (i.e., how is the role of citizen performed)?

A final frame treats youth and citizen as a single entity, a single social role. In this frame, questions focus attention and study on youth civic engagement projects/programs as civic space for being and acting as citizens as a lived reality: Youth/

young person/citizen are one. There is no age-graded citizen; rather, there are citizens of different sizes, shapes, colors, and ages. For example:

- How do participating young people show themselves as citizens in their everyday lives?
- What do participating young people say about themselves as being and acting as citizens?
- What have young people learned about the challenges for them and the strategies available to them to being and acting as citizens in the here and now?

In this book, our bias is toward the fourth orientation, whereas the case studies show that each of these orientations is legitimate and can lead to quality evaluation.

Questions Orientation	Case Example
Foreground citizen	Have young people met politicians before? How has the program supported young people's civic agency?
Foreground youth	How have young people's attitudes toward helping others changed? How has this group impacted you?
Two entities	How have young people learned to work together? What opportunities have you gained from being part of this group?
Single entity	What do young people say about themselves as they become and perform as citizens?

Other simple analyses not undertaken but useful would be examination of the dependent, independent, and intervening variables proposed and used in the evaluation design. Another is how each variable, output, or outcome was defined, operationalized, and measured. A final is to examine data collection tools.

■ EVALUATION USE

The purpose of evaluation is to be useful. Most commonly, evaluation is used for program improvement, policy making, accountability, and decision making (Weiss, 1998), along with conceptual clarity and programmatic reflection (Patton, 2008). In this section we analyze the case studies to learn how the evaluator in each conceptualizes use, both during and after completion of the study. Interestingly, some authors do not make clear how the evaluation was to be used, by whom, for what, and how. Although use is basic within professional evaluation practice, it may be an afterthought when a case study is written. Based on an analysis of the case studies, most orient toward program improvement and accountability. Only Kwame-Ross talked about decision making, although this was implicit in many of the other case studies, and only a few discussed policy making as an example of use.

Most of the civic youth work evaluation case studies used the evaluation study for program improvement. For some this was an explicit orientation, as in Mattessich et al.'s case: "How can WIMPS improve?" For others it was more implicit, with examples of how the evaluation provided some evidence that could be used for program improvement and program expansion.

Another clear use of evaluation in most of the cases was for accountability. Today, funders require, even demand, accountability-focused evaluations for both initial and ongoing funding. Given that most civic youth work programs are externally funded, most evaluations produced data that demonstrated they had positive impact; that is, positive changes were found. Again, much of these data were on program impact on young people, a typical funder priority.

Fewer of the case studies discuss how the evaluation was used for decision making, although some did mention how it was used by program staff to make decisions. Boyte described how the evaluation supported a university decision to expand the engagement experience to all preservice teachers. Shumer et al. clearly advocate for a participatory evaluation design based on the results of their evaluation case study, and that is an example of another type of decision. Kwame-Ross describes how the evaluation influenced decisions made in the school. Of interest is that none of the case studies described decision making as a primary focus for how the evaluation was designed and conducted. None located the study in the broader frame of evaluation capacity building (Compton et al., 2004) or "continuous program improvement."

Very few of the evaluation case studies reported that what was learned could be useful for policy making. Except for Baizerman, these civic youth work evaluation case studies did not indicate or discuss how what was learned could inform policy around youth civic engagement and civic youth work, and about the "condition of youth." Through analyzing how the case studies conceptualized use, another theme emerged: To what end were the CYW case studies directed?

■ USE ORIENTATION

The emphasis on program improvement was the priority, and studies tended to neglect other possible uses for the work, including the improvement of youth work practice, policy development, and youth program advocacy. Overall, the different case studies produced data to improve program efforts or to satisfy accountability demands. Often missing from the case examples were "lessons learned" about the different types of youth work practice necessary to carry out the program, and given what was learned, what policies might better support overall programmatic and practice efforts to support a robust and vibrant youth citizenry. The following table maps the evaluations across these three use orientations:

Program oriented	Mattessich et al.
	Shumer et al.
	Boyte
	Baizerman
	Kwame-Ross
	Richards-Schuster & Timmermans
Youth work oriented	Baizerman
Policy oriented	Baizerman
Nation building	Baizerman
Condition of youth in society	Baizerman

We have data that demonstrate how program evaluations are often conceptualized to meet local funder and other internal reporting demands, as well as other uses. Often missing from the evaluation design is the understanding that "youth can surmount great odds and make significant contributions, but it is not reasonable to expect them to become civically engaged in communities and societies that fail to support them (Yates & Youniss, 1999, p. 273). The evaluation case studies described here are remarkable in that they all conclude that young people became more engaged in civic life. Surprisingly, most of this is related back to the program, rather than to the larger context and the policies that support civic youth work and the individual program in the evaluation. In that sense, these case studies had a smaller and narrower focus and were in that sense acontextual, in comparison to larger topics, issues, problems, environments, and programs.

Finally, the evaluation case studies do not focus on what is often taken for granted and hence (almost) invisible within CYW initiatives: the practitioner, the civic youth worker (youth worker, teacher, minister, recreation worker). Given that much of the programs described often rely on volunteers and on professionals other than youth work broadly named (Mattessich's case example is the exception here), how adults support young people through these programs is often ignored (see al-Bakri [2014] and VeLure Roholt & Baizerman [2013] on this). The evaluations often reveal some technical changes for the program (such as described in Shumer et al. as improving the website), but a more refined understanding of what goes on everyday and how it goes on to constitute a program, and how adults can animate youth civic engagement, has not been well documented and remains underdescribed and maybe overtheorized both in youth work and surely in these evaluation case studies. Reading these case studies teaches little about civic youth work as such, and what about its practices that (may) result in youth becoming (or not) public civic actors, more often, in more life spaces, more effectively, more deeply, and the like.

■ YOUTH INVOLVEMENT IN EVALUATION

A common feature among many of the case studies was the involvement of young people in the evaluation process, from designing the overall evaluation to assisting in data collection, analysis, the reporting of results, and use of findings. Over half of the case studies included here have youth-led evaluation design features. Some were solely youth-led evaluation designs (Hubbard), whereas others incorporated elements of youth-led evaluation into a larger design that also included traditional elements (for example, Mattessich et al.; Richard-Shuster & Timmermans; Shumer et al.). These case studies illustrate effective ways youth-led practices can be incorporated into CYW evaluation designs and, by doing so, how the evaluation itself became richer, more valid, more credible, and itself more effective in use.

Youth-led evaluation is a relatively newly named evaluation approach, with efforts to describe its elements (Sabo-Flores, 2008; Shumer, 2007) and the practice (Checkoway & Richards-Shuster, 2003; Checkoway et al., 2003) all gaining momentum within the last 10 years. Early on, this work connected directly to other collaborative and participatory approaches (Fetterman, 2001). Now it is an emerging evaluation approach with an expanding literature, rich practice illustrations, and a topical interest group in the American Evaluation Association (youth-focused evaluation). The case studies demonstrate how it has spread and the ways it can be used to both support programmatic ethos and high-quality, informative, and useful evaluation studies.

Criticisms remain about the involvement of young people in the evaluation enterprise. These case studies provide strong arguments for young people's inclusion. They not only demonstrate a capacity (Lansdown, 2004) for doing this work but also add value to the evaluation design by raising important questions often not considered by adults and other experts (Richards-Schuster & Timmermans); support further data collection (Shumer et al.), and deepen insights useful for the evaluation and its use throughout the process (Mattessich et al.). These case studies add to the building of evidence that not only do young people have the ability to participate in the evaluation enterprise, they also contribute significantly to the overall evaluation process and the quality and utility of the evaluation and actual use.

■ DISCUSSION

CYW continues to evolve, raising the question: Will evaluations of these efforts also change? Although the case studies in this volume do not represent a generalizable sample, they do provide exemplars of how evaluations can be done of CYW initiatives and programs. In analyzing within each and across the entire case samples included in this volume, several ideas emerge related to CYW evaluation. The case studies provide rich examples of how the evaluation process can be democratizing (Mathison, 2000). This may be especially important when evaluating programs and practices that aim to develop and strengthen democratic processes and understanding democratic civic engagement and democratic roles for youth. Through supporting more democratic approaches, the case studies also begin to challenge conventional images of young people—quietly but often deliberately providing opportunities for others to see and understand young people as capable, competent, and creative. Finally, this reading of the case studies raises questions about how much we know about the practices supportive of youth civic engagement. Rarely, both in these cases and in evaluations of civic youth work is this youth practice an evaluation focus.

Democratizing Evaluation

Youth civic engagement and civic youth work challenge authoritarian and adult expert approaches to youth development and youth work. The underlying values and practices in CYW are democratic, creative, and critical (VeLure Roholt et al., 2009). An ultimate goal is the creation and sustentation of "free space" (Evans & Boyte, 1992) for youth civic agency. The evaluation design should, in our view, reinforce a group's capacity "to take action, negotiate and promote change"(Johnson, 2010, p.155). The case studies included provide numerous ways to design an evaluation to support young people's rights (Johnson, 2010) and deepen the democratic spirit of an organization, agency, or program (Mathison, 2000). Here again is our philosophy and ideology of civic youth work.

As these case studies illustrate, there is not a choice between rigorous and objective evaluations and participatory evaluations. Instead, the evaluation process can support and deepen youth civic engagement through emphasizing young people rights and aligning these with an overall participatory spirit of a program or youth group. These case studies all advocate for advancing the strategy of participatory evaluation within CYW. Indeed, this approach has promise to be used to also challenge unrelenting public negative images of young people.

What all of the case studies accomplish is a reimagining of what it means to be and to act as a young person in each of these studies and in each of the program settings. Often young people are described as victims or perpetrators, developing and "not yet ready for prime time," but rarely as competent, caring, and contributing members of society (Checkoway & Richards-Schuster, 2003). The case studies challenge these images of young person/youth by inviting them into roles and responsibilities and then describing how their involvement strengthens an evaluation and supports their personal development and civic skill building. Without seeing young people as competent and insightful about the social conditions they live in and as wanting to make a difference in these, evaluations may unintentionally work to perpetuate misrepresentations of young people or, in effect, erase their presence in studies except as data sources or objects to be studied.

Developing methods and approaches to adequately capture young people's experiences and their learning requires challenging the ageist ways of making sense of their experiences (Checkoway, 1998). When this framework shifts, new insights can emerge about young people's capacities, interests, competencies, imagings, and abilities. For example, Ginwright (2010) describes how youth civic engagement initiatives involving African American youth should focus on "radical healing." Often, young people are seen as apathetic by a wider public, and this image has been reinforced by large-scale quantitative studies documenting low levels or participation of certain political activities (Putnam, 1995). Missing from such discussion are the ways organizations, social structures, and agency policies work to disenfranchise young people from political work (VeLure Roholt et al., 2009). Also missing are the nontraditional ways young people are engaged in civic and civil life (Ginwright, 2010). CYW evaluations have to consider how young people come to understand civic engagement in their local communities and youth institutions (schools and parks) and how this understanding can change dramatically depending on young people's life experiences (Rubin, 2007). As the case studies show, when invited into the evaluation process, young people have much to teach about civic engagement, evaluation, and how they should be seen and studied.

What remains hidden even within these case studies are the practices that support civic youth work. Very few evaluation studies consider adult practice worthy of attending to and clarifying. Is the practice so simple that it requires no further attention? We don't think so (VeLure Roholt & Baizerman, 2013). Practice, even civic youth work, constantly evolves (Higgs, 2010). The evolution of civic youth work and related practices to support youth civic engagement are undernoticed and poorly documented, understood, and evaluated.

This creates a disadvantage for the youth civic engagement field, as "practice needs to know (our fore knowings and prejudgements) before we can conceptualise and imagine the questions we want to ask of practice" (Higgs, 2010, p. 1). High-quality youth civic engagement cannot flourish without an understanding of the adult practices that bring it into existence and sustain it over time. A critical need in youth civic engagement and civic youth work is for evaluations to begin to document these practices. What are these based in and on what knowledge and what type of knowing? Greater clarity of practice can strengthen practice and lead to additional questioning of it that focuses on ethical, culturally responsive, and efficacious practices with different youth populations, communities, and neighborhoods. All of this is essential to better understand what efforts need to be done how with whom and when to best support a vibrant, active, and nonviolent youth citizenship. Civic youth work is not ineffable; it can be described and understood. Evaluation studies of civic youth work must engage this primordial need.

■ **CONCLUSIONS**

Reviewing these case studies discloses questions for the youth civic engagement/civic youth work evaluation enterprise. Do we know enough about what outcomes these efforts can accomplish? As the case studies illustrate and the literature review confirms, most CYW evaluations focus on individual youth outcomes, often taking for granted how young people are constructed in a local program area. Reading across the case studies, additional outcomes emerge, which demonstrate the breadth of outcomes CYW could support. Further work to document an expansive range of outcomes remains. Second, can the use of CYW evaluations expand beyond the local and the internal program? As an emerging field of youth work practice within a semiprofession (youth work), documenting and sharing evaluation data further supports the naming and diffusion of quality practice. Like many practice fields, evaluation data have much to teach beyond the local and particular, yet typically their use is conceptualized only in the narrowest terms. Finally, how can the diffusion of youth-led evaluation practice be supported and broadened? Although the case studies document the value of youth-led evaluation efforts and elements to support high-quality evaluations of CYW, much is missing. One focus should be on the expertise required to facilitate high quality youth-led efforts. Another should be on how these practices can be effectively taught and the practice diffused. To youth workers, the problem in such efforts is often adults who cannot or will not see young people as competent creators and implementors: It's the adults and adult expertise that too often prevent or detract youth inclusion in evaluation processes.

The case studies included in this volume sensitize the reader/evaluator to what and how such studies can be undertaken. They provide rich exemplars of the skill and expertise needed. Together, they show how well-designed evaluations have value not only for the study agency staff and stakeholders but also for broader audiences interested in and concerned about young people and their civic development and efficacy. A first task is to make visible examples of this work; this is what we did here.

10 Evaluation Practice to Enhance Civic Youth Work

■ ROSS VELURE ROHOLT AND
MICHAEL BAIZERMAN

The vocation of evaluation is intended to be practical, and this means it is to be used for a variety of purposes (Baizerman et al., 2014). Evaluation is an intervention and not only an applied research process. The case studies illustrate some of the ways evaluations can be put to work as intervention. For example:

- Boyte advocates for a conception of youth civic engagement outcomes that move beyond the traditional paradigm and includes more complex understandings of individual agency.
- Baizerman describes a comprehensive framework for evaluating youth civic engagement that moves from individual youth to policy, articulating the different foci an evaluator and an evaluation could take.
- Mattessich et al. provide a rich case of the practical ways an evaluation can learn what funders ask for, while also stretching everyone's understandings of what the project includes, for example, its influence on social capital and a changed social image of "young person."

Of course, our sample of case studies is biased because we selected them and from a limited pool. Especially so when compared to recent reviews on youth civic engagement (Center for the Study of Social Policy, 2011; Hollander & Burack, 2009). These reviews, unlike our case studies, suggest that youth civic engagement evaluations are not living their vocation; that is, they are neither practical nor used.

Certainly many evaluation studies are used within organizations, often for accountability purposes. Yet civic youth work evaluation studies typically do not provide an expansive conception and understanding of what youth civic engagement evaluations could be. This final chapter is our framework for such a broader conception. We begin by providing four questions to keep in mind when designing a youth civic engagement evaluation.

■ DESIGNING CIVIC YOUTH WORK
EVALUATIONS: FOUR ORIENTING QUESTIONS

Many good tools to support high-quality evaluations are easily available (for example, Stufflebeam, 2004). Missing are questions specific to civic youth work initiatives, programs, and activities. Too often in this field, the evaluation design and product are high quality, but the civic youth work evaluation is not. By this we mean that it does not get at the core elements, practices, and outcomes of true civic youth work practice. To this end, we suggest four questions for evaluators to consider when studying civic youth work initiatives, programs, and practices:

- Does the evaluation design and the way that it is implemented support and reinforce the civic youth work program strategy?
- Does the evaluation design support youth voice?
- How will learning be shared from the evaluation study and with whom?
- What is the conceptual understanding of youth civic engagement, young person, and youth citizen?

Does the Evaluation Design Support and Reinforce the Program Strategy?

High-quality youth civic engagement efforts provide meaningful opportunities for young people to participate directly in community and civic work. Our own research on civic youth work discusses the connection between their involvement in directly addressing a public issue which is personally meaningful and youth civic learning and youth civic development (VeLure Roholt et al., 2009). It seems reasonable to expect the evaluation design and practice to support the overall democratic ethos of civic youth work, thereby further reinforcing the values, practices, and knowledge of democratic inquiry, deliberation, and knowledge for action.

It is already understood by evaluators that "evaluation, if done well, is democratizing" (Mathison, 2000, p. 237). Several of the case studies in this volume describe in part how to support a democratic evaluation. Mattessich et al. and Shumer et al. both describe how high-quality evaluations were designed with young people, including the data collection and analysis. See also the piece by Kwame-Ross. Resources to support youth participatory and youth-led evaluations are available (Checkoway & Richards-Schuster, n.d.; Sabo-Flores, 2008; Shumer, 2007). Given these resources and evidence to suggest that youth involvement in the evaluation process both supports their civic development and also contributes to high-quality evaluations and to its uses for practical program obligations and change, it is reasonable to expect that more civic youth work evaluation designs will include the ethos and practice of participatory evaluation practice. If this is done, the next question may be less central, but still is an important reminder.

Does the Evaluation Design Support Youth Voice?

In our own practice of evaluating civic youth work initiatives, we often found that stakeholders differ in what they want to know and have told us about the program, as expected. Typically, funders want to have a clear understanding of whether the program achieved youth outcomes (e.g., Winter, 2003), whereas young people want to emphasize and tell others what they have done and what it means to them to have done this work. Although not always at odds, the different points of view could easily become displaced or submerged if the funder's perspective is given higher priority. Add in management, staff, and the larger community and the issue becomes more complicated.

High-quality evaluation responds to stakeholder input (Patton, 2008). In civic youth work programs, young participants are clearly stakeholders, and as participants, young people are often highly qualified to offer advice to evaluators. A common feature of civic youth work programs is a focus on the development of their own ideas and informed actions and on young people gaining confidence to express these to others. Thus, it is reasonable to expect that most youth participants within a relatively short time will be able, if not fully, to be comfortable telling an evaluator what "outcomes" should be included, how the evaluation could be designed in ways that don't violate program expectations and values, how practice and process can be assessed/"measured" and importantly, what for them is significant and important about the program and about the opportunity to be involved in the program. Young people must have the opportunity to provide input to the evaluator of a study of youth involvement: This is a moral a priori. But the imperative goes further. They must, we argue, be full (and appropriate) participants in the evaluation process (e.g., Paris & Winn, 2014).

Youth voice may also challenge simplistic and standardized evaluation designs and practices. Civic youth work is a social innovation, and "evaluating social innovations is a complex problem" (Cambell-Patton & Patton, 2010, p. 601). As a social innovation, civic youth work initiatives focus on multiple outcomes. They are interrelated rather than distinct and separate, and support highly individualized outcomes on the levels of young people, youth program, and agency (Cambell-Patton & Patton, 2010). Clarifying these outcomes and the overall process that supports this work seems impossible without directly asking young people to participate in the development and (often) the implementation of the evaluation. When consulted, young people share issues and questions that many evaluations of youth civic engagement often miss: How does race, class, gender, sexual orientation, and so on impact what is done? How has the community responded to what the group did, and how might this relate to the issue they are working on and who belongs to the group? What challenges have they encountered, and how have they worked through these? When done, the next question an evaluator should attend to is: How can what is learned be shared with audiences beyond the program studied?

How Will What Is Learned Be Diffused?

In completing the literature review for this book, a common feature of civic youth work evaluations was found: These studies were not in the litera-ture. Although there are good reviews of how to evaluate civic youth work initiatives (e.g., Cambell-Patton & Patton, 2010), we found little about the designs and other practices, or findings from civic youth work evaluations. We know hundreds, if not more, evaluation studies have been completed, but few organizations make them available to the general public (Public Achievement Northern Ireland; Mattessich et al. [Chapter 7] did so and deserves recog-nition for this). Most of the studies remain part of the gray literature, with lessons and findings not widely shared beyond agency staff and stakeholders. Too often, the use of evaluation studies remains local and internal, making it nearly impossible "to stand on the shoulders of giants" (Merton, 1965) to build a solid base for and practice of evaluating this type of youth work and civic informal education.

Telling the findings of a study may be a moral good as well as good evaluation practice; its value is in part through facilitating use (Patton, 1993). Professional evaluators plan from the beginning of a study how the evaluation will be shared and used and offer models to enhance the uses of a study. A study of whether, how, and to whom findings are diffused should be done with specific attention to civic youth work. This is not only about evaluation; it is about enhancing democratic civic life and using evaluation to that end.

What Is the Conceptual Understanding of Youth Civic Engagement and the Young Person?

Most youth civic engagement evaluations should start with an understanding of the program and practice. Although important when evaluating civic youth work, we recommend that the evaluator also clarify his or her own understanding of "young person" and what it means to be "civically engaged" (VeLure Roholt & Baizerman, 2013). These clarifications can be shared with program participants and staff, and the differences can be worked out. This is important for several reasons, including these are subjects about which all citizens likely have personal views and feelings, and these could show up unannounced in an evaluation. Remember that these are socio-moral and politico-moral activities, and as such are not value neutral. They invite passion. This allows the evaluator's framework to be negotiated, and in this way it can democratize aspects of the study, which teaches civic skills. We know that what we bring to and how we look at a situation shape what we perceive. This is sa-lient for evaluating civic youth work: Young people are simply not seen as political, as citizens, as civically efficacious, as potential civic contributors. In effect, they are invisible.

Young people are most often seen as "becoming adults with political will rather than being children without political voice" (Aitken, 2001, p. 23). This image may no longer be supported in many youth civic engagement programs, especially those that invite, welcome, and support young people in becoming directly involved in community change. Clarifying and developing a common language around how the program understands young people and what it means to be civically engaged is a minimum step in evaluating this work.

At minimum, we recommend that evaluators designing civic youth work evaluation attend to these issues. They are an introduction to the expanded framework we propose next to guide civic youth work evaluations.

■ AN EXPANDED FRAMEWORK FOR EVALUATING YOUTH CIVIC ENGAGEMENT

We now describe an expanded vision of how civic youth work initiatives can be evaluated. This framework intentionally focuses on civic youth work as a complex social innovation (Cambell-Patton & Patton, 2010), and on the imperative to understand, along with program-level outcomes, the process by which young people become citizens (Hollander & Burack, 2009). And also on the basic practices of civic youth work as a practice (van Manen, 2015). This framework describes the multiple ways civic youth work evaluations can be designed to meet these ends.

Provided are four evaluation logic models based on four different units of analysis: individual, group, community, and practice. Although we agree with Cambell-Patton and Patton (2010) that logic models often oversimplify a complex and dynamic process, we choose this framework to describe the multiple possible ways evaluation could be framed because it is one that most evaluators, even novices, understand. We have complicated the model by using questions rather than statements within each of the logic model categories: inputs, activities, outputs, and outcomes.

The use of questions is intentional; open questions frame possibilities for how an evaluator could look and what this way of looking might allow him or her to see. Questions also emphasize the different choices that can be made when designing a civic youth work evaluation. Rather than use standardized measures and standard outcomes, the questions prompt reflection and consideration of what could be evaluated and how; deciding what to evaluate is part of the evaluator's responsibility and something that can (should) be negotiated with and among stakeholders. A good evaluation design can be useful internally and locally. When constructed more broadly, it can also support general knowledge building as well. Often this requires expanding our understanding of what can be learned from a well-designed program evaluation.

Our framework shows the different units of analysis for an evaluation. We begin with the most common unit of analysis: the individual. Here we want to complicate the evaluation slightly by including questions that emphasize how civic youth work initiatives often have unique, one-time outcomes rather than use standardized outcomes for participants (Cambell-Patton & Patton, 2010). The second table introduces different questions that can support designing an evaluation on group-based outcomes. It is surprising that we did not find group outcomes to be a focus in the youth civic engagement evaluation literature, even though a common methodology for civic youth work is group work and most of the practice models and approaches emphasize group work, group building, and learning in and by a group—the core of civic practice. The third table presents guiding questions to document community-level changes supported by youth civic engagement initiatives. Many of these projects invite and support young people trying to have a community-level impact. Thus, it is reasonable to evaluate community-level efforts, for example, having a traffic light installed, retro fixing smoke detectors in senior citizen homes, developing a storefront library. The final table raises basic questions about civic youth work evaluation: what practices support a vibrant and active youth civic engagement experience. Typically, youth civic engagement evaluations focus on the program. We also suggest a focus on practices (Higgs & Titchen, 2001). Here additional questions are provided that encourage an evaluator to consider how an evaluation of practice might be incorporated into an overall evaluation design. Knowing more about the practices and the related processes of youth civic engagement remains understudied, and it clearly is one area where youth civic engagement evaluations could make a significant contribution to the field. The study of practice(s) as such is an emergent field (van Manen, 2015).

▪ EVALUATION LOGIC MODEL: INDIVIDUAL

Most civic youth work evaluations focus on individual outcomes; that is, changes in a young person. The following table provides questions that can lead to how evaluations can be designed when the program focus is change on the level of individual youth. Here the focus is on unique, study-specific outcomes rather than on standardized outcomes, such as youth voting, knowing their political representatives, or reading or watching daily news. Often the outcome is a youth's personal, social, or political development—on youth development. This table introduces the ways citizenship can be not only learned but lived (VeLure Roholt et al., 2009). It also introduces how young people live as political persons in contrast to those who assume that they are apolitical or apathetic in general or in relation to a specific program outcome, or public issue. Rarely have we worked with a young person who did not care deeply about at least one local public issue in their community.

Level: Individual Young Person

Logic Model Category	Examples of Questions to Guide Evaluation
Inputs	• What issue compelled them? Addressed them?
	• How does this group or set of individuals define a particular issue? Why this topic?
	• What connection do young people have to this issue?
	• What did each young person contribute to the work? How often? Did this change over time?
	• What of this was new to them? How well did they do each?
	• What knowledge did each young person bring to the group? Did these change? To what?
	• What attitudes/values toward citizenship? Did these change? To what? Toward the issue? Toward the group? What skills did each young person bring to the group? Did these change? To what?
Activities	• What roles did each young person take on during the work? Why this? Was it new to them? How was it learned? How well did it go?
	• What knowledge did each young person use during the work?
	• What values did each young person show/live during the work?
	• What skills did each young person use during the work?
	• How well did they use each, in their own opinion?
	• How well did they use each, in the opinion of others?
	• How well did they use each, in the opinion of civic youth workers?
	• What did each young person learn doing the work?
	o Self-report
	o Group report
	o Civic youth worker report
Outputs	• How often did young people contribute to the group? On what topic?
	• How often did the young people attend the group?
	• What information or data did they provide to the project?
	• What information or data did they learn from others?

Logic Model Category	Examples of Questions to Guide Evaluation
Outcomes	• Did each young person have an enhanced grasp of and live citizen roles? • Did the program support an enhanced civic literacy among each participant? • Did each young person experience self as citizen? • Are all young persons now actively, regularly engaging in public citizen work? • Has each young person's attitudes changed about voting, participating in politics, and his or her commitment to democratic values and dispositions? • Has each young person learned skills to support his or her ongoing involvement in democratic practice/governance?

■ EVALUATION LOGIC MODEL: GROUP

In reviewing the literature on both civic youth work and evaluation of civic youth work, most remarkable is what is missing: Almost no attention is paid to group-level understandings and outcomes. A common (almost universal) approach to civic youth work and to youth work of other types in all setting is group work, with adults supporting groups of young people in learning about and then working as a group on a public issue they find personally compelling, one that addresses them and to which they choose to respond. Even with this standard approach, most of the evaluation and research on youth civic engagement has focused on individual change, using standardized outcomes. The following table introduces questions to guide youth civic engagement evaluations for group-level outcomes.

Logic Model Category	Examples
Inputs	• Who were the individuals who wanted a group to form/be in? • How did the group originally define the issue? • What knowledge, attitudes/values/beliefs, skills about the issue did the group collectively possess? • What other resources did the group know they collectively had access to?

Logic Model Category	Examples
Activities	• What did they do to build a group? • What activities on the issue did the group undertake as a group? • Why this? How did they do it? With what effectiveness? • How did what they do contribute to the group's work? To the group's effectiveness as a group? To the group's cohesion? • How did they participate as a group member?
Outputs	• How did the group assign tasks? • How did the group resolve conflicts? • Do individuals act in ways to support group cohesion and group effectiveness?
Outcomes	• Does the group identify as a group? • Does the group, as a group, identify and agree to work on an issue as a group? • Does the group do its work democratically? • How does each member contribute to the overall group's action? (member roles)

■ EVALUATION LOGIC MODEL: COMMUNITY

Youth civic engagement initiatives focus on creating impact in, on, and for a community, whether neighborhood, school, place of worship, or sport. Research and evaluation reports have documented the importance of having young people involved in meaningful and significant work for their community, and this has become a common practice in civic youth work initiatives. Remarkably, evaluating community impact is rarely found in civic youth work evaluations. Even when young people demand that research and evaluation focus on what they have accomplished in, with, and for their community, this is often ignored in favor of a focus on how their achievement supports their own personal, individual, healthy youth (civic) development. Attending to community-level impacts is more complicated, especially on how to attribute contributions. But when included, it provides a broader description of the civic youth work and its social importance. It is as if the failure to include these outcomes works to deny their very existence, surely their importance. And by extension, it denies the accomplishments of the young activist citizens not just in the future but also at the present moment.

Logic Model Category	Example
Inputs	• What existing local community group focused on this issue? • Did you approach any of these groups and did they contribute useful knowledge, attitudes, skills, or other resources? • What partnerships did you develop with community groups? Which? Why them? • What was community history on this issue? • What was community position on this issue?
Activities	• What alliances did the group make with same/different issue groups? • Who has the group asked to consult on this issue? • Where have group members sought information on this issue? • What research has the group done on the public issue? • What planning, with whom, have they done? • What strategy or approach have they chosen to make a change on this issue?
Outputs	• How many contacts has the group made? • Who knows about the group's work and about individual members? • How many of these contacts have resulted in assistance or connections, or other forms of alliance and/or help? • What do they now know about the issue that they didn't know previously? • What actions have they taken to implement the plan they created?
Outcomes	• Has the group educated or expanded community interest in this issue? Who? Which groups? • How have group members been received by other community groups? • How has their work on this public issue affected others in the community? • Did they achieve their action goals? • What action did they take on the issue and to what result?

Evaluation Logic Model: Practice, Practices, and Process(es)

Recent reviews of civic youth work research and evaluation shows little attention to the transformational processes that support strong and robust youth civic engagement (Hollander & Burack, 2009), and so too on practices supportive of youth civic engagement (VeLure Roholt & Baizerman, 2013). Most of the attention remains on program effectiveness. A result is that the black box remains: We know what goes in and we can describe outcome, but we often have little if any description or understanding of what happens in between, when staff and young people are together working. That is, we don't really know what is going on, and of that, what works (and why). Of all of this we know very little.

Logic Model Category	Example
Inputs	• How were participants recruited? • Who are participants? • Who are facilitators? • Who are practitioners? • What is the framework for practice? • What is the value base of the practice?
Activities	• How do adults and young people interact before group meeting? During group meeting? In between group meetings? • What did practitioner do in/before/after and between group meetings? How? Why? Did it work? How so? • What do youth say about youth work done with them? • What did the youth participants do in/before/after and between group meetings? How? Why? Did it work? How so?
Outputs	• What decisions have young people helped to make? • What shared understanding among participants has developed? • What roles do young people have and skill developed? • Who speaks for the group? When? • What was the practitioner trying to accomplish? Did it happen? How come? • Do participants regularly come to the meetings? • How do young people describe their experience in the group? • How do young people talk about working with the youth worker?

Logic Model Category	Example
Outcomes	• What did the practitioner contribute to the group's mastery of democratic, nonviolent, inclusive practice?
	• What did the practitioner contribute to the group's civic involvement?
	• Did the participants become a group?
	• Does the group have ownership over the issue and the process to address the issue?

Discussion

These are suggestive and incomplete listings of types of evaluation questions that we think are important, useful, and practical. A more complete listing gets close to the boundaries of where evaluation and social/behavioral/human science research touch. For example, what are youth and adult meanings of "enhanced mastery of citizen/civic roles" and "when did the group members decide/sense/feel that they were a "group?" These boundary issues can be resolved during the negotiations leading to the hiring of the outside evaluator or the assignment of the inside (agency/staff) evaluator, and also during discussions and negotiations on evaluation outcomes, design, and the rest.

There is a dual responsibility here for program and evaluator to open to light and air the taken-for-granted ethos, assumptions, practice, and practices and structures, which together constitute "program"—what it is, what it wants to accomplish, how it works, and whether it was effective. In youth civic engagement programs, these become critical, as few agree on common definitions for central concepts within the field (Sherrod et al., 2002): coming to an agreed understanding of terms and a clear understanding of program and outcomes (both intentional and unintentional), and also developing appropriate ways to measure these that do not violate program ethos and practices. This is surely true in the United States and even more important when discussing youth civic engagement as an international practice.

We are aware that much of this book is US-centric, more so in the discussions than in the case studies. This is important to remember because youth civic engagement practice(s) and civic youth work are socially, politically, and culturally bound to ways of naming and understanding the implicit contract between citizen and the state, the practices that are its citizen and institutional ideals, and the safety of individuals living these as part of their active citizenship. This is true especially for young people who in their society may not be seen as citizens. This brings us back to the Preface.

Conclusion: Preface Revisited

Youth civic engagement can get a young person killed in some communities and nations. Elsewhere it is invisible and/or meaningless to most adults. In some places, it is framed as a moral panic.

Evaluation calls for the practical, both concrete and abstract, both specific and general—all can be practical, even when "theoretical" (Judge & Bauld, 2001). In its typical practice worldwide, evaluation is local, concrete, specific, and time-bound to a particular intervention put in a box called program, project, or initiative. Rarely are interventions like this treated to large, public, high-cost, "sophisticated" evaluations because these are "small things," complex small efforts costing little in funds and other resources. This is odd given that governments and nations want their social institutions to produce their local version of citizen—adult citizen. Most governments leave this work to schools, to religious institutions, to civic groups, and to the family. Most simply do not want robust citizens who are youth; this is for adults, for later "when they are ready—wiser" (maybe more compliant?).

Youth civic engagement and civic youth work are challenges to governments and governance where/when youth are not actively invited to and supported in their citizen participation. The initiatives/programs discussed here and in our other work (Velure Roholt et al., 2013; VeLure Roholt & Baizerman, 2013) can be read as challenges to such dismal views (or fear) of young citizen and youth civic action by government and "the system." And it also challenges formal education, which owns this domain of learning about civics: This work is in multiple contested spaces.

It is a political act to do this work, and a moral act, too. It is this way for the evaluator. This individual needs technical expertise, political courage (and stamina), and a moral compass.

This book is a soft GPS guide to that.

11 Alternative Frameworks for Evaluating Complex Youth Civic Engagement Programs

■ CHARMAGNE CAMPBELL-PATTON

After reading through the many case studies in this book, two things should be clear: There is no one way to engage youth in civic life, and there is no one way to evaluate such efforts. Instead, what seems to be emerging are a set of principles for youth civic engagement programming and evaluation that can guide the field toward greater impact and continued learning and development. For example, there is general agreement that each civic engagement program must take into account the specific needs, goals, and desires of the youth as well as the community. Furthermore, most evaluation designs have appropriately prioritized youth participation and voice. Yet both youth civic engagement programs and their evaluations are often still based on an assumption of a linear, logical framework that can be tested and assessed for impact. Indeed, that is the model most familiar to funders, and often required by them, so many programs adopt them for compliance. In this chapter, I invite practitioners and evaluators of youth civic engagement programs to think beyond this linear model for youth programming and consider alternatives based on complexity science and systems thinking. In particular, I will call out the possibility of applying developmental evaluation to support the editor's call for a more refined understanding of the process of youth civic engagement. Finally, I will provide some guidance for practitioners and evaluators in balancing the requirements of evaluation for accountability and impact with the need for evaluation for learning and development to move the field toward a deeper understanding of what works, for whom, and under what conditions.

■ PROGRAM THEORIES AND DESIGN IMPLICATIONS

When designing an evaluation, it is important to understand how the initiative or intervention is conceptualized. This is sometimes called the "IT" question in evaluation. When it is said that something works or doesn't work, what is the *IT* that works or doesn't work? Answering this question involves conceptualizing *the theory of change*. The idea that evaluators should be involved in creating and testing theories of change emerged in the 1970s as part of a more general concern about assessing a program's *readiness for evaluation*. The basic notion was that before undertaking an evaluation, the program should be clearly conceptualized as some identifiable set of activities that are expected to lead to some identifiable outcomes. The relationships between those activities and outcomes should be both logical and testable. This process is sometimes called evaluability assessment: "Evaluability assessment is a systematic process for describing the structure of a program and for analyzing the plausibility and feasibility of achieving objectives; their suitability for in-depth evaluation; and their acceptance to program managers, policymakers, and program operators" (Smith, 2005, p. 137).

One primary purpose of an evaluability assessment for youth civic engagement programs would be explaining the underlying logic (cause-and-effect relationships) of the program, including what resources and activities are expected to produce what results. This is often referred to as the program's theory. Some of the questions that need to be asked in developing a youth civic engagement program's theory include the following:

- What resources will be available for working with young people?
- What activities will participating youth undertake?
- What will be the outcomes for the young people as well as others in the community with whom they may engage?

An evaluability assessment would ideally also gather various stakeholders' perspectives on the program theory and assess their interest in evaluation. Questions include the following:

- What do the young people think?
- How do program staff, parents, teachers, community members, policy makers, and funders understand and perceive the youth civic engagement program?

An evaluability assessment would also explore capacity and readiness for evaluation by asking:

- What is the capacity to undertake an evaluation?
- Is the program ready for rigorous evaluation (e.g., is the program's theory sufficiently well conceptualized and its outcome measures adequately validated to permit a meaningful summative evaluation)?

Finally, an evaluability assessment would also examine what research and knowledge the program designers used to inform their program model. In the case of youth civic engagement, they would examine the extent to which a program is grounded in research and knowledge about *the craft of youth civic engagement* (Roholt, Hildreth, & Baizerman, 2009). Consider, for example, four different approaches to youth civic engagement highlighted in this volume: civic education, service learning, social organizing, and youth development. Civic education engages youth to increase their knowledge about society. Service learning aims to develop youth's sense of social responsibility. Social organizing engages young people in actual social change. Youth development approaches aim to build the competence, confidence, character, and connections of young people. As our editors have highlighted in the previous chapter, these different approaches emphasize different outcomes and, therefore, invite different evaluation questions. They are also rooted in different theories of change. To understand the intended outcomes, a situation assessment would ask:

- What literature and research informs the approach?
- In what ways does the program apply shared values and fundamental principles in the field of youth civic engagement?

An evaluator, working with program designers, would examine the program's theory of change and help program managers design a program model that can be evaluated based on the program's theory of change. It is important that all stakeholders involved in the design, implementation, and evaluation of each program understand the program's underlying theory of change.

In effect, evaluability assessment puts evaluators in the business of facilitating design of the program in order for it to be evaluated. For already existing programs, this means redesigning the program because the original program model was insufficiently specified to be evaluated. As evaluators became involved in working with program people to more clearly specify the program's model (or theory), it became increasingly clear that evaluation was an *up-front activity*, not just a back-end activity. That is, traditional planning models laid out some series of steps in which planning comes first, then implementation of the program, and then evaluation, making evaluation a back-end, last-thing-done activity. But to get a program plan or design that could actually be evaluated meant involving evaluators—and evaluative thinking—from the beginning. Evaluative thinking, then, becomes part of the program design process, including, especially, conceptualizing the program's theory of change: How will what the program does lead to the desired results?

What is especially important about this for our purposes is that the very process of conceptualizing the program's theory of change can have an impact on how the program is implemented, understood, talked about, and *improved*. This means that evaluators have to be (1) astute at conceptualizing program and policy theories of change and (2) skilled at working with program people, policymakers, and funders to facilitate their articulation of their implicit theories of change. Given the importance of these tasks, it matters a great deal what theory of change frameworks the evaluator can offer.

■ COMPLEX YOUTH CIVIC ENGAGEMENT MODELS

Let us consider two opposing models for a program's theory of change. The first is a top-down model that conceptualizes the challenge of development as disseminating around the world-proven and standardized "best practices." Proven best practices are those that have been validated by randomized, controlled trials. This approach to change draws on pharmaceutical and agricultural metaphors, conceptualizing effective social interventions to be the equivalent of vaccinations or drugs in the health arena, or like new varieties of plants in the agricultural arena.

The second model, in stark contrast, conceptualizes social change as a bottom-up process of adaptation in which an idea and intervention like civic engagement must be adapted and attuned to local culture, priority concerns, history, capacity, and politics. This model eschews standardized practices and universal "best practices." Instead, guided by shared values and fundamental principles, initiatives are customized collaboratively with local partners to create an approach that is appropriate to the local setting and sensitive to local needs, concerns, priorities, and hopes. The second approach is driven by adaptation and innovation on the ground.

Given the participatory nature of youth civic engagement programs, practitioners tend to prefer this second approach because it necessitates that programs are designed with regard to local circumstances. Although the program may be informed by similar programs in other locations, no single youth civic engagement program can be implemented exactly the same in two different locations. This is particularly true in the context of developing countries, where differences between communities are likely to be even more significant that in the developed world. For example, I have been working with an international non-governmental organization that has developed a model for youth civic engagement that they plan to apply to develop new programs in several communities around the world. Beginning in Jackson, Mississippi, I have worked with a team on the ground that is deeply familiar with the local situation to conduct a situation assessment, which will provide the basis for the program's theory of change. In the future, the nongovernmental organization plans to replicate this process in India, Mexico, and the Philippines, among other countries.

The contrasting top-down and bottom-up approaches to change also involve fundamentally different evaluation designs. When change is conceptualized as top-down dissemination of best practices, randomized, controlled trials are appropriate and the critical program implementation issues are standardization and fidelity. Typical evaluation questions include: How closely must implementation of a program in new localities follow an original blueprint? How much can implementation vary from the original ideal and still be considered the same program? These questions point to one of the central issues in implementation: *adaptation versus fidelity as a premier evaluation criterion of excellence.*

In contrast, the bottom-up, adaptive management model emphasizes and attends to the uncertainty and unpredictability of social change and innovation processes. As we consider the implications of this type of model, it is useful to distinguish simple from complex approaches. A *simple* problem is how to bake a cake following a recipe. A recipe has clear cause-and-effect relationships and can be mastered through repetition and developing basic skills. The steps in baking a cake can be standardized and a recipe written with sufficient detail that even someone who has never baked has a high probability of success. Best practices for programs are like recipes in that they provide clear and high-fidelity directions since the processes that have worked to produce desired outcomes in the past are generalized as highly likely to work again in the future. Assembly lines in factories have a "recipe" quality as do standardized school curricula. Part of the attraction of the 12-Step program of Alcoholics Anonymous is its simple and standardized formulation.

Evaluating social innovations is a *complex problem* (Westley, Zimmerman, & Patton, 2006). Parenting is *complex*. Unlike the recipe for baking a cake, there are no clear books or rules to follow to guarantee success. Clearly, there are many experts in parenting and many expert books available to parents. But none can be treated like a cookbook for a cake. In the case of the cake, the intervention is mechanical. The flour does not suddenly decide to change its mind. On the other hand, children, as we all know, have minds of their own. Hence, our interventions are always in relationship with them. There are very few stand-alone parenting tasks. Almost always, the parents and child interact to create outcomes. *Any highly individualized program has elements of complexity.* The outcomes will vary for different participants based on their differing needs, experiences, situations, and desires.

Like parenting, youth civic engagement is a complex process that cannot be achieved by following a simple recipe. As noted previously, youth civic engagement programs can take a number of different forms, and there is no agreement about a single model that achieves the "best results." There is general agreement, however, that each civic engagement program must take into account the specific needs, goals, and desires of the youth as well as the community, just as the youth civic engagement model I described earlier is doing. Though they have identified a set of principles for youth civic engagement, what those mean in practice in each local community, as well as which are most important, will vary.

Simple formulations invite linear logic models that link inputs to activities to outputs to outcomes like a formula or recipe; the evaluation measures and design can, likewise, be standardized. Complex problems and situations invite adaptation and individualization. Evaluation, in such cases, requires a design that is flexible, emergent, and dynamic, mirroring the emergent, dynamic, and uncertain nature of the intervention or innovation being evaluated.

A complex, dynamic systems model of youth civic engagement stands in stark contrast to the more typical linear logic model that evaluators have become used to conceptualizing. In Chapter 4, WIMPS presents a traditional linear logic model for a youth civic engagement program. This is a classic education model that begins with inputs of young people, staff, and resources. These inputs are funneled into activities, which generate immediate outputs, and short- and long-term outcomes. For example, knowledge and skills are attained through participation, leading to attitude and behavior change, and ultimately to positive community outcomes. The advantage of this classic logic model for evaluation purposes is that it focuses attention on outcomes. What knowledge and skills are acquired? What attitudes are changed? What behaviors are developed and sustained? What community outcomes are attained? The focus on outcomes reinforces the search for a standardized "best practice" intervention that can produce those outcomes reliably and validly. The classic counterfactual question is also highlighted: What would have happened in the absence of the intervention? Asking that question leads to a randomized, controlled trial as the evaluation design of choice. The focus of such an evaluation is to answer the simple question: Did it work?

In contrast to simple linear logic models, which show causation flowing in only one direction, from intervention to outcomes, complex dynamic models make the process part of the outcome and include attention to system dynamics in which feedback loops come into play. The process is aimed at building the long-term capacity for and commitment to youth civic engagement, and both capacity and commitment depend on the bottom-up, authentic involvement of local leadership and youth. A systems model balances attention to both processes and outcomes, and depicts their interactions as inherently dynamic.

Figure 11.1 displays a sustainable reinforcing dynamic system for youth civic engagement. The intervention offers meaningful youth engagement that leads (in the theory of change) to positive youth outcomes and positive community outcomes,

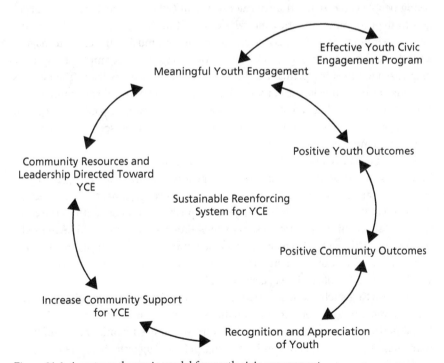

Figure 11.1 A systems dynamic model for youth civic engagement.

but as those outcomes are realized, the meaningfulness of youth engagement is also enhanced (as shown in the feedback loops from outcomes to engagement). In the dynamic model, positive outcomes lead to recognition and appreciation of youth, which deepens youth engagement and enhances outcomes (again depicted in feedback loops). Attaining outcomes increases community's support for youth engagement, which feeds back to increase recognition and appreciation of youth. These dynamics, in interaction and combination, generate additional resources for youth civic engagement and attract more leadership, which produce still more meaningful opportunities for youth service. The evaluation challenge is to inquire into and document these complex system dynamics and interactions, which will be different in different contexts.

In the previous chapter, the editors highlight the lack of attention to the greater context within which programs are operating in many of the case studies they compiled for this volume. Indeed, a narrowly focused, linear logic model tends to treat a program's impact in isolation from other institutional and societal factors. An effort to more accurately capture and reflect program realities would involve the creation of a systems map that shows the youth civic engagement program as one potentially strong influence on participating teenagers but also takes into account the important influences of the youth culture, the school system, and other community-based youth programs. Moreover, the participating young person may be affected by other systems: the legal system (laws governing what young people can do), the transportation system (which affects how the teenager gets to the program's activities and where opportunities can be offered), and the pervasive influences of the media (television, movies, music) that affect teenagers' attitudes and behaviors. Figure 11.2 shows one (simplified) example of a systems map that identifies the primary influences on young people's lives. The systems map may also include larger contextual factors like the political environment; economic incentives that can affect a teenagers' participation in youth service; and social norms and larger cultural influences that affect how society responds to civic engagement by young people.

Figure 11.3 adds a layer of description of what the connections between these influences would be in an environment of positive youth civic engagement. For example, in an environment conducive to youth civic engagement, the connection between youth and the media would generate positive views of youth in the community. Taking this connection a step further, the relationships could be mutually reinforcing, with youth also using media as a platform for civic engagement. In the arena of out-of-school time activities, the connection between these activities and youth should promote civic engagement skills.

Constructing such a systems map with a civic engagement initiative may lead the program to consider a more collaborative effort in which various institutional partners come together to work toward the desired youth and community outcomes. A systems map of youth civic engagement suggests that a civic engagement program by itself, focusing only on the teenager and only on its own delivery

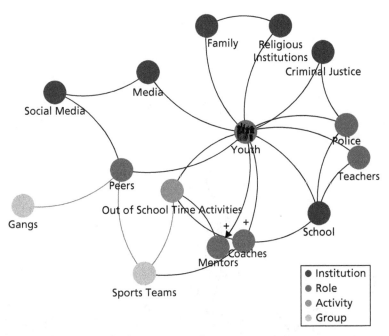

Figure 11.2 Systems map of influences on youth.

of knowledge to the teenager, is less likely to achieve the desired outcome than a model that takes into account the influences of other people in the teenager's system (the teenager's world) and collaborates with other institutions that can have an effect upon the attainment of desired outcomes.

This section has provided just a few of the possibilities for incorporating systems perspectives in evaluation of youth civic engagement programs (Williams & Iman, 2006). In the case of youth civic engagement, this means looking at the entire system in which the youth civic engagement program operates and how it impacts not just the participants or the community individually but also the complex interactions and interconnections between the different participants, beneficiaries, and stakeholders. The next section explores the implications for this approach on the framing of evaluation questions, design, and use.

▪ IMPLICATIONS FOR EVALUATION QUESTIONS

In the previous chapter, the editors highlight some of the different types of evaluation questions they found in the case studies they compiled for this volume. Most focused on student impact, and a few focused on the impact of the adults or the broader community. Yet once a systems approach is applied, it becomes clear that various desired outcomes may be interdependent. Outcomes like life skills, employment skills, increased educational attainment, prevention of risky behaviors, and civic engagement are interdependent rather than isolated and autonomous.

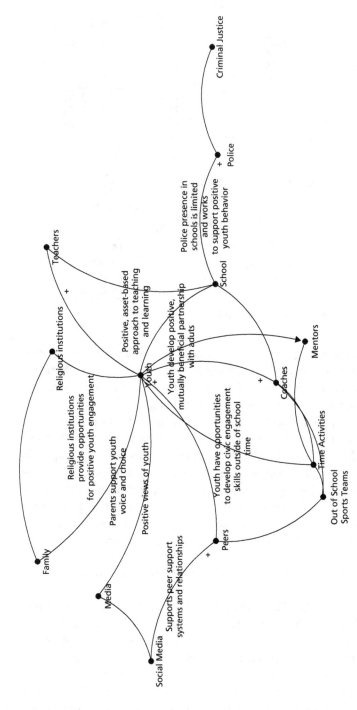

Figure 11.3 Systems map of youth civic engagement.

The following labels appear within the figure:

- Criminal Justice
- Police
- Teachers
- School
- Religious institutions
- Youth
- Mentors
- Coaches
- Out of School Time Activities
- Sports Teams
- Peers
- Family
- Media
- Social Media

- Police presence in schools is limited and works to support positive youth behavior +
- Positive, asset-based approach to teaching and learning +
- Youth develop positive, mutually beneficial partnership with adults +
- Religious institutions provide opportunities for positive youth engagement
- Parents support youth voice and choice
- Positive views of youth +
- Youth have opportunities to develop civic engagement skills outside of school time +
- Supports peer support systems and relationships +

This directs the evaluation to look at *the relationship among outcomes* rather than treating them simply as distinct and separate entities. The precise nature of this interdependence will vary by young person, which directs us again to the challenge of individualized outcomes in both theory of change formulations and evaluation.

Rather than ask the question "What was the impact on students?" or even, "What was the impact on the adults or the community?," the systems approach assumes that different young people will experience and attain different outcomes depending on their situations. Evaluations that take into account the complexity of the intervention would instead ask: What elements work for which youth in what ways and in what context? How do the civic engagement elements and dimensions interact with different young people in particular contexts to produce what variations in outcomes?

Implications for Evaluation Focus

After framing the most common evaluation questions from the case studies, the editors go on to identify four categories for the evaluations questions with regard to the relationship between the concepts of youth and citizen. The narrowly focused, linear model focuses entirely on a program's effects and ignores the rest of the young person's world. Using the complexity lens, a broader context would have to be taken into account in which youth are seen as actors within a *system*, both impacting and impacted by this system. When we ask about that larger world, we are inquiring into the multitude of relationships and connections that may influence both the nature of a young person's civic engagement and the outcomes of that engagement. We know, for example, that teenagers are heavily influenced by their peer group. The traditional linear, narrowly focused logic model targets the individual teenager. A systems perspective that considers the influence of a young person's peer group might ask how to influence the knowledge, attitudes, and behaviors of the entire peer group. This would involve changing the subsystem (the peer group) of which the individual young person is a part.

Likewise, the system's web of potential influences invites us to ask about the relative influence of the young person's parents and other family members, or teachers and other adults, as well as the relationship to the staff of the civic engagement program. In effect, this systems perspective reminds us that the behavior of a young person will be affected by a number of relationships and not just participation in the civic engagement program. In working with such a model with program staff, the conceptual elaboration of the theory of change includes specifying which direction arrows run (one way or both ways, showing mutual influence), which influences are strong (heavy solid lines) versus weak (dotted lines), and which influences are more dominant (larger circles versus smaller circles). This conceptualization then guides the evaluation data collection, which will have to include case studies to capture variations in participants' individualized experiences and outcomes. The systems approach raises some system relationship questions, including:

- What relationships in a young person's life influence that youth's attitudes and behaviors?
- How are the world and the systems we work in changing, and how do we understand those changes so as to learn, adapt, and develop?
- What are the interrelationships and interconnections between and among youth and others in the community?

Implications for Evaluation Design

Given the preceding implications, the evaluation cannot be simply a pre-post design focused on standardized and predetermined outcomes attainment because the outcomes are emergent and dynamic as the engagement process unfolds. No standardized recipe will be implemented or emerge because each locality, and the leaders and young people in that locality, will design a process that fits their situation. Adherence to principles and values can be evaluated (e.g., to what extent is there democratic input throughout the process?), but part of the purpose of the evaluation is to support monitoring and interpretation of how various principles and values are applied in the adaptive management and development process.

One approach to evaluation that I believe is particularly well suited for youth civic engagement is *developmental evaluation*. Developmental evaluation guides "adaptation to emergent and dynamic realities in complex environments" (Patton, 2011, p. 1). This approach supports innovative initiatives in a state of continuous development and adaptation by bringing data to bear to inform and guide emergent choices. In my experience, developmental evaluation provides a useful alternative for conceptualizing what evaluation can contribute to youth civic engagement initiatives.

In Chapter 9, Harry C. Boyte describes how developmental evaluation was used in the effort to evaluate civic agency. Developmental evaluation differs from typical program improvement evaluation (making a program better) in that it involves changing the program model itself as part of innovation and response to changed conditions and understandings. Developmental evaluation doesn't render overall judgments of effectiveness (traditional summative evaluation) because the program never becomes a fixed, static, and stable intervention. This is an especially critical point for youth civic engagement programs if one thinks about ever-changing political dynamics within communities, including changes in participating young people, for example, in their political efficacy and their relationship to their community if they have a civic victory, and changes in the community's stereotypes about teenagers when teens engage in community improvement projects. These impacts are dynamic and interacting. Developmental evaluation of youth civic engagement initiatives supports social innovation and adaptive management. Evaluation processes include asking evaluative questions, applying evaluation logic, and gathering real-time data to guide program, product, and/or organizational *development*. The evaluator is often part of a development team whose members collaborate to conceptualize, design, and test new approaches in a long-term, ongoing process of continuous improvement, adaptation, and intentional change. The evaluator's primary function in the team is to infuse team discussions with evaluative questions, data, and thinking to facilitate data-based reflection and decision making in the developmental process (Patton, 2016a, 2016b).

Developmental evaluation is an alternative to formative and summative evaluation (Patton, 2008). The formative-summative distinction was first conceptualized by Scriven (1967) in discussing evaluation of a school curriculum. Summative evaluations are those conducted after completion of the program for the benefit of some external audience or decision maker to determine whether to continue, expand, or disseminate the program or curriculum. Formative evaluations, in contrast, serve the purpose of getting ready for summative evaluation by helping work through implementation problems and get the program (or curriculum) sufficiently stabilized to be ready for a summative assessment. Over time, formative evaluation came to refer to any evaluation aimed at improving an intervention or model, but the implication has remained that such improvements are supposed to lead to a stable, fixed model that can be judged as worthy or unworthy of continued funding and dissemination.

But suppose an innovative youth civic engagement intervention is using a bottom-up approach and is being implemented in a highly dynamic environment where those involved are engaged in ongoing trial-and-error experimentation, figuring out what works, learning lessons, adapting to changed circumstances, working with new participants—and they never expect to arrive at a fix, static, and stable model. They are adapting principles and values rather than following a recipe. They are interested in and committed to ongoing development. Developmental evaluation supports this kind of ongoing change in a program, adapting it to changed circumstances, and altering tactics based on emergent conditions and youth responses and feedback. It includes the possibility of actively involving the young people themselves in the evaluation in a participatory evaluation approach (Delgado, 2006; Flores, 2003, 2007).

Complexity science offers insights into the changed role that evaluation can usefully play in highly innovative and dynamic circumstances. Studying how living systems organize, adapt, evolve, and transform challenges the largely mechanistic models of most programs—and most evaluations. Complexity science reveals that the real world is not a machine. Complex systems like young civic engagement systems are too dynamic, emergent, and, yes, complex, to be reduced to simple cause–effect recipes. Social innovators are often driven not by concrete goals but by possibilities, often ill-defined possibilities expressed as values, hopes, and visions. In the early days of innovation, when ideas about possibilities are

Traditional Evaluations	Complexity-Based, Developmental
Render definitive judgments of success or failure	Provide feedback, generate learnings, support direction, or affirm changes in direction
Measure success against predetermined goals Position the evaluator outside to assure independence and objectivity.	Develop new measures and monitoring mechanisms as goals emerge and evolve. Position evaluation as an internal, team function integrated into action and ongoing interpretive processes with external evaluation support and feedback.
Design the evaluation based on linear cause-effect logic models Aim to produce generalizable findings across time and space.	Design the evaluation to capture system dynamics, interdependencies, and emergent interconnections Aim to produce context-specific understandings that inform ongoing innovation.
Accountability focused on and directed to external authorities and funders.	Accountability centered on the innovators' deep sense of fundamental values and commitments—and learning.
Accountability to control and locate blame for failures	Learning to respond to lack of control and stay in touch with what's unfolding and thereby respond strategically
Evaluator determines the design based on the evaluator's perspective about what is important. The evaluator controls the evaluation.	Evaluator collaborates with those engaged in the change effort to design an evaluation process that matches philosophically and organizationally.
Evaluation engenders *fear of failure*.	Evaluation supports *hunger for learning*.

Figure 11.4 Alternative approaches to evaluation.

just being formed, the innovative process can actually be damaged by forcing too much concreteness and specificity.

This contrasts with how traditional evaluators typically approach these situations. Evaluators are trained to insist that hoped-for changes and visions be specified as clear, specific, and measurable goals, and the process for attaining those goals must be mapped in a linear logic model. That is typically all the evaluator has to offer, the only conceptual tool in the evaluator's toolkit. This is a classic case of *when all you have is a hammer, everything looks like a nail*. It is the opposite of methodological appropriateness and responsiveness in evaluation. In contrast, developmental evaluation offers an opportunity to conceptualize an initiative as a complex, dynamic system with individualized and interdependent outcomes. Figure 11.4 summarizes distinctions between traditional evaluation and developmental evaluation.

Implications for Evaluation Use

Most of the case studies in this book orient toward program improvement or accountability. Traditionally accountability has focused on and been directed to external authorities and funders. Complexity-based developmental evaluation shifts the locus and focus of accountability. In values-focused, principles-driven civic engagement, the highest form of accountability is internal. Are we walking the talk? Are we being true to our values and vision? Are we dealing with reality? Are we connecting the dots between here-and-now reality and our vision? And how

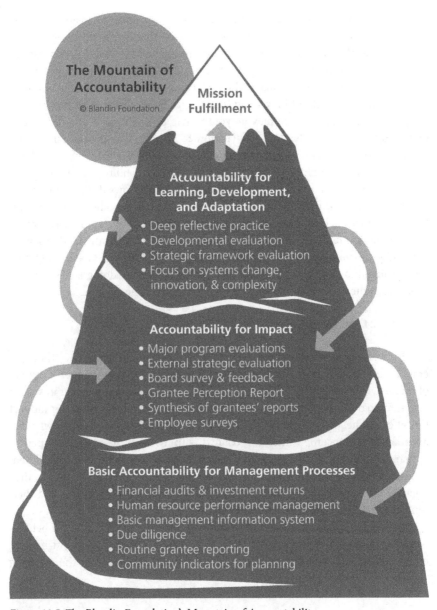

Figure 11.5 The Blandin Foundation's Mountain of Accountability.

would we know? What are we observing that's different, that's emerging? What are we learning? These become internalized questions, asked ferociously, continuously, because those involved want to know. In the context of youth civic engagement, those questions become: What do we really know about youth civic engagement? How are we adapting as new generations of children enter their youth and become engaged?

Asking such questions and engaging the answers, as uncertain as they may be, is not easy. It takes courage to face the possibility that one is deluding oneself. When this works, each individual's sense of internal and personal accountability connects with the group's sense of collective responsibility and ultimately connects broader questions of institutional and societal accountability. One of the resources I have found most helpful in making the case to those who are seeking a simple recipe for something as complex as youth civic engagement is the "Mountain of Accountability" (see Figure 11.5) (Patton & Blandin Foundation, 2014). This resource from the Blandin Foundation clarifies the relationships between basic accountability, accountability for impact, and accountability for learning and development—where developmental evaluation sits. It allows decision makers to see the connections between the different levels of accountability and highlights the importance of engaging in evaluation for learning and development as a way to achieve mission fulfillment. Rather than simply ensuring that you are doing what you said you would do and having the impact you said you would have, evaluation for learning and development will ensure that what you are doing is relevant and adapting to the ever-changing landscape of youth civic engagement.

■ CONCLUSION

Youth civic engagement models are as varied as youth themselves. They operate in an ever-changing context and are influenced by and influence a myriad of factors. To be effective in this reality, youth civic engagement programs must take into account the systems in which they are operating. Evaluation can support this effort by helping programs to articulate their program theories in a way that acknowledges the complexities and context within which the programs operate. Systems thinking and developmental evaluation can help youth civic engagement programs be adaptive and responsive to the changing landscape in which they operate. Implementing this type of approach will take many programs and their funders outside of their comfort zones, forcing them to acknowledge, address, and respond to the complex realities in which they operate. But the result, I believe, will be much more effective youth civic engagement programs and much more useful data to help these programs continue to improve and adapt to the changing world in which they operate.

■ NOTES

▮ Chapter 4

1. Clark quoted in Charles Payne, *I've Got the Light of Freedom: The Organizing Tradition and the Mississippi Struggle* (Berkeley: University of California Press: 1965), p. 68.

2. This is the theme of a report commissioned by Gary Cunningham of the Northwest Area Foundation, Harry C. Boyte, *The Empowerment Gap: Rethinking Poverty Reduction Strategies* (Minneapolis: CDC/Augsburg, 2014). This essay draws on the report. The importance of a "noninstrumental" understanding of civic agency is made with considerable force by David Hoffman in his recent phenomenological study of students who have become agents of change at UMBC, *Becoming Real: Undergraduates' Civic Agency Journeys* (Baltimore: UMBC, 2013). In a related argument, Paul Dragos Aligica, a long-time colleague of Nobel Prize–winning political theorist Elinor Elinor and her husband, Vincent Ostrom, argues that the "ontological" quality of their approach, emphasizing agency, intentionality, and co-creation has been overlooked in the Ostroms' work on citizen-centered governance of common pool resources. Algica writes, "If we manage to avoid 'brute empiricism,' Ostrom argued, and 'if political experience is conceived to be artifactual (i.e., created by reference to human knowledge),' then the focus changes. The social sciences and the study of governance are not about 'covering laws' or 'natural regularities,' but rather they are about how 'intentionality and knowledgeable calculations' generate the 'living realities' of the social and political realm." Quote from "Citizenship, Political Competence, and Civic Studies: The Ostromian Perspective," in Peter Levine and Karol Soltan, *Civic Studies* (Washington, DC: AAC&U/Bringing Theory to Practice, 2014), p. 41.

3. Martin Luther King, "Letter from a Birmingham Jail," April 16, 1963, quotation from text at http://www.africa.upenn.edu/Articles_Gen/Letter_Birmingham.html

4. Dudley Cocke, co-founder of the Roadside Theater, a part of Appalshop, in the Appalachian region and a long-time champion of empowering cultural work, recounted this conversation he had with a gathering of foundation program officers at a national conference in Philadelphia (May 26, 2014, email correspondence).

5. Bill Doherty interview with Harry Boyte, January 19, 2014, St. Paul, Minnesota.

6. For instance, in K-12 education, anthropologist Annett Lareau has explored the split between community values and individualist, competitive school cultures in her study of what she calls "the cultural logic" of poor and working-class families compared to schools and educators. Educators, whether in suburbs or inner cities, are trained in what Lareau calls a "dominant set of cultural repertoires about how children should be raised," including highly individualist, competitive, and achievement-oriented norms. In contrast, for working-class and poor families, there is an emphasis on sustaining relationships with family and friends. Annette Lareau, *Unequal Chidhoods: Class, Race and Family Life* (Berkeley: University of California Press, 2003), pp. 4 and 5.

Recent research sponsored by the Kellogg School of Management at Northwestern, "Unseen Disadvantage," finds similar dynamics in much of higher education, showing how individualist achievement norms generate inequality through their effects on undergraduates. Thus, the achievement norms such as "doing your own thing," "paving your own path," and "realizing your individual potential" make college "the ultimate symbol of independence" for middle- and upper-class students. But such norms are experienced far differently by students from working-class families. For the latter, "expectations for college center around interdependent motives such as working together, connecting to others, and giving back," Nicole Stephens reports. In four studies, Stephens and her fellow researchers found that as working-class students were exposed to the message of individual success and independence, a strong social class performance gap emerged. Rebecca Covarrubias, Stephanie Fryberg, Camille S. Johnson, Hazel Rose Markus, and Nicole Stephens, "Unseen Disadvantage," at http://www.kellogg.northwestern.edu/news/unseen_disadvantage.htm.

7. Conversation with Nan Skelton, St. Paul, Minnesota, June 19, 2014.

8. Seethe YouTube video on "Public Achievement—Transforming Special Education in Fridley" for background on this story http://www.youtube.com/watch?v=VaRimtavig8

9. Quotes from Blood and Ricci about their teaching from Harry Boyte and Jen Nelson, "A 21st Century Freedom Movement," *Huffington Post*, June 12, 2013, at http://www.huffingtonpost.com/harry-boyte/a-21st-century-freedom-mo_b_3421977.html

10. See http://swampland.time.com/where-in-the-world-is-joe/; quote from Joe Klein, "On the Road," *Time*, October 18, 2010, p. 38.

■ Chapter 7

1. Information here appears for illustrative purposes and derives solely from the surveys of crew members, not from the other data collection instruments.

2. Statistically significant differences demonstrated through t-tests, at $p \leq .05$.

■ REFERENCES

Aitken, S. (2001). *Geographies of young people: The morally contested spaces of identity.* London, UK: Routledge.

Alkin, M. C. (Ed.). (2004). *Evaluation roots: Tracing theorists' views and influences.* Thousand Oaks, CA: Sage.

Allan, J., & Catts, R. (2012) (Eds.). *Social capital, children and young people.* Bristol, UK: Policy Press.

Ansley, F., & Gaventa, J. (1997). Researching for democracy and democratizing research. *Change: The Magazine of Higher Learning, 29*(1), 46–53.

Baizerman, M. (1975). Evaluation research and evaluation: Scientific social movement and ideology. *Journal of Sociology and Social Welfare, 2,* 277.

Baizerman, M., McDonough, J. J., & Sherman, M. (1976). *Self-evaluation handbook for hotlines and youth crisis centers.* St. Paul, MN: Center for Youth Development and Research, University of Minnesota.

Baizerman, M., & VeLure Roholt, R. (2016). Youth worker professional development: Moving from practicing the symbolic to working substantively. In K. Pozzoboni & B. Kirshner (Eds.). *The changing landscape of youth work: Theory and practice for an evolving field* (Ch. 3). New York, NY: Information Age Publishing.

Baizerman, M., VeLure Roholt, R., & Fink, A. (2014). Evaluation advisory groups. *Research on Social Work Practice, 24*(2), 186–187.

Baizerman, M., VeLure Roholt, R., Korum, K., & Rana, S. (2013). From lessons learned to emerging practices. *New Directions for Youth Development, 139,* 121–146.

Ballet, J., Biggeri, M., & Comim, F. (2011). Children's agency and the capability approach: A conceptual framework. In M. Biggeri, J. Ballet, & F. Comim (Eds.), *Children and the capability approach* (pp. 22–45). Hampshire, UK: Palgrave Macmillan.

Bell, Z., & Student Nation (2013, February). Is the international student movement the future of global organizing? *The Nation,* Available online at: http://www.thenation.com/blog/172746/international-student-movement-future-global-organizing

Bellah, R., Madsen, R., Sullivan, W. M., Swidler, A., & Tipton, S. M. (1985). Habits of the heart. *Social Psychology Quarterly, 49,* 103–109.

Bennett, S. (1997). Why young Americans hate politics, and what we should do about it. *Political Science and Politics, 30*(1), 47–52.

Bessant, J., Sercombe, H., & Watts, R. (1998). *Youth studies: An Australian perspective.* Longman, Australia: South Melbourne.

Blood-Knafla, A. (2013). Experiences of students with special needs in public achievement (unpublished master's thesis). Augsburg College, Minneapolis, Minnesota.

Boyte, H. C. (1999). *CommonWealth: A return to citizen politics.* New York, NY: Free Press.

Boyte, H. C. (2008). Against the current: Developing the civic agency of students. *Change: The Magazine of Higher Learning, 40*(3), 8–15.

Boyte, H. C. (2011). Constructive politics are public work: Organizing the literature. *Political Theory, 39*(5), 630–660.

Boyte, H. C., & Scarnati, B. (2014). Transforming higher education in a larger context: The civic politics of public work. In P. Levin & K. Soltan (Eds.) *Civic studies* (p. 85). Washington, DC: AAC&U.

Bradford, S., & Cullen, F. (2012). *Research and research methods for youth practitioners.* New York, NY: Routledge.

Bryan, A. (2014). *Black's law dictionary.*Union, NJ: West Group.

Buber, M. (1975). *The way of response.* N. N. Glatzer (Ed.). New York: Schocken Books.

Cambell-Patton, C. & Patton, M. Q. (2010). Conceptualizing and evaluating the complexities of youth civic engagement. In L. Sherrod, J. Torney-Purta, & C. Flanagan (Eds.), *Handbook of research on civic engagement in youth* (pp. 593–620). Hoboken, NJ: John Wiley & Sons.

Cammarota, J., & Fine, M. (2008). Revolutionizing education: Youth participatory action research in motion. New York, NY: Routledge.

Center for Disease Control (2011). *Introduction to program evaluation for public health programs: A self-study guide.* Atlanta, GA: Centers for Disease Control and Prevention.

Center for the Study of Social Policy. (2011). *Results based public policy strategies for promoting youth civic engagement.* Washington, DC: Center for the Study of Social Policy.

Chawla, L. (2002). *Growing up in an urbanising world.* London, UK: UNESCO.

Checkoway, B., Dobbie, D., & Richards-Schuster, K. (2003). Involving young people in community evaluation research. *Community Youth Development, 4*(1), 7–11.

Checkoway, B., & Richards-Schuster, K. (2003). Young people's participation in research and evaluation. *American Journal of Evaluation, 24*(1), 21–33.

Checkoway, B., & Richards-Schuster, K. (2004a). Youth participation in evaluation and research as a way of Lifting New Voices. *Children, Youth and Environments 14*(2), 84–98.

Checkoway, B., & Richards-Schuster, K. (2004b). *Participatory evaluation with young people.* Battle Creek, MI: W. K. Kellogg Foundation.

Checkoway, B., & Richards-Schuster, K. (2011). Youth participation in community research for racial justice. In Nyden, P., Hossfield, L., Nyden, G. (Eds.), *Public sociology: Research, action and change* (pp. 169–175). Thousand Oaks, CA: Pine Forge Press/SAGE.

Checkoway, B., Richards-Schuster, K., Abdullah, S., Aragon, M., Facio, E., Figueroa, L., Reddy, E., . . . White, A. (2003). Young people as competent citizens. *Community Development Journal: An International Forum, 38*(4), 298–309.

Coles, R., & Scarnati, B. (2015). Transformational ecotones in higher education. In H. C. Boyte (Ed.), *Democracy's education: Public work, citizenship, and the future of colleges and universities* (pp. 115–125). Nashville, TN: Vanderbilt University Press.

Collected Works of Tao Xingzhi. (1985). 2nd volume. Changsha, China: Hunan Education Press.

Compton, D., & Baizerman, M. (2009). Managing program evaluation: Towards explicating a professional practice. *New Directions for Evaluation, 121.*

Compton, D., Baizerman, M., & Stockdill, S. (Eds.) (2004). *The art, craft, and science of evaluation capacity building. New Directions for Evaluation, 93.*

Compton, D. W., & Baizerman, M. (2007). Defining evaluation capacity building. *American Journal of Evaluation, 28*(1), 118–119.

Cotton, D. (2012). *If your back's not bent: The role of citizenship education program in the civil rights movement.* New York, NY: Simon and Schuster.

Coussee, F. (2009). The relevance of youth work history. In G. Verschelden (Ed.), *The history of youth work in Europe: Relevance for youth policy today* (pp. 7–13). Strasbourg, France: The Council of Europe.

Dahler-Larsen, P. (2012). *The evaluation society.* Palo Alto, CA: Stanford University Press.

Delgado, M. (2006). *Designs and methods for youth-led research.* Thousand Oaks, CA: Sage.

Delli Carpini, M. X. (2000). Gen.com: Youth, civic engagement, and the new information environment. *Political Communication, 17*(4), 341–349. http://dx.doi.org/10.1080/10584600050178942

Driskell, D. (2002). *Creating better cities with children and youth: A manual for participation.* London, UK: Earthscan.

Evans, S., & Boyte, H. (1992). *Free spaces: The source of democratic change in America* (2nd ed.). Chicago, IL: University of Chicago Press.

Fetterman, D. (2001). *Foundations of empowerment evaluation.* Thousand Oaks, CA: Sage.

Fitzpatrick, J., Sanders, J., & Worthen, B. (2010). *Program evaluation: Alternative approaches and practical guidelines* (4th ed.). New York, NY: Pearson.

Forss, K., Marra, M., & Schwartz, R. (Eds.). (2011). *Evaluating the complex: Attribution, contribution, and beyond.* New Brunswick, NJ: Transaction.

Fusco, D. (2012). *Advancing youth work: Current trends, critical questions.* New York, NY: Routledge.

Garza, P., & Stevens, P. (2002). *Best practices in youth philanthropy.* Basehor, KS: Coalition of Community Foundations for Youth.

Gerth, H. H., & Mills, C. W. (1958). *From Max Weber: Essays in sociology.* New York, NY: Oxford University Press.

Gharabaghi, K., Skott-Myhre, H., & Kreuger, M. (2014). *With children and youth: Emerging theories and practices in child and youth care work.* Waterloo, Ontario: Wilfrid Laurier University Press.

Gibson, C. (2001). *From inspiration to participation: A review of perspectives on youth civic engagement.* New York, NY: Carnegie Corporation of New York.

Ginwright, S. (2010). Peace out to revolution! Activism among African American youth: An argument for radical healing. *Young, 18*(1), 77–96.

Ginwright, S., Noguera, P., & Cammarota, J. (2006). *Beyond resistance! Youth activism and community change: New democratic possibilities for practice and policy for America's youth.* New York, NY: Routledge.

Groopman, J. E., & Prichard, M. J. (2007). *How doctors think* (Vol. 82). Boston, MA: Houghton Mifflin.

Hart, R. (1992). *Children's participation: From tokenism to citizenship.* Florence, Italy: UNICEF International Child Development Centre.

Hehir, T., & Wilkens, C. (2008). Deaf education and bridging social capitol: A theoretical approach. *American Annals of the Deaf, 153*(3), 275–284. http://library.ncrtm.org/pdf/J305.1533.01A.pdf

Higgins-D'Alessandro, A. (2010). The transdisciplinary nature of citizenship and civic/political engagement evaluation. In L. Sherrod, J. Torney-Purta, & C. Flanagan (Eds.)., *Handbook of research on civic engagement in youth* (pp. 559–592). Hoboken, NJ: John Wiley & Sons.

Higgs, J. (2010). Researching practice: Entering the practice discourse. In J. Higgs, N. Cherry, R. Macklin, & R. Ajjawi (Eds.). *Researching practice: A discourse on qualitative methodologies* (pp. 1–8). Rotterdam, the Netherlands: Sense Publishing.

Higgs, J., & Titchen, A. (2001). *Practice knowledge and expertise in the health professions.* Oxford, UK: Butterworth-Heinemann.

Hoffman, D. (2013). *Becoming real: Undergraduates civic agency journeys.* University of Maryland, College Park, Baltimore County.

Hoffman, D. (2015). Fostering civic agency by making education (and ourselves) real. In H. C. Boyte (Ed.), *Democracy's education: Public work, citizenship, and the future of colleges and universities* (pp. 154–160). Nashville, TN: Vanderbilt University Press.

Holland, J. (1998). *Emergence: From chaos to order.* Cambridge, MA: Perseus Books.

Huiying, X. (2012). *Service-learning model of civic service education in primary school.* China Philanthropic Education Research Center, Institute of Culture Innovation and Communication. Beijing: Beijing Normal University.

Hunter, K. M. (1991). *Doctors' stories: The narrative structure of medical knowledge.* Princeton, NJ: Princeton University Press.

Introduction to process evaluation in tobacco use prevention and control (February, 2008). Atlanta, GA: Office on Smoking and Health, Centers for Disease Control and Prevention, US Department of Health and Human Services. http://www.cdc.gov/tobacco/publications/index.htm

James, A. (2011). To be (come) or not to be (come): Understanding children's citizenship. *The Annals of the American Academy of Political and Social Science, 633*(1), 167–179.

James, T. (2003). Democratizing knowledge: The role of research and evaluation in youth organizing. *Community Youth Development, 4*(1), 33–39.

Jeffs, T., & Smith, M. (1999, 2005). *Informal education. Conversation, democracy, and learning.* Ticknall, UK: Education Now.

Jeffs, T., & Smith, M. (2010). *Youth work practice.* New York, NY: Palgrave McMillian.

Johnson, V. (2010). Rights through evaluation and understanding children's realities. In B. Percy-Smith & N. Thomas (Eds.), *A handbook of children and young people's participation: Perspectives from theory and practice* (pp. 154–163). New York, NY: Routledge.

Jolly, E., Campbell, P., & Perlman, L. (2004). Engagement, capacity and continuity: A trilogy for student success. Retrieved from http://www.campbell-kibler.com

Judge, K., & Bauld, L. (2001). Strong theory, flexible methods: Evaluating complex community-based initiatives. *Critical Public Health, 11*(1), 19–38.

Keeter, S., Zukin, C., Andolina, M., & Jenkins, K. (2002). *The civic and political health of the nation: A generational portrait.* The Center for Information and Research on Civic Learning and Engagement. Online at: http://www.civicyouth.org/research/products/Civic_Political_Health.pdf

Kirby, P., Lanyon, C., Cronin, K., & Sinclair, R. (2003). Building a culture of participation: Involving children and young people in policy, service planning, delivery and evaluation. Retrieved from http://www.gyerekesely.hu/childpoverty/docs/involving_children_report.pdf

Knowlton, L., & Phillips, C. (2013). *The logic model guidebook: Better strategies for great results.* Thousand Oaks, CA: Sage.

Lansdown, G. (2005). *The evolving capacities of the child.* Florence, Italy: Innocenti Research Center.

Lave, J., & Wenger, E. (1991). *Situated learning: Legitimate peripheral participation.* Cambridge, UK: Cambridge University Press.

Lerner, R. (2004). *Liberty: Thriving and civic engagement among America's youth.* Thousand Oaks, CA: Sage.

Magnuson, D., & Baizerman, M. (2007). *Work with youth in divided and contested societies.* Rotterdam: Sense Publishing.

Mangcu, X. (2015). The promise of black consciousness. In H. C. Boyte (Ed.), *Democracy's education: Public work, citizenship, and the future of colleges and universities* (pp. 226–234). Nashville, TN: Vanderbilt University Press.

Manser, A. (1967). Games and family resemblances. *Philosophy, 42*(161), 210–225.

Mark, M., Henry, G., & Julnes, G. (2000). *Evaluation: An integrated framework for understanding, guiding, and improving policies and programs.* San Francisco, CA: Jossey-Bass.

Mathison, S. (2000). Promoting democracy through evaluation. In D. Hursch & E. W. Ross (Eds.), *Democratic social education: Social studies for social change* (pp. 229–242). New York, NY: Falmer Press.

Mattessich, P. (2003). *Managers guides to program evaluation.* Saint Paul, MN: Wilder Publishing Center.

Mayeroff, M. (1971). *On caring.* New York, NY: Harper Collins.

McIntyre, A. (2000). *Inner city kids: Adolescents confront life and violence in an urban community.* New York, NY: New York University Press.

Merton, R. K. (1965). *On the shoulders of giants: The post-Italianate edition.* Chicago, IL: University of Chicago Press.

Mitchell, T. (2008). Traditional vs. critical service-learning: Engaging the literature to differentiate two models. *Michigan Journal of Community Service Learning, 14*(2), 50–65.

Morality and Life Course Standard, drawn by the Ministry of Education of the People's Republic of China. Beijing: Beijing Normal University Press, 2011.

Morrell, E. (2004). *Becoming critical researchers: Literacy and empowerment for urban youth.* New York: Peter Lang.

Morss, J. (1990). *The biologising of childhood: Developmental psychology and the Darwinian myth.* London, UK: Lawrence Erlbaum.

Moss, P., & Petrie, P. (2002). *From children's services to children's spaces: Public policy, children and childhood.* London, UK: Routledge Falmer.

National Service Programs: AmeriCorps. http://www.nationalservice.gov/programs/americorps/americorps-state-and-national

Niemi, R., & Junn, J. (2005). *Civic education: What makes students learn.* New Haven, CT: Yale University Press.

Noble Smith, S. (2011). "Lessons I wish I'd learned in college." In N. Longo & C. Gibson (Eds.), *From command to community: New approaches to leadership education in colleges and universities* (pp. 234–246). Boston, MA: Tufts University Press.

Noguera, P, Ginwright, S., & Cammarota, J. (Eds.) (2006). *Beyond resistance: Youth activism and community change. New democratic possibilities for policy and practice for America's youth.* New York, NY: Routledge.

Owen, J., & Alkin, M. (2006). *Program evaluation: Forms and approaches.* New York, NY: Guilford.

Paris, D., & Winn, M. (2014). *Humanizing research: Decolonizing qualitative inquiry with youth and communities.* Thousand Oaks, CA: Sage.

Patton, M. Q. (2008). *Utilization-focused evaluation* (4th ed.). Thousand Oaks, CA: Sage.

Patton, M. Q. (2011). *Developmental evaluation.* New York, NY: Guilford.

Patton, M. Q. (2016a). The developmental evaluation mindset: Eight guiding principles. In M. Q. Patton, K. McKegg, & N. Wehipeihana (Eds.), *Developmental evaluation exemplars: Principles in practice* (pp. 289–312). New York, NY: Guilford.

Patton, M. Q. (2016b). What is essential in developmental evaluation. *American Journal of Evaluation, 37*(2), 250–265.

Patton, M. Q., & Blandin Foundation (2014). *Mountain of Accountability: Pursuing mission through learning, exploration and development.* Grand Rapids, MN: Blandin Foundation.

Payne, C. (1965). *I've got the light of freedom*. Berkeley: University of California.

Percy-Smith, B., (2007) You think you know? . . . You have no idea: Youth participation in health policy development. *Health Education Research, 22*(6), 879–894. http://her. oxfordjournals.org/content/22/6/879.full.pdf+html

Polkinghorne, D. (1988). *Narrative knowing and the human sciences*. Albany, NY: State University of New York Press.

Reid, R., Gonzalez, J., Nordness, P., Trout, A., & Epstein, M. (2004). A meta-analysis of the academic status of students with emotional/behavioral disturbance. *The Journal of Special Education, 38*(3), 130–143.

Richards-Schuster, K., & Checkoway, B. (2009). Youth participation in public policy at the local level: New lessons from Michigan municipalities. *National Civic Review, 98*(4), 26–30.

Rogers, P. (2011). Implications of complicated and complex characteristics for key tasks in evaluation. In K. Forss, M. Marra, & R. Schwartz, R. (Eds.), *Evaluating the complex: Attribution, contribution, and beyond* (pp. 33–52). New Brunswick, NJ: Transaction.

Rogoff, B. (1990). *Apprenticeship in thinking: Cognitive development in social context*. Oxford, England: Oxford University Press.

Rosen, D. (2007). Child soldiers, international humanitarian law, and the globalization of childhood. *American Anthropologist, 109*(2), 296–306.

Royse, D., Thyer, B., & Padgett, D. (2010). *Program evaluation: An introduction*. Belmont, CA: Wadsworth, Cengage Learning.

Rubin, B. (2007). There's still not justice: Youth civic identity development amid distinct school and community contexts. *Teachers College Record, 109*(2), 449–481.

Sabo Flores, K. S., ed. (2003). Youth participatory evaluation: A field in the making. *New Directions for Evaluation, 98* (Summer). San Francisco, CA: Jossey-Bass, 1–112.

Sabo Flores, K. S. (2008). *Youth participatory evaluation: Strategies for engaging young people*. San Francisco, CA: Jossey-Bass.

Sandermann, P., & Neumann, S. (2014). On multifaceted commonality. Theories of social pedagogy in Germany. *International Journal of Social Pedagogy, 3*(1), 15–29.

Scriven, M. (1967). The methodology of evaluation in perspective of curriculum evaluation. In R. W. Tyler (ed.), *AERA Monograph series on curriculum evaluation, 1* (pp. 39–83). Chicago, IL: Rand McNally.

Sercombe, H. (2010). *Youth work ethics*. London, UK: Sage.

Sherrod, L., Flanagan, C., & Youniss, J. (2002). Dimensions of citizenship and opportunities for youth development: The what, why, when, where, and who of citizenship development. *Applied Developmental Science, 6*(4), 264–272.

Sherrod, L., Torney-Purta, J., Flanagan, C. (2010). Introduction: Research on the development of citizenship: A field comes of age. In L. Sherrod, J. Torney-Purta, & C. Flanagan (Eds.). *Handbook of research on civic engagement in youth* (pp. 1–22). Hoboken, NJ: John Wiley & Sons.

Shier, H. (2001). Pathways to participation: Openings, opportunities, and obligations. *Child & Society, 15*(2), 107–117.

Shumer, R. (2007). *Youth-led evaluation: A guidebook*. Clemson, SC: National Dropout Prevention Center.

Smith, M. F. (2005). Evaluability assessment. In S. Mathison (ed.) *Encyclopedia of evaluation* (pp. 136–139). Thousand Oaks, CA: Sage.

Sommer, B. (2008). *Hard work and a good deal: The Civilian Conservation Corps in Minnesota*. St. Paul, MN: Minnesota Historical Society Press.

Spencer, J. (2009). *Toward a unified theory of development: Connectionism and dynamic system theory reconsidered*. Oxford, UK: Oxford University Press.

Strasser, S. (1985). *Understanding and explanation: Basic ideas concerning the humanity of the human sciences*. Pittsburg, PA: Duquesne Press.

Stufflebeam, D. L. (2004). *Evaluation design checklist*. Kalamazoo, MI: Western Michigan University. The Evaluation Center. Retrieved from http://www.wmich.edu/evalctr/archive_checklists/evaldesign.pdf

Tavernise, S. (2015, February 12). Few health systems studies use top method, report says. *The New York Times*. Retrieved from http://nyti.ms/1J3uhac).

Valle, J. W., & Connor, D. J. (2011). *Rethinking disability: A disability studies approach to inclusive practices*. New York, NY: McGraw Hill.

van Manen, M. (1990). *Researching lived experience: Human science for an action sensitive pedagogy*. New York, NY: Suny Press.

van Manen, M. (2015). Phenomenology of practice: Meaning-giving methods in phenomenological research and writing. Walnut Creek, CA: Left Coast Press.

VeLure Roholt, R. (2005). *Democratic civic practice: A training curriculum for teachers and youthworkers*. Belfast, Northern Ireland: Public Achievement (funded by United States Institute of Peace). Retrieved from http://www.publicachievement.com

VeLure Roholt, R., & Baizerman, M (Eds.) (2013). Evaluation advisory groups. *New Directions for Evaluation, 136*, 1–127.

VeLure Roholt, R., & Baizerman, M. (2013). *Civic youth work primer*. New York, NY: Peter Lang.

VeLure Roholt, R., & Baizerman, M. (Eds.) (2012). Special section on "Evaluation in Contested Spaces." *Evaluation and Program Planning, 35*(1), 139–218.

VeLure Roholt, R., Baizerman, M., & Hildreth, R. (Eds.). (2013). *Civic youth work: Co-creating democratic youth spaces*. Chicago, IL: Lyceum.

VeLure Roholt, R., Baizerman, M., & Hildreth, R. W. (2009). *Becoming citizens: Deepening the craft of youth civic engagement*. New York, NY: Routledge.

VeLure Roholt, R., Rana, S., Baizerman, M., & Korum, K. (Eds.) (2013). Transforming youth organizations to support healthy youth development. *New Directions for Youth Development, 139*.

Weiss, C. (1998). *Evaluation: Methods for studying programs and policies* (2nd ed.). Upper Saddle River, NJ: Prentice Hall.

Westley, F, Zimmerman, B., & Patton, M. Q. (2006). *Getting to maybe: How the world is changed*. Toronto, Canada: Random House.

Williams, A., Ferguson, D., & Yohalem, N. (2013). Youth organizing for educational change. Retrieved from http://forumfyi.org/files/Youth_Organizing_for_Education_0.pdf

Williams, B., & Iman, I. (2006). *Systems concepts in evaluation: An expert anthology*. AEA Monograph. Point Reynes, CA: EdgePress.

Winter, N. (2003). Social capital, civic engagement and positive youth development outcomes. Retrieved from http://www.policystudies.com/studies/community/Civic%20 Engagement.pdf

Yarbrough, D., Shulha, L., Hopson, R., & Caruthers, F. (2011). *The program evaluation standards: A guide for evaluators and evaluation users*. Thousand Oaks, CA: Sage.

Yates, M., & Youniss, J. (Eds.). (1999). *Roots of civic identity: International perspectives on community service and activism in youth.* Cambridge, UK: Cambridge University Press.

Yiyung, X. H. (2012). Service-learning model of civic service education in primary school. China Philanthropic Education Research Center, School of Social Development & Public Policy, Beijing Normal University.

Youniss, J., & Yates, M. (1997). *Community service and social responsibility in youth.* Chicago, IL: University of Chicago Press.

■ INDEX

Note: Tables and figures are indicated by an italic "*t*" and "*f*" respectively.

enhancing use. *See* Use and Share Lessons
     Learned step
ethicomoral self, 81
evaluability assessment, 155
evaluation
     adaptation vs. fidelity criterion, 157
     American Evaluation Association's
          Program Evaluation
          Standards for, 2
     both-and evaluation processes, 48
     choosing what to evaluate, 25
     of civic agency, 60–70
     community engagement in, 89–100
     defined, 2–4
     democratizing effect of evaluation,
          137–139, 142
     design process, 129–140
     determining study type, 21–23
     developmental evaluation, 164–165
     effective vs. scientific, 28
     embedded in ongoing activity, 115
     enhancing civic youth work through
          community logic model, 149–150
          evaluation as intervention, 141
          expanded framework for evaluation,
               145–146
          group logic model, 148–149
          individual logic model, 146–148
          practice and processes, 151–152
          questions regarding, 141–145
          responsibility of program and
               evaluator, 152
     evaluator knowledge level, 18–19
     as extension of civic engagement, 49
     fantasy evaluation plan for Northern
          Ireland, 71–88
     meeting structures as form of,
          121–122
     mixed-method evaluations, 62, 91
     as a nonlinear process, 7
     as opportunity for citizen-making, 125
     outcome evaluation, 23–24
     as a process, 1–2
     process evaluation, 23
     reflective questions guiding, 19–20,
          142–145

     socio-political aspects of, 32–35
     traditional vs. complexity-based,
          164–166, 166*f*
     of WIMPS program, 101–113
     of youth civic engagement, 154–168
     youth roles in, 11–13
     See also civic youth work: evaluating;
          youth-led evaluation
Evers, Medgar, 62–63

fantasy evaluation plan, 71–88
Fine, M., 18
First Year Learning Initiative, 68–69
Focus Evaluation Design step
     conflict exhibit evaluation example,
          6, 20–25
     overview of, xiii
     public achievement fantasy plan for
          Northern Ireland, 71–88
     short description, 4*t*
focus groups, youth-driven, 42–45
freedom spirit, 61
Fridley Middle School, 65–68
fugitive material, x

Gather Credible Evidence step
     community engagement in
          assessment, 89–100
     conflict exhibit evaluation example,
          6, 25–29
     overview of, xiii
     short description, 4*t*
Gibson, C., 17
gray literature, x, 28
group level questions, 23
group logic model, 148–149

Hart, Roger, 12
Hart's ladder of participation, 10, 12
Hbrabowski, Freeman A., 69
Henry, Aaron, 62–63
Highlander Folk School, 62
Hildreth, Roudy, 77
Hoffman, David, 69–70, 169n2
Horton, Miles, 62–63
Humphrey Institute, 60, 63–65, 77